The Coloniality of the Secular

The Coloniality of the Secular

An Yountae

RACE, RELIGION, AND POETICS OF WORLD-MAKING

DUKE UNIVERSITY PRESS
Durham and London
2024

© 2024 DUKE UNIVERSITY PRESS
All rights reserved
Project Editor: Bird Williams
Designed by A. Mattson Gallagher
Typeset in Garamond Premier Pro by Westchester Publishing Services

Library of Congress Cataloging-in-Publication Data
Names: An Yountae, author.
Title: The coloniality of the secular : race, religion, and poetics of world-making / An Yountae.
Description: Durham : Duke University Press, 2024. | Includes bibliographical references and index.
Identifiers: LCCN 2023016231 (print)
LCCN 2023016232 (ebook)
ISBN 9781478025108 (paperback)
ISBN 9781478020127 (hardcover)
ISBN 9781478027096 (ebook)
Subjects: LCSH: Postcolonial theology. | Religion and politics. | Racism—Religious aspects—Christianity. | Decolonization—Religious aspects. | Postcolonialism—Religious aspects—Christianity. | Religion—Philosophy. | Imperialism. | Hispanic American theology. | BISAC: RELIGION / General | PHILOSOPHY / Religious
Classification: LCC BT83.593 .A5 2024 (print)
LCC BT83.593 (ebook)
DDC 201/.72—dc23/eng/20231106
LC record available at https://lccn.loc.gov/2023016231
LC ebook record available at https://lccn.loc.gov/2023016232

Cover art: Joaquín Roca Rey, *Study Figure for Unknown PoliticalPrisoner* , 1952. Bronze, 13 x 9 x 10 inches. Collection OAS AMA | Art Museum of the Americas. Artist's permission courtesy of Archivi Joaquín Roca Rey.

Contents

vii Acknowledgments

1 Introduction
   A Decolonial Theory of Religion

   PART I. GENEALOGIES

25 1. Modernity/Coloniality/Secularity
   The Cartography of Struggle

57 2. Crisis and Revolutionary Praxis
   Philosophy and Theology of Liberation

   PART II. POETICS

97 3. Phenomenology of the Political
   Fanon's Religion

113 4. Phenomenology of Race
   Poetics of Blackness

139 5. Poetics of World-Making
   Creolizing the Sacred, Becoming Archipelago

177 Conclusion

181 Notes
205 Bibliography
223 Index

Acknowledgments

I would like to thank the College of Humanities at California State University, Northridge (CSUN), for the various grants that supported the writing of the book. I also want to thank Rick Talbott and Mustafa Ruzgar, the chairs of the Department of Religious Studies, for their continuous support during the process. The College of Humanities Research Lab helped me advance initial research for the project with the help of students who participated in the lab during 2018 and 2019. Special thanks to my research assistants, Menen Basha and Michael Meeks. In many ways, the initial questions and concerns that inspired the project were born at the National Endowment for the Humanities Summer Institute, which took place at Macalester College in 2017. I thank James Laine and everyone who participated in the institute for helping me deepen my interests on the issue of method and theory for the study of religion.

Thanks to the many conversations I had with Jeffrey Robbins, Mayra Rivera, Eleanor Craig, and Santiago Slabodsky, what was once a vague idea in my head evolved into a concrete project. Those who read parts of the book and offered critical feedback enriched the writing process tremendously. I thank Mayra Rivera, Rafael Vizcaino, Justine Bakker, Benjamin Davis, and Eleanor Craig for reading the chapters. I'm also greatly indebted to Beatrice Marovich who read the entire manuscript and offered feedback. I was extremely lucky to share part of this process with Beatrice (also writing her own book), whose friendship and support was invaluable to the journey.

This book was written in conversation with many people whom I encountered at various academic events. I want to thank the following people and institutions for inviting me to share different parts of this work: Delia Poppa and Vincent Lloyd (Villanova University), Anya Topolski (Religion-Race-Secularism Network), Alda Balthrop-Lewis and David Newheiser (Australian Catholic University), Joshua Ramey (Haverford College), Rafael Vizcaino (DePaul University), Beatriz Cortez and Douglas Carranza (Central American Studies Symposium at CSUN), Lucie Robathan (Concordia University and McGill University), Nicolas Panotto (Otros Cruces), Shela Sheikh (International Symposium in Phenomenology), Jeffrey Robbins (Westar Institute), Roberto Sirvent (Political Theology Network), and the Kroc Institute at Notre Dame University. I also remain grateful to the following interlocutors who helped me shape my ideas through the years: Atalia Omer, David Kline, Catherine Keller, Filipe Maia, Noelle Vahanian, Karen Bray, J. Kameron Carter, and Clayton Crockett. Finally, I thank the editorial team at Duke University Press. I'm particularly grateful to the editors, Sandra Korn (who's now joined Wayne State University Press) and Courtney Berger, for shepherding the project with great care and love.

Where are your monuments, your battles, martyrs?
Where is your tribal memory? Sirs, in that gray vault.
The sea. The sea has locked them up.
The sea is History.
First, there was the heaving oil,
heavy as chaos;
then, like a light at the end of the tunnel,
the lantern of a caravel,
and that was Genesis.
Then there were packed cries,
the shit, the moaning.

—DEREK WALCOTT, "The Sea Is History"

INTRODUCTION
A Decolonial Theory of Religion

Hailed as a landmark text in twentieth-century anticolonial thinking, Aimé Césaire's *Notebook of a Return to the Native Land* (*Cahier d'un retour au pays natal*) is an epic poem that denounces the devastating historical reality of colonial violence. Written in a caustic tone, the poem calls for the old colonial order, with its "Aged poverty rotting under the sun, silently... [that points at] the awful futility of our raison d'être," to be destroyed. The call for abolishing the existing order ushers in, at the same time, the possibilities of imagining a new order. As the Saint Lucian poet Derek Walcott observes, Césaire's poignant cry is preserved as a poetic sensibility, a "sensibility of walking to a New World."[1] Discussing the differences between the Guadeloupean poet Saint John Perse and Aimé Césaire, Walcott brings attention to the shared sensibility of these two Caribbean poets. Despite their different views of the colonial Antilles, Walcott writes, "The deeper truth is that both poets perceive this New World through Mystery."[2] If religion, in its dominant form, has historically accommodated systems of colonial and racist ideology, these poets signal how there are unnamable experiences, affective registers, and imaginaries—often akin to religion—that play an instrumental role in undoing the unjust order and envisioning a new world. These registers elude words and concepts. The poets often struggle to find a name for them. With the term *religion* not being an option, they recurrently turn to the figure of the sacred. In their view, mystery or the mystical does not signal a simple retreat to the inner world (or the otherworldly) but the undoing of the self that necessarily involves the dissolution of the old world and the rebuilding of a new world, new modalities of being and relationality.

The Coloniality of the Secular probes the wide-reaching influence of religion that constitutes the historical sediments of culture and mobilizes sociopolitical institutions, norms, and practices. We witness religion's broad implication in the world not only as a system of power that sanctions violence but also as the driving motor behind counterhegemonic forces that seek to build a new order. I want to bring attention to the latter, because the various alternative figures substituting the category of religion are often mislabeled as secular iterations of the sort, distinctive from religion. The presumably secular thinkers I read in the following do not simply turn away from religion, nor do they hastily attempt to rehabilitate it as a countersecular recipe. They do, however, signal that their decolonial ideas and visions persistently attend to the efforts to reconceive the sacred, often regardless of their intention and awareness. I pay close attention to the underelaborated link between these thinkers' decolonial visions and their efforts to resignify the sacred. In doing so, I seek to incorporate the work of decolonial thinkers, who were heretofore unconsidered, into the archive of the study of religion.

Césaire's work points to the complex imbrication of religious and secular sediments that jointly form the historical layer of colonial modernity in the Americas. Theorizing colonial modernity requires thinking beyond the boundaries set by binary categories of the secular and the religious. In both *Discourse on Colonialism* and *Notebook*, Césaire draws on numerous theological metaphors to diagnose colonialism as symptomatic of political theology. The deep roots of colonialism, in Césaire's analysis, lay in the religious foundation underpinning the modern West. For Césaire, religion anchors the genesis of the modern colonial world by facilitating the dialectical sublation of the colonial other.[3] If the colonial world is predicated on a certain political theology, countercolonial discourse must attend to the problem of religion underpinning the colonial order. In this sense, Césaire's decolonial poetics carries significant religious dispositions. The second half of *Notebook* displays a sudden change of tone in which the narrative takes an overtly religious character. The progression of the poem suddenly shifts into a confession and a manifesto in which Césaire claims his negritude to be an incorrigible dissent of the Christian-colonial worldview: "I declare my crimes and that there is nothing to say in my defense. Dances. Idols. An apostate."[4] Negritude and the colonial abject signify refusal: a refusal of the Christian-colonial world and its metaphysics. However, the reconstruction of a countercolonial order does not take a secular path for Césaire. Bringing down the colonial political theology calls for a counterpolitical theology. The remainder of the poem walks the reader through Césaire's ritual of re-creating himself (negritude) in which the newly cast self eventually displaces the metaphysical edifice of the old colonial order. That is, Césaire's poetic journey of becoming, his *poiesis*, takes place through the reconstruction of the symbolic and religious foundation underlying the colonial order. Césaire's decolonial poetics, aimed at theorizing of the new being, winds up, in a way, reconceptualizing religion.

Aside from Césaire, many important thinkers invested in decoloniality have suggested that we must traverse the secularist categories that prevent us from reaching down to the deep reserve of aesthetic, spiritual, and affective sensibilities that shape the intellectual traditions of the Americas. The works of Aimé Césaire, Derek Walcott, Sylvia Wynter, Édouard Glissant, Enrique Dussel, and Gloria Anzaldúa all complicate the boundaries of the religious and the secular for theorizing decoloniality. What happens when theory operates and circulates through secularist categories that disregard the religious foundation of colonial modernity? What if the various theories of decoloniality are significantly more informed by religious imaginations than we often think?

Commenting on postcolonial theory and religion, Nelson Maldonado-Torres notes that, despite its important contribution to the study of race, modernity, and colonialism, postcolonial theory "has tended to side with modern secularism in its characterization of religion," thus privileging "Third world secular authors."[5] Theory is often associated with secular categories and worldviews. As Wendy Brown, Judith Butler, and Saba Mahmood write in their preface to *Is Critique Secular?*, the common assumption that critique is secular presupposes that "the secular worldview is altogether different from a religious one" when in reality "secularism is inherently generative and suffused with religious content."[6]

The different voices emerging in the Americas against colonial modernity trouble the binary categories of the religious and the secular. Such categories impede a fuller grasp of the breadth and depth of both decolonial thinking and religion—including the ways they might be mutually co-constitutive. Discussing the genealogy of Caribbean poetics, Sylvia Wynter comments on the sense of Antillean history the Martinican poet and philosopher Édouard Glissant grapples with. Wynter notes that, for Glissant, this history is "nothing less than the struggle against the imposed role, that of the lack of being to the first secular model of being in human history."[7] Caribbean poetics, as Wynter sees it articulated by Glissant, signals the refusal of the colonial-secular iteration of the human. She traces this tradition of decolonial poetics back to Césaire, whose *Notebook* "was the founding counterdiscourse of the Antilles."[8] Both Fanon's and Glissant's works "were the continuation of the act of poetic uprising against" the imposed mode of being in which the Black population represents ontological lack—as the mirroring other of the modern secular mode of being.[9] Wynter and other Caribbean thinkers commonly point to coloniality's collusive link with the secular. What happens when theory, the theory that articulates new being and new order against colonial modernity, is intrinsically critical of the secular? And what if the re-envisioning of the new order entails a spiritual dimension? Whereas contemporary scholarship has been challenging the "myth" of the secular and the secularist categories that reduce religion to a narrow concept, religion is still often misconceptualized by many scholars who theorize race, modernity, and colonialism.

The Coloniality of the Secular explores how decolonial theory can open ways to theorize religion in the Americas. It locates a genealogy of critical inquiries that have challenged the normative and often violent doctrine of the secular in the (post)colonial Americas. Whereas secularism's connection to colonialism has recently become a popular area of academic inquiry, the conceptual category of the secular's role in the constitution of coloniality has been rather underattended—in both the study of religion and the field of decolonial theory more broadly. The tight linkage between the secular and the concept of religion, race, and coloniality, I submit, is crucial for theorizing modern religion.

The purpose of this book is twofold. First, it places religion at the center of decolonial scholarship by reading religion as one of the constitutive elements of (de)coloniality. Many contemporary decolonial theorists acknowledge religion's place in decolonial thinking, and some elaborate on it to a certain extent. As I show in chapter 1, many of the twentieth-century thinkers who inspired contemporary decolonial scholarship (José Carlos Mariátegui, Gloria Anzaldúa, Gustavo Gutiérrez, Enrique Dussel, Aimé Césaire, Sylvia Wynter, to name a few) viewed religion as a vehicle of both colonial politics and the decolonial otherwise. However, this connection has not yet been adequately explored in contemporary conversations about decolonial theory. This is because religion's substantial role in the historical trajectory of modernity/coloniality is often obscured by secularist epistemic frameworks, often resulting in an awry understanding of religion shared by many outside the field of the study of religion. I pay particular attention to the unmarked predominance of the secularist framework in the academic study of religion that in a way reinforces the Eurocentric episteme. Undoing the intricate tie between modern religion (the secular), race, and coloniality remains an important task yet to further develop. This book is an attempt to reconceptualize religion and clarify its relation to (de)coloniality. I do not offer a prescriptive redefinition of what religion is and what it is not, but I interrogate the narrow conception of religion that misplaces it in both colonial relations of power and various iterations of decolonial thinking. Reconceptualizing religion in broader terms allows me to attune to vital spiritual and affective dynamics fueling decolonial thinking, such as the figure of the sacred that conjures decolonial imaginations in the works of the various poets named above.

Second, *The Coloniality of the Secular* seeks to demonstrate what decolonial thought offers to the study of religion, race, and coloniality in the Americas. It discusses the challenges and insights that decolonial thought provides when considering questions about method, texts, sites, and conceptual frameworks. In other words, *The Coloniality of the Secular* explores the possibility of a decolonial theory for the study of religion by insisting on the need to consider the Americas and the transatlantic historical experience as primary sites for theorizing modern religion.

The study of non-Western religions has been a vital area of inquiry in the study of religion since its founding in the nineteenth-century European academy. But rarely have these studies been crafted with theories and conceptual frameworks produced in the global south. The conceptual and theoretical tools of investigation in modern and contemporary academic discourses are usually reserved for the global north. Theory belongs to the West. In *Out of the Dark Night,* Achille Mbembe shares his observation of the current geography of reason sustained by "a Yalta-like division of the world between the global North, where theory is done, and the 'Rest,' which is the kingdom of ethnography."[10] The primary function of marginalized geographies in this imperial cartography of reason is "to produce data and to serve as the test sites of the theory mills of the North."[11] Mbembe's analysis resonates with Dipesh Chakrabarty who, more than twenty years ago, pointed out the inherently exclusive Westernness of theory. In *Provincializing Europe*, he writes, "Only 'Europe' . . . is theoretically (that is, at the level of the fundamental categories that shape historical thinking) knowable; all other histories are matters of empirical research that fleshes out a theoretical skeleton that is substantially 'Europe.'"[12] Western theory—that which is presented simply as "theory"—is understood to transcend locale (place).

When considering Western theory's co-constitution or entanglement in the formation of colonial modernity, it is necessary to reconsider its capacity to disarticulate the complex knots of coloniality. Theory, articulated in its secular-colonial iteration, presents us with various inadequacies for aptly grasping the depth and the extent of diverse forms of knowing that precisely contend the very secular-colonial foundations of European modernity. Numerous thinkers outside or at the margin of colonial modernity who articulated a different world (future) did so through conceptual frameworks that are often entirely different from the current Western framework that dominates global knowledge production. The vital geohistoric differences of these heterogeneous narratives are often subsumed by the normative conception of theory and its universalizing categories. The notion of religion and the concomitant category of the secular are among the many problems that surface in contemporary academic conversations, which often tend to apply homogeneous theories and methods to capture radically heterogeneous worldviews and forms of knowing.[13] Rather than taking the secularity of theory (hence, its coloniality) for granted, we need to reconsider theory in its relation to religion's place in the configuration of colonial modernity, including the production of its own presumably secular sciences that inform theory.

The Coloniality of the Secular probes the presumed secularity of theory. Here, I draw a distinction between secularism/religion as a lived experience, and the conceptual category of the secular/religion that informs the modern Western epistemic framework. Religion as a lived experience has persistently inspired anticolonial thinking in various communities of the (pre)colonial Americas, despite the rise and the rule of secularism. Both Indigenous and

Afro-Caribbean intellectual traditions, for instance, have staunchly resisted Western binary categories that segregate religion from the realm of the intellect that mobilizes thinking and imagination. However, the dominant Western epistemic framework that informs both colonial knowing and, to some extent, contemporary decolonial theory tends to subsume the vibrant reality of these various religious (spiritual-poetic-creative) sensibilities to secularist categories. Of course, the field of decolonial theory is vast in its scope and orientation. The term *decolonial theory*, or *decolonial thought*, carries, in this sense, a certain risk of generalization. I must acknowledge that *The Coloniality of the Secular* is particular in its scope and approach. I do not, by any means, seek to represent the vast geography of decolonial thinking in its entirety, nor do I attempt to essentialize particular discourses I engage here as the only brands of decolonial thought.

While this book broadly aims to tackle issues of race, coloniality, and the categories of religion/secular in the Americas, the key thinkers who take the central stage are mostly from the Caribbean intellectual tradition. Also important for my reading is the place of the South American tradition of philosophy and theology of liberation. Overall, the primary analytic framework I employ is based on the discourses that emerged from the conversations between Latin American thinkers and US-based Latin American theorists, often dubbed as "the decolonial turn" or the analytic framework of modernity/coloniality. In chapter 1, I offer a broader map that points to the diverse genealogies of decolonial thought stretching across the Americas beyond the particular conversations I focus on in the remainder of the book.

The modern notion of religion can be viewed as a product of the emergence of modernity/coloniality, with the secular being the mirror twin of modern religion that welds together the two ends of modernity/coloniality. As numerous important works have recently suggested, the modern categories of race and religion are mutually co-constitutive.[14] The invention of race—as a constitutive element of coloniality—cannot be articulated apart from the history of the emergence of the concept of religion as the traditional lines demarcating ontological difference between people shifted from religious language (religious difference) to the secular language of scientific reason (racial difference).[15] In other words, Europe's colonial imaginary was constituted by the newly emerging racial categories that now replaced religion's role of drawing lines of hierarchical difference between diverse populations. From the fifteenth-century Spanish Inquisition to the sixteenth-century Valladolid debates, from the missionary activities in the New World to the rise of comparative study of religion in nineteenth-century Europe, religion—and its twin mirror, the secular—has been instrumental in marking off ontological differences along the racial lines that aligned with Europe's colonial interests.[16] Put differently, the co-emergence of race and religion in modern Europe required its enterprises in the colonial frontier in which the control (production) of race and religion was crucial for colonial governance.

The works of Willie Jennings and Nelson Maldonado-Torres explore the European construction of religion in tandem with race during the colonial encounters in the Americas by examining early colonial writings and reports about Indigenous religions.[17] The basic premise for my claims here lies adjacent to their works. However, *The Coloniality of the Secular* takes a different route. Many of the materials I engage with are not religious but are "secular" sources. My concern is not limited to the historical sites and archives of knowledge inscribed in precolonial or colonial religions. Rather, my interest stretches to the constructive visions and insights offered by anticolonial thinkers who were writing from outside the parameters of religion. I suggest that these secular-political texts complicate the problematic binaries reified by the modern concept of religion. My reading demonstrates that these thinkers viewed religion as an important metaphysical axis that sustains the colonial worldview and order—despite the alleged secularity of coloniality. Many of these thinkers viewed secular modernity as an ideological platform of coloniality. I demonstrate that their critical reading of colonial modernity harbors important critiques of religion. In their view, the normative universal of secularism imposed by the West signifies, essentially, a transmutation of the hegemonic Western (Christian) worldview. Such critical reading of religion's place in colonial modernity is evident in Wynter's oeuvre, which helps us draw the lines of connection between, race, religion. and colonial modernity in the works of various twentieth-century Caribbean thinkers. Interestingly, she includes Frantz Fanon (along with Glissant) in a Cesairean genealogy of the poetic revolt—a revolt against the imposed violence of the secular. Wynter's reading might seem to conflict with the widespread perception of Fanon as a staunch secular humanist. However, as my reading shows in chapters 3 and 4, Fanon's relationship with religion is much more complex and complicated than we often realize. It is precisely the various secularist categories informing theory—which at times shape Fanon's own views—that lead us into an awry reading of religion's place in Fanon's work. My reading shows that, while Fanon seems to denounce religion and often pits religion against decoloniality, his critique of religion somehow reveals his attachment to the sacred, rather than its renouncement. Like Césaire, Fanon understood that the re-creating of the self (and of a new order) involves resignifying the symbolic and religious grammar that ratifies the existing order. In this sense, Fanon's decolonial poetics, often associated with secular humanism, winds up reconceptualizing religion.

The Coloniality of the Secular probes the co-constitutive linkage between modernity/coloniality/secularity. To unpack modernity/coloniality/secularity, I navigate a diverse range of academic discourses that span across disciplines. These conversations are not necessarily all connected or adjacent to each other. Bringing these different discourses together, however, allows me to zoom in to the important point of connection that cuts across the compound modernity/coloniality/secularity.

Decolonial theorists call for careful reconsideration of the Eurocentric nature of universalizing epistemic frameworks informing knowledge and knowledge production.[18] Various scholars working from within this tradition take Aníbal Quijano's notion of coloniality of power as the departing point of their analyses. The notion of coloniality highlights the polychronic nature of power operative in colonialism. Coloniality manifests beyond the historical institution of colonialism. Colonialism is tied to the specific historical event and period; coloniality outlasts decolonization.

The decolonial turn has in many ways invigorated the critical study of religion not only by carrying on the critical projects advanced by postcolonial studies but also by revisiting and refining many of the key theses that postcolonial studies has advanced. Acknowledging postcolonial theory's important contributions, Latin American—and US-based decolonial theorists point out some key differences that distinguish the two. First, whereas postcolonial theory's focus tends to be on nineteenth- and twentieth-century European colonialism in Asia and Africa, decolonial theory uses the fifteenth-century colonial encounter in the Americas as the primary point of reference. The former renders colonialism a derivative of modernity while the latter views colonialism (or, rather, coloniality) as constitutive of modernity. Second, decolonial theorists point out postcolonial theory's penchant for European theory. Countercolonial thinking and discourse have existed all along since the first colonial encounter. When considering the importance of knowledge and knowledge production in the formation and the circulation of coloniality, grounding countercolonial discourse in European theoretical framework presents visible limitations.[19]

Charting the connection between religion and decoloniality is important not only for the study of religion but also for those who investigate coloniality across interdisciplinary boundaries. That religion's place is often omitted or reduced in these academic conversations of decolonial theory indicates that the broad extent of religion's role—however unmarked and understated it may be—in the formation of the colonial regime of power and knowledge has been underattended. As Sylvester Johnson comments in *African American Religions, 1500–2000*, the lack of interest that various theories of modernity show in religion indicates a failure to understand religion's constitutive role in the formation of the mechanism of power.[20] Briefly speaking, the failure to closely probe the link between religion and decoloniality leaves three large blind spots in the ongoing conversations about power and coloniality in the Americas.

First, many writings of "secular" decolonial thinkers often hint at nuanced readings of religion beyond the critique of prevalent colonial religions, as I show through the book in conversation with various Caribbean thinkers (Aimé Césaire, Frantz Fanon, Sylvia Wynter, Édouard Glissant). The generative political visions that these thinkers offer are often intertwined with their attempt to reconfigure religion, or the sacred. In other words, there are diverse forms of religion-making that take place in and through various alternative forms of decolonial critique and imagination. These different forms of decolonial thinking and imagination invite us to reconceptualize the rather narrow notion of religion (as well as the concept of the secular) that pervades many academic conversations.

Second, this aforementioned failure underestimates the role of religion (Christianity, to be more specific) that underpins the secular colonial order. Numerous scholars have already pointed out the inextricable connection between colonialism and secularism by exposing the mechanism of colonial governance and enterprises informed by religious (Christian) worldviews and agendas.[21] But the presence of religion in the colonial Americas extends far beyond the well-known history of Christianity's missionary activities. Since the first colonial encounter, religion has served as the metaphysical backbone of coloniality, not just as an imposition of political structures and cultural norms, but as a cosmological rupture.[22]

Third, a long tradition of anticolonial resistance and critique emerging from religious communities across the Americas has been overlooked.

When these movements are studied, the full depths of their significance are not entirely grasped without properly unpacking the complexities inscribed in (anti)colonial religions. More important, the complex relation between religion and (coloniality of) power raises a more fundamental question regarding the emergence of modern religion. Underlying the historical phenomenon of the interaction between religion and coloniality in the Americas is perhaps the problem of the category of religion, which was conceived in tandem with the emergence (invention) of race in the global colonial matrix of power.[23]

The complex relationship between the categories of religion, the secular, and the problem of power has been articulated by many scholars in the field of the study of religion. Charles Long has articulated lucidly the intricate connection between the construction of religion as a category and the reality of conquered and marginalized people. The signification (invention) of the former is linked with the signification of the latter as the process involves the reification of certain oppositional norms (e.g., rationality versus irrationality) as defining characteristics of each group that is the West and its "Other."[24] In his genealogical study of the modern category of religion, Talal Asad situates the modern category of religion in the historical trajectory of the emergence of Western liberal secularism by tracing the process of privatization of religion.[25] The reification of the category of religion is predicated on its compatibility with the universalizing norm of secular rationality. Many argue, after Asad, that the construction and essentialization of the category of religion (as opposed to the secular) is itself a problematic endeavor that reinforces the colonial regime of knowledge.[26] More specifically, the emergence of the modern category of religion was directly informed by the colonial encounter in which the notion of religion played a key role in the anthropological enterprises that served Europe's colonial interests.[27]

Recent debates about secularism question the rigid binary of the religious and the secular by pointing toward the mutual imbrication between modernity and secularism. These conversations interrogate the modern concept and category of religion, probing the enduring influence of religion in the formation of Western modernity. These critical voices complicate the classical secularist discourse that traces its roots back to Karl Marx and Max Weber's claim of the disenchantment of modernity.[28] In his influential work *A Secular Age*, Charles Taylor charges the mainstream secularist discourse for its reductive tendency. The secular age, Taylor argues, does not indicate the decline or emptying of religion from the public space. Rather, it points to the change in the condition of belief: the transition from a society where belief is unchallenged to one in which it is viewed as one option among others. The traditional secularization thesis subscribes to the binary that positions religion as the opposing concept of Enlightenment rationality and progress while reinscribing a privatized notion of religion. Taylor and his interlocutors point out that the ongoing presence of religion, regardless of its visibility, troubles the simplistic association of modernization with secularism. For some, critical intervention in the (post)secular debate rests on unsettling its simplistic narrative, that is, the actual reality of the transition or prominence of one (either religion or the secular) over the other (Jürgen Habermas, Charles Taylor); others attend to the ideological mechanism of the secular that accommodates certain universalizing normative claims (José Casanova, Talal Asad, William Connolly). As William Connolly summarizes, the problem of secularism "is not merely the division between public and private realms that allows religious diversity to flourish in the latter. It can itself be a carrier of harsh exclusions. And it secretes a new definition of 'religion' that conceals some of its most problematic practices from itself."[29] Many contemporary critics of secularism point out that, historically, secularism has been more often about policing religious difference than fomenting it.[30] They argue that advocates of secularism overlook the strong Christian roots of the normative categories it has reinforced. Historically, secularism often regulated religious difference with its normative categories, a process that played a formative role in Europe's colonial enterprises. Some of its key critics (such as Taylor and Habermas), however, treat secularism largely as an inner-European phenomenon, thus disregarding the inseparable link between secularism and colonialism.

The broad extent of secularism's significance cannot be grasped without considering its role in the constitution of the modern colonial world. Many scholars insist that a critical study of secularism must attend to the structure of power configuration and exchange in (neo)colonial governance. These power exchanges both inform the construction of the secular and obscure the normativization of Western liberalism at the same time. Their works demonstrate how the secular has been employed as a device to police and suppress colonial difference, whereas Europe's understanding of secularism has been substantially informed by the colonial encounter and governance. Put differently, the secular has been serving as the ideological banner of modern Western universalism by preserving the Western/Christian hegemony while depoliticizing (the notion of) religion.[31]

The modernity/secularity constellation is further complicated when we extend the analytic lens from secularism to the conceptual category (and imaginary) of the secular. The discourse of political theology that emerged alongside the critical study of secularism probes the genealogical trajectory of the secular, a category that is distinctive from secularism and secularization. Overall, the resurgence of political theology in recent academic conversations tends to take on a particular conception or stream of political theology, one that developed from the work of the early twentieth-century German jurist Carl Schmitt. Schmitt placed the concept of sovereignty at the heart of the modern political system and political life, a concept that he attributes to Western theological roots. Political theology, for Schmitt, probes the ways in which old theological concepts condition secular political ideas and systems.[32]

The most relevant and pressing insight that political theology brings to the decolonial study of religion is its focused attention on the tight connection between violence and sovereignty. Contemporary debates in political theology are broadly centered around the critique of the political system that legitimizes the violence sanctioned by the said system. To draw a typological contrast, critical study of secularism dislocates the dominant narrative of secular modernity as the guarantor of religious difference (freedom) by pointing out that secularism regulates difference rather than fomenting it and that it regulates violence rather than eliminating it. Political theology takes a step further and argues that the secular *enacts* violence (a violence rooted in the sacred), that violence is constitutive of the political. It insists on the inseparable nexus of theology/modernity. Despite its important contribution to the critical examination of secular modernity, however, political theology (at least in accounts advanced by continental philosophy and radical theology) has rarely extended its analysis toward historicizing of secular modernity outside of the Western (Euro-American) framework. These dominant streams (largely Schmittian) of political theology have overlooked the colonial-modern nexus (hence, the analytics of race) in the past. As a result, their analyses of violence often leave out the abjects of political life, those whose existences do not register in the index of Western political life. Whereas political theology's inquiry offers an incisive understanding of the intricate tie between modernity and the secular (modernity/secularity), it has overlooked the nexus of modernity/coloniality. Likewise, the important analytics of modernity/coloniality advanced by decolonial theorists largely overlook the nexus of modernity/secularity as many take the presumable secularity of modernity for granted. I argue that modernity, coloniality, and secularity (the secular) must be examined in relation to each other.

I do not situate my approach in the early twentieth-century European genealogy that traces its origin back to Carl Schmitt and his interlocutors such as Karl Lowith and Hans Blumenberg. Nor do I take on the conversations about political theology initiated by contemporary continental philosophers such as Jacques Derrida, Giorgio Agamben, or Slavoj Žižek. I don't want to offer yet another genealogical study of the secular, a genealogy that often traces its origin to the aforementioned European thinkers. Rather, *The Coloniality of the Secular* follows the various critical interventions that emerged in the Americas. These thinkers do not offer a coherent intervention on the problem of political theology. In this sense, the focus of *The Coloniality of the Secular* does not center narrowly on the thematics of political theology. Rather, it proposes a broader theory and method for the study of religion, a theory of religion that is situated in decolonial thinking and method. Therefore, my intention is not to borrow the insights from decolonial thinkers to offer a better answer to the ongoing conversations in political theology and vice versa. Rather, I borrow from political theology the insights born out of its focused articulation of the conceptual problem of the secular, a problem that carries critical implications for a decolonial study of religion. In other words, this book is *not* a book about political theology in that it does not engage primarily with the writings of political theology, Schmittian or otherwise. Yet this book *is* about political theology to the extent that it attends to the large problem of the theology (a secular theology of coloniality and whiteness) that organizes the modern-colonial worldview and mobilizes political concepts. In doing this, I follow the grammar of political theology and unfalteringly call the secular a *theology*—as must be evident from my previous sentence. The secular is as theological as any confessional Christian theology in that it is equally as normative, doctrinal, sectarian, exclusionary (and simultaneously universalizing), and redemptionist (messianic). Secularism is the name of the concrete juridico-political manifestation and political theology that the secular enacts. Beyond Schmitt and the conversations that grew out of his work, the politico-theological problem, in the broad sense that I articulate, largely looms in colonial modernity, and my argument is that numerous anticolonial thinkers articulate this problem in different forms—and often not in the name of political theology as I demonstrate with Frantz Fanon, for instance.

A slightly different yet useful way to situate this book in the ongoing conversations about the modern concept of religion and the secular would be to draw on the typology that Markus Dressler and Arvind-Pal Mandair offer in their introduction to *Secularism and Religion-Making*. The editors classify contemporary postsecular scholarship in three different strands: (1) social philosophers who examine liberal secularism (Taylor and Habermas); (2) philosophical and theological critique of ontotheology (political theology); and (3) a historical approach (and discourse analysis), associated with Asad, that focuses on genealogies of power. Discussing the first two groups that draw on the philosophical method, Dressler and Mandair point out that these two groups share a common assumption, that is, religion as a cultural universal.[33] The important debates these two groups advance are at times partly eclipsed by their adoption of universalizing categories of religion that confine religion to the realm of belief and thought. More important, the editors of *Secularism and Religion-Making* raise critical questions regarding the historical formation of secular modernity, a question I echo and also use as the departing point of this book. My observation about the crucial place of coloniality in the critical study of secular modernity finds a significant resonance in Dressler and Mandair's articulation of secular modernity as a comparative imaginary of the modern West vis-à-vis its colonial other.[34] The third group in their typology includes scholars who historicize the central place of colonialism in the formation of secular modernity. These scholars have contributed to a growing stream of conversations that complicate various normative assumptions about the category of religion. Central to their analysis is the problem of power. The study of religion cannot be done without a critical analysis of power from which it emerges. Religion in this sense is, at least to a certain extent, a product of production and regulation. These scholars provide crucial insights about the intricate relationship between power, colonialism, and the study of modern religion.[35] *The Coloniality of the Secular* builds on many of the important theoretical contributions these scholars of religion and history have made (that is, those who belong in the third group). At the same time, many of these works point toward eighteenth- and nineteenth-century colonialism as the primary reference for understanding the connection between colonialism and the study of religion. Although the modern discipline of the academic study of religion was deeply informed by the more recent imperialist enterprises of Europe, there is a much older and more important point of reference for understanding the symbiotic relation between the simultaneous invention of the colonial other and the modern imaginary of the West: the colonial encounter of 1492.

The Coloniality of the Secular is situated between the two different conversations I discussed above, that is, scholars of religion who historicize modernity and colonialism, and those who theorize diverse iterations of decoloniality in the Americas. These two important streams share significant differences as well as similarities. Aside from the different historical reference between the two, one probes colonial modernity from the Americas (decolonial theorists) whereas the other one does so primarily with a focus on Asia and Africa (scholars of religion and colonialism). Both groups theorize alternative modernities beyond the narrow confines of Europe, and they both view the axis of knowledge and power as central to their analysis. Decolonial theory offers scholars of religion and colonialism a broader framework for thinking about the formation of secular modernity as a Western imaginary whereas the latter helps the former to think more critically (and constructively) about the place of religion (and the secular) in the making of not only colonial modernity but also alternative modernities.

Decolonial theory helps to locate the place of religion in the constitution of modernity/coloniality. It helps clarify the historical continuity that cuts through the various events constituting the making of the Western imaginary: the continuity of the theological ethos that has continuously shaped its making since the early Roman Christendom to the present secular order of neoliberal globalization.

In his article "Secularism," Gil Anidjar joins the much-contested debate about Edward Said's secularism by adding that Said must have forgotten the important lesson his book *Orientalism* has taught us: "that Orientalism *is* secularism."[36] Considering that, for Said, orientalism operates across boundaries and disciplines, keeping a distance or indifference to religion is "effectively abandoning religion to scholars of religion ... leaving them perhaps in the pre- or ahistorical, indeed 'sacred' sphere."[37] Consequently, what is overlooked is not only the role of religion, but also the complex intellectual genealogies that inform and inspire diverse forms of anticolonial ideas and movements. In this sense, engaging with secular texts and thinkers deserves as much attention as the study of religious texts and practices of religious communities in the Americas. The fact that the study of Latin American and Caribbean Black and Indigenous religions is primarily dominated by the study of local communities' "practices" while there is scarce interest in their intellectual production (theory) raises questions about the problem of knowledge and knowledge production, as well as the dominant category of religion largely informing the field—even when many are already highly critical of such categories. Religion and secularism have already been widely scrutinized by contemporary scholarship. Such critiques have yet to extend to other adjacent theoretical-methodological frameworks that determine the process of identifying artifacts, texts, theories, thinkers, and sites for the study of religion. When considering the mutual imbrication of religious/aesthetic/cultural sensibilities and political visions in the Americas, it is highly imperative that we reconsider these secular texts as critical sources for theorizing religion. Failure to do so results in the continuous loss of nuanced critiques and readings of religion in those texts as well as the full implication of their political vision. The secular, as the twin mirror of religion, is a key fabric constitutive of modernity/coloniality. Throughout the book, I interrogate the problematic disciplinary practices and theoretical assumptions that reinforce colonial-secularist forms of knowing (and knowledge production), which reproduce the narrow category and concept of religion. Rethinking the dominant theoretical tendency and secularist frameworks in the field is a crucial element of the decolonial theory of religion that I propose.

While I take a comprehensive approach and make certain categorical generalizations, *The Coloniality of the Secular* does not pretend to be all-comprehensive. The analyses that follow engage thinkers and texts rather than movements. Following Walter Mignolo's dictum "I am where I think," I acknowledge my own site of enunciation and therefore recognize the particularity and limitations of my own approach.[38] My reading and intervention focus particularly on the possible connections between the radical intellectual movements and Christian traditions in the Americas, while my interlocutors are mostly theorists with literary and philosophical inclinations who have rarely made direct interventions in the study of religion and religious thoughts. In this sense, the connections and implications I explore here offer a mere glance at the diverse emerging conversations that are yet to take form.

The central questions that drive my inquiry go beyond the critique of religion and its formative role in the constitution of colonial modernity in the Americas. Equally important to me is the task of locating and theorizing various sites of the enunciation of a decolonial otherwise. World-making struggles that emerged against the tyranny of colonial modernity offer crucial resources for rethinking the conversations about modern religion, race, and coloniality. The chapters that follow show my attempt to elaborate on the link between these generative visions of decoloniality and the possible reconception of the sacred that they signal.

Overall, part 1 presents theoretical analyses that locate and amplify the problem of the religious/secular underpinnings of colonial modernity. The introduction and chapter 1 provide preliminary theoretical backgrounds in which I situate my argument. Chapter 1 builds on the primary points I elaborate in the introduction. I further discuss key themes, topics, and questions by locating the various decolonial interventions in religion that often go underrecognized and underexplored due to their presumably secular orientation. I map out both the different sites of enunciation of colonial secularity and the sites of anticolonial resistance by reviewing a broad range of literature that extends across the twentieth-century Americas. These diverse voices point to different locations (North America, South America, Caribbean) and interrogate different issues (gender, class, indigeneity, Blackness). The brief review of an ever-expanding cartography of struggle reveals the complex topography of power in which religion is entangled. It also hints at various points of possibility for exploring and further theorizing the nexus of modernity/coloniality/secularity.

Chapter 2 captures the intellectual history of twentieth-century Latin America with a focus on two important adjacent movements: philosophy of liberation, and liberation theology. Despite their partly shared root and trajectory, these movements occupy contrasting positions in contemporary decolonial scholarship. The former (philosophy of liberation) serves as a crucial resource for contemporary decolonial thought whereas the latter (liberation theology) is largely left out of the conversation on decoloniality. While acknowledging the historical significance of LALT (Latin American liberation theology) as an authentic Latin American intellectual intervention, decolonial theorists have seldom engaged with LALT. I argue that the omission of LALT is likely due to the dominant secularist framework operative in decolonial theory. I locate the important common historical trajectories that were shared by both LALT and decolonial theory as seen in the works of key Latin American philosophers such as José Carlos Mariátegui and Enrique Dussel, both of whom viewed religion as a powerful tool for decolonial critique and resistance. The first part of the chapter illustrates the intellectual landscape in which philosophy of liberation emerged in mid- to late twentieth-century Latin American intellectual circles. It traces the advancement of philosophy of liberation as an important form of decolonial thinking. It also re-illuminates the ways in which religion informed some of its key figures. I pay particular attention to their critique of secularism as a project of colonial modernity. The second half of the chapter reads liberation theology through the lens of (de)coloniality by examining its limits and possibilities. Liberation theology breaks away from the traditional Western theological method by situating knowledge in geopolitics and by breaking down the binary of knowledge and praxis. Liberation theology also presents a strong critique of imperialist capitalism and the problem of class, an area that remains rather underattended in decolonial scholarship. Taken together, the chapter sheds light on the seeds of decolonial thinking and its inseparable connection to religion that existed all along in modern Latin American intellectual traditions.

Part 2 consists of three chapters that explore constructive possibilities for rethinking the existing terms and theoretical frameworks used for theorizing religion in conversation with Caribbean decolonial poetics. Chapter 3 probes the complex place of the secular in colonial epistemology in conversation with Frantz Fanon. It brings to light Fanon's complicated relation with religion. Against the prevailing narrative that emphasizes Fanon's antagonism toward religion, I argue that Fanon does not simply dismiss or turn away from religion in search of a secular decolonial future. I demonstrate that Fanon's phenomenology of the political hints at the significant place of religion in Fanon's critique of colonial modernity. I read his critique of colonial modernity as a critique of the political theology of coloniality (whiteness). Chapter 4 extends my close reading of Fanon's phenomenology to racial embodiment. In addition to offering an acute observation of the way Black bodies are registered in space (and time), his phenomenological reflection also allows us to think about the possibility of life, revolt, and world-making in the face of immeasurable violence. I explore how Fanon's struggle to reconfigure his body (Blackness) winds up resignifying religion. Fanon employs the French philosopher Maurice Merleau-Ponty's work on phenomenology as he reflects on the ways his own body is co-constituted by the world and others who inhabit it. I argue that his phenomenological reflection on race (Blackness) offers the possibility of rethinking the sacred. The secular humanist's staunch rejection of Western religion and metaphysics unfolds, paradoxically, alongside the unnamed figure or moment that evokes a certain sense of the sacred, a sacred presented as antithesis to the sacred. I suggest that Fanon's struggle to decolonize and restore his humanity can be read as an attempt to recode, that is, decolonize, the sacred.

The stream of decolonial thought that chapter 5 explores is informed by philosophical and poetic reflections on the transatlantic experience of displacement, namely, the Middle Passage and (post)plantation life. The chapter deepens discussions about the problem of secularist methods and disciplinary practices that often segregate religion in decolonial thinking and poetics. The chapter focuses on Édouard Glissant, one of the key thinkers who shaped the Caribbean poeticist tradition. With his constructive philosophical vision, Glissant seeks to rethink being in relation to place(lessness). Decolonizing being and place requires rethinking them completely anew, as creative movements of encounter, exchange, and becoming. While Glissant rarely evokes religion explicitly, the notion of the sacred occupies a significant place in his philosophical vision. The poetics of creolization, central to Glissant's thoughts, indicates a constant morphing, becoming, and re-creating of the sacred. In conversation with his Caribbean interlocutors such as Aimé Césaire, Derek Walcott, and Sylvia Wynter, I seek to identify the central place of the sacred in Glissant's generative visions.

Theory's allusive secularity entices us into embracing certain epistemic norms that dislocate various intellectual genealogies that have for a long time sought to articulate complex and heterogeneous worldviews. Reflecting on the confining effects the secularist presumption has on feminist epistemic capacity, M. Jacqui Alexander writes, "Experience is a category of grand epistemic importance in feminism but we have understood it primarily as secularized as if it were absent spirit and thus antithetical to the sacred."[39] The modern notion of religion (and the subsequent bias that pits religion against decoloniality) reifies binary categories that make us lose sight of the equally ideological nature of the secular while precluding a deeper understanding of the possibilities (of a different world) that these murky (quasi)religious figures may signal. Meanwhile, a related yet slightly different figure, namely, the sacred, surfaces in the writings of different anticolonial intellectual traditions of the Americas. The notion of the sacred figures prominently in the Caribbean intellectual tradition. Where religion signifies an imposed category perhaps inadequate to capture the complex ambiguity of religion in the archipelago, the sacred is often employed as a vessel that holds the space for articulating the creative capacity and imagination for creating new worlds.

The figure of the sacred is one that is not without its own complicated history and problems in the study of religion and colonialism. Whereas nineteenth- and early twentieth-century anthropologists viewed the sacred as an archaic code that holds together various "exotic behaviors" of "primitive" communities, phenomenologists of religion uplifted it as a postmetaphysical signifier that attests to the universality of religion (as an inner phenomenon that is belief), thus reinforcing the Christian-centric definition of religion. Despite these complicated histories, I want to pay attention to the murky figure of the sacred that surfaces in various works of Caribbean thinkers. In my observation, this is not a figure that signals an overtly mystic (spiritual) dimension transcending history. The sacred here functions as an alternative figure to religion where the notion of religion engraves strong boundaries that miscategorize the complex modalities of thinking and being in the archipelago. I must clarify, however, that I am not suggesting the sacred as an alternative or a competing figure in relation to the concept of religion. Rather, the murky figure of the sacred allows us to glimpse myriad unrealized possibilities that the conventional notion of religion would have otherwise signified. That many of these thinkers have buried the figure of religion does not mean that the dreams, visions, practices, and affective registers associated with it have been interred as well. The absence of (the figure of) religion is still haunted by religious imaginations of the sort. In this sense, the sacred functions as a kind of boundary object that complicates and unhinges the link between decolonial poetics and decolonial politics, as well as the link between decolonial politics and religion. These various tropes of the sacred form, this way, a certain vernacular resource for the study of religion.

Working with vernacular sources signals a form of thinking and theorizing from the vernacular space in which the object (religion/sacred) and its theorization are profoundly woven into the vast mundane texture of social life.[40] It is at the burial site of religion that we catch sight of the overlooked figure of the sacred that continuously evokes the ghosts that never cease to make demands: the unrealized dreams, the unfulfilled visions, the unthinkable and the unimaginable, and ultimately, unknowable forms of world-making.[41] Where lives and dreams are buried alive, the ocean as an "open water grave" represents not only the symbol of a painful memory, but also the horizon from which unimaginable and unknowable forms of worlds are yet to emerge. Poetics and the figure of the sacred at its center might be an activating force that mobilizes these unspoken words, unrealized dreams, and unfulfilled hopes and despairs that have been muted by the secular modern. In this sense, Caribbean decolonial poetics might hint at a "counter-ritual" that disarticulates the colonial "unritual." As Valérie

Loichot has recently articulated in the context of Caribbean arts and literature, the colonial unritual deprives the sacred. It deprives mourning the open water grave.[42] Poetics grapples with the question of how to attend to the drowned and muted voices that do not cease to make claims on the present. But it also seeks to reckon with the equally difficult question of new beginnings and how to begin again after trauma. Life and future are not determined by endless narratives of pain and grief. Caribbean decolonial poetics is born in this middle, the middle of the ocean: between the abyssal depth of the ocean in which dreams are drowned and the shoreline on which life begins again. Where foundation has been evacuated, the thin and murky figure of the sacred that emerges in Caribbean decolonial poetics gestures at a new ground, a groundless ground on which unthinkable and unknowable forms of worlds are to be made.

PART I

Genealogies

1

MODERNITY/COLONIALITY/SECULARITY
The Cartography of Struggle

This chapter builds on the central arguments I laid out in the introduction, in which I advanced the theoretical discussions and the methodological implications for a decolonial theory of religion that investigates the nexus of modernity/coloniality/secularity. This chapter seeks to locate the specific sites for theorizing the nexus of modernity/coloniality/secularity in the Americas. Here I map out the different sites of enactment of the colonial secular, which are the various sites of struggle and contestation that were crucial in the formation of the colonial Americas. More importantly, I pay close attention to the sites from which generative anticolonial visions and struggles have emerged. The many thinkers and discourses I discuss here offer a mere glimpse of the numerous interventions and critiques that potentially point toward crucial resources for theorizing religion (and race) in the Americas. These resources not only shed light on the complex entanglement of modernity/coloniality with the secular but also re-illuminate the complex religious-cultural layers of generative anticolonial thinking that have continuously inspired a decolonial otherwise.

In what follows, I offer a brief overview of the wide-ranging literature that maps out the cartography of struggle stretching across the Americas. Some of these sites have already begun to shape conversations about religion and (de)coloniality, although a deeper examination of these connections is yet to be realized. I show how these diverse interventions to disarticulate coloniality commonly point at the secular as the ideological edifice that underpins coloniality. The wide breadth of discussed materials in this chapter does not signal any pretense of offering an all-comprehensive narrative of religion and (de)coloniality. Rather, the broad scope of my genealogies indicates the relevance and the gravity of the inquiry that I am pursuing. It demonstrates the persisting yet nuanced presence of religion in the diverse forms of anticolonial thinking and critique. While this brief review gives only a limited glimpse of an extensive archive of religion and (de)coloniality in the Americas, it also points toward numerous pathways and possibilities that the study of religion, race, and (de)coloniality may take. These accounts raise important questions that challenge dominant theoretical and methodological frameworks shaping the study of modern religion, which often tend to disarticulate modern religion from the constellation of race/coloniality/secularism.

The jointly marked categories of religion, race, and the secular often operate in conjunction with the normativity of whiteness.[1] The intellectual cartography that these categories construct presents us with a map of normative ideas that derives from the West, a map in which countless ideas and practices that exist outside its normative white-secular (that is, Christian) parameter remain illegible. As Jonathan Kahn and Vincent Lloyd observe, the normative secularist framework manages race and religion. The secularist framework that presumably transcends race and religion domesticates the often-disruptive and radical messages of Black religion that speak directly to issues related to race and religion.[2] What I attempt to do in this chapter is to identify and illuminate the various intellectual endeavors that remain illegible within the cartography of the current epistemic order. Many of the figures I discuss here do not make an explicit intervention in religion. However, their powerful critique of the present order recurrently hints at certain aesthetic, spiritual, and philosophical registers that religion often signals. In this sense, their decolonial critique often implicates the reconfiguration of religion (or the sacred), which is usually obscured by the secularist theoretical grammar. As Aaron Kamugisha notes in regards to Caribbean intellectual history, "Caribbean theorists' profoundly multidisciplinary and metatheoretical approach to expressing ideas also belies the scholarly distinctions of the Western academy, producing works that defy any easy categorization and require an intellectual inventiveness for a true appreciation of its value."[3] A close and careful look at the nuanced connection between religion and power may re-illuminate the "constellation of ideas, practices, and relationships currently illegible but potent and potentially transformative."[4] In this sense, these thinkers and texts constitute the body of a vernacular archive for the study of religion.

The following survey points at various locations of anticolonial critique and resistance that uncovers the constellation of race, religion, and the secular. Some of the questions that guide my inquiry are as follows: What are the specific social and geohistoric locations that were pivotal for both the enactment of coloniality and the rise of decolonial resistance? What are the issues and questions specific to these locations that interrogate the coloniality of the secular and the link between race and religion? What are the imaginaries specific to these locations that give rise to decolonial visions capable of disarticulating the nexus of modernity/coloniality/secularity? In what ways do their endeavors to articulate decoloniality reconceptualize religion? Reversely, how does the resignified religion (or the sacred) reconceptualize decoloniality? Who are some of the thinkers who have pursued the above-mentioned questions?

The nuanced critique of religion that these figures offer troubles the notion of religion as their critique signals neither a simple rejection of religion nor a rehabilitation. What we witness is persisting nuanced efforts to reconfigure the sacred at the center of their decolonial visions. In other words, these secular critics of colonialism insist that to reconceive being and thinking radically anew involves the resignification of the sacred. In their critique and rejection of colonial modernity, these thinkers suggest the possible remaking of religion. Reversely, their critique of religion enriches our understanding of the broader critique of colonial modernity they point at. The overall scarcity of attention to the link between the generative visions of decolonial thinking and the sacred (whichever form they may be) is precisely symptomatic of the coloniality of knowledge.

*Theorizing Coloniality: Western Modernity
and the Religious Other*

The long history of anticolonial critique and resistance in Latin America and the Caribbean dates back to the first colonial encounter, initiated by Bartolomé de las Casas and taken over by Inca Garcilaso de la Vega, Guamán Poma de Ayala, Francisco Bilbao, José Carlos Mariátegui, Aimé Césaire, José Martí, Frantz Fanon, Sylvia Wynter, and Gloria Anzaldúa, among many others. The genealogy of decolonial thought is extensive and long. Aside from key thinkers, there are countless movements that have inspired and nourished the streams of decolonial thought such as the Tupac Amaru rebellion, the Haitian Revolution, the Cuban Revolution, the fugitives of North America and maroons of the Caribbean, the Muslim slave revolt in Brazil (Revolta dos Malês), and the Zapatistas. Examples are numerous. One could also add twentieth-century dependency theory and liberation theology to the list. It is, however, in the recent works of the Argentinean-Mexican philosopher Enrique Dussel and the Peruvian sociologist Aníbal Quijano that a clearer notion of decolonial thinking emerges in ways that parallel and complement postcolonial studies. The brief genealogy I lay out here highlights some of the early key conversations that were instrumental for contemporary discourse of decolonial theory with a particular focus on the intersection between modernity/coloniality, religion, and the secular.

The notion of *la colonialidad del poder* (the coloniality of power) advanced by Quijano offers a compelling conceptual tool for articulating the colonial relations of power that exceeds the historical event of colonization.[5] Central to Quijano's analysis is the colonial use or invention of race as a category of social classification with the end of maintaining domination through the control of labor. Race functions as the main tool to demarcate colonial difference; in other words, colonial difference is enforced by the racist distribution of social identities. After social identities are codified by racial hierarchy, labor is distributed accordingly, thus consolidating the mechanism of exploitation of labor and resources, which is crucial for the management of colonial capitalism.[6] Colonial power works not only through social relations that determine economic production, but also, more fundamentally, through knowledge. Commenting on the coloniality of knowledge, Walter Mignolo writes that "knowledge has a privileged position: it occupies the level of the enunciated, where the content of the conversation is established, and it occupies the level of enunciation, which regulates the terms of the conversation."[7]

The crucial place of knowledge was already emphasized by Dussel, whose philosophy of liberation has insisted on the critique of Eurocentric epistemology since the early 1970s. Influenced by Emmanuel Levinas's critique of totalitarian metaphysics, Dussel deconstructs modernity as a totalitarian myth. He provincializes modernity by labeling it "European," while situating the Americas in the place of alterity. Against the myth of European modernity that views itself as the sole agent of scientific rationality, Dussel, in conversation with Immanuel Wallerstein, situates modernity within the global matrix of a world-system.[8] Modernity, Dussel argues, was born in 1492 with the birth of the Americas as the other of Europe without whose forced labor and resources Europe's global hegemony would not have been possible. Wallerstein's world-system theory helps us to clarify the intimate connection between the emergence of a modern world-system and Europe's colonial expansion. The emergence of the core (Europe and its modernity), as Wallerstein calls it, is heavily dependent on the existence of the periphery (Europe's colony).[9]

If Levinas locates the exteriority of totalitarian metaphysics in the historical experience of his own Jewishness as the internal otherness of Europe, Dussel locates it in the Americas, the external otherness of Europe. Exteriority originates from a place other than European modernity. Despite exclusion and denial, it has existed and persisted all along (and outside) modernity. Exteriority signals that which cannot be contained by the sweeping force of totalitarian metaphysics.[10] It signals an otherwise. In this sense, as Catherine Walsh writes, Abya Yala (an Indigenous name for the Americas) testifies to the long history of decolonial struggles "that give possibility and concretion to a decolonial otherwise."[11]

A systematic theorization of (de)coloniality in its relation to modernity takes place in the work of Mignolo, who refines the ideas advanced by Quijano and Dussel. Mignolo follows Dussel's lead in pointing out the limits of Wallerstein's theory for understanding the inception of European modernity. Wallerstein's work helps us understand the rise of Western hegemony in conjunction with (as a consequence of) colonial expansion and accumulation. Wallerstein made visible the operating platform of Western capitalism as a modern world system emerging through the Atlantic commercial circuit. However, Wallerstein views modernity as derivative of the Enlightenment, particularly the French Revolution.[12] Wallerstein views the sixteenth century as the inception of the capitalist world economy but he argues that it operated for three centuries (up until the French Revolution) "without any established geo-culture." He thus fails to catch the "constitutive character of the Americas for the imaginary of the modern/colonial world."[13] Decolonial theorists view modernity and coloniality as mutually co-constitutive. As Mignolo writes, "If modernity is a narrative (or, better still, a set of narratives), coloniality is what the narratives hide or disguise, because it cannot be said explicitly."[14]

Implicit in Mignolo's analysis is the observation that religion laid down the metaphysical foundation of the modern/colonial imaginary. The Ibero-Imperial vision of what Dussel calls the first modernity (1492)—built on the philosophico-theological worldview—faded away with the rise of orientalism during the second modernity (eighteenth century), but it did not vanish. The theological worldview that underlies the emerging modern/colonial vision of Renaissance Europe can be summed up in the ethical question that was central to the Valladolid debates: the rights of the people. The question carries a double meaning, as it refers to the rights of Europeans on foreign land as well as the rights of the natives in the New World. Mignolo rightly observes the ironic juxtaposition between the sixteenth-century debates on the rights of people and the 1789 declaration of the "Rights of the Man and of the Citizen," which came out of the French Revolution. The sixteenth-century colonial imaginary behind the question of rights of people is obliterated in the eighteenth-century modern imaginary.[15]

Such forgetfulness indicates the erasure of colonial difference. In other words, colonial difference is sublated by the universalizing claims of Western modernity. Its central philosophical principle of rationality finds a potent platform of articulation in the secularist grammar. The secular serves as an efficient denominator of both epistemic and political frameworks for nesting a value-neutral sense of objectivity. It purportedly divorces reason from the old theological worldviews with the end of accommodating the ever-progressing scientific rationality and the universal value of egalitarianism it advocates.

However, historically, secularism has seldom been—if ever—a space from which religion was successfully disarticulated. Rather, it has often served as the medium through which the normative Western worldview—a worldview rooted in its traditional religious values—was enacted through scientific languages of objective rationality. Mignolo finds the transfer of the theological language into the rhetoric of secular scientificism in the historical juxtaposition of the sixteenth-century "purity of blood" principle in the aftermath of the Inquisition and the nineteenth-century scientific language of "the color of skin." The former draws the dividing line in religion whereas the latter resorts to secular science.[16] Here Mignolo points out the theological root of the modern science and discourse of race. The secular category of race overtook the religious rhetoric of "blood," a key marker that would distinguish Christians from Moors and Jews prior to the reconfiguration of their relationship in 1492. This way, "blood as a marker of race/racism was transferred to skin."[17] Religion was certainly a powerful arbiter that classified people in premodern Europe, but it does not mean that different kinds of classificatory identifiers based on racial phenotype and skin color did not exist. In *The Invention of Race in the European Middle Ages*, Geraldine Heng presents a comprehensive historical survey that troubles the simple narrative of racism as entirely derivative of modern scientific racism. The grammar of scientific racism, in its various prototypical forms, was already co-constitutive of the language of religious difference in premodern Europe. Reversely, this could imply that the modern-secular language of race bears the imprint of religious signification. In this sense, race is a theological disposition to a certain extent. In *Race: A Theological Account*, J. Kameron Carter offers a compelling account of how Christianity has been, since its early roots, a racializing narrative of whiteness; a theological foundation has centered (on) whiteness in the Western imaginary.

The emergence of the modern idea of Europe as an imaginary of whiteness is inseparable from its continuous construction and configuration of religious identities from its premodern days to the present. The comparative imaginary that emerges alongside colonial modernity vis-à-vis the colonial other predates the fifteenth-century colonial encounter, an imaginary that was co-constituted "in necessary relation to the Jew and/or the Arab."[18] Gil Anidjar draws on the politico-theological concept of the enemy as a central element at the heart of the process that involved the reconfiguration of racial identity, which led to the emergence of the European imaginary. Arabs and Jews are the necessary enemy of the Christian (and its presumably secular variant: white) Europe: Islam being the external enemy while Judaism represents the internal enemy.[19] Christian Europe's anti-Jewish and anti-Muslim campaigns, such as the Crusades and the Spanish Reconquista, that predate its fifteenth-century overseas expansion are its visible examples. Scholars have pointed out the process of religious-racial reconfiguration that leads up to 1492 in the Iberian Peninsula, which was initiated by the long process of Reconquista, culminating in the fifteenth-century Inquisition. This process indicates an important historical reference or moment that signals the dawn of the project of colonial modernity. Europe's colonial imaginary was not initiated out of a vacuum through an accidental encounter with the colonial other. Europe's overseas campaign is in direct continuity with its long history of political and military campaigns against its religious-racial others. Examining these histories of entanglement (between Jews, Muslims, and the emergence of the Western imaginary) suggests important perspectives for re-illuminating the complex geohistorical configuration of global race dynamics in which Islam often signifies an adversary of the rational values of the secular, democratic West.[20]

Aside from the entangled history of race and religion in (pre)modern Europe, the place of religion in colonial modernity cannot be underestimated when considering, first, its explicit role as the theological motivation driving the early colonial enterprises, and second, its continuing presence informing the modern juridico-political system. Despite acknowledging the critical role of religion and secularism in the formation of modernity/coloniality, Mignolo does not pursue this question further. He insinuates religion's far-reaching role in the formation of European modernity, but it dissipates as he advances his investigation of (de)coloniality.[21] Beyond the visible presence of Christianity during colonization, religion constitutes the multifaceted matrix on which power forms and circulates in the Americas, including in secularist iterations of colonial modernity. Probing the nexus of modernity and coloniality requires a rigorous investigation of the mechanism through which religion enacts the coloniality of power. Pointing out the regrettable divide between scholars of race/coloniality and scholars of religion, Nelson Maldonado-Torres observes the failure of scholars of religion to consider race and coloniality as critical components of religion as well as race scholars' equally problematic uncritical reception of the category of religion.[22]

The European colonial expansion cannot be separated from the secularist-humanist reinvention of Europe's selfhood. As Sylvia Wynter points out, the birth of the modern Western imaginary was inaugurated with the affirmation of its autonomous political subjectivity against the theocratic rule of the Church: an affirmation that necessitated the colonial imaginary of the irrational and enchanted natives.[23] Coloniality, I submit, requires theology—including its secularized iterations. Since its inception, the modern/colonial imaginary has consistently been, in a way, a theological enterprise. For the natives, the Spanish colonial enterprise in the Americas signified the reconfiguration of cosmology, which included one's relationship to land.[24] The continuing regime of coloniality from the fifteenth century to today is in a way characterized by the replacement of one particular theology by another. The newly imposed theology of the secular places the notion of the human—a particular conception of the human—at its center. This is why the central questions and propositions that drove the Valladolid debates still remain deeply relevant. The Valladolid debates demonstrate colonialism's constitutive role in the evolution of modern Western humanism. The impact of these debates cannot be underestimated as they were heavily instrumental in advancing the juridico-political notions of sovereignty, just war, international law, and cosmopolitanism. More broadly, they were formative in establishing the basic foundational concepts that inform modern liberal political concepts such as rationality, freedom, property ownership, and equality.

Central to these debates was the question of Indians' humanity since at stake was the legitimacy of the Spanish Crown's activity in the New World. Against Bartolomé de las Casas, who defended Indians' humanity and rights, Juan Ginés de Sepulveda denied their humanity, thus justifying the war against the Indians when it was deemed necessary: "Applicable to those barbarians vulgarly called Indians, whose defense you seem to have taken up, is as follows: That those whose natural condition is such that they must obey others, if they refuse that lordship and there is no other recourse, may be subdued by arms; and that this war is just according to the opinion of the most eminent philosophers."[25]

Sepulveda bases his view in Aristotelian Natural Law. In *Politics*, Aristotle advances the notion of Natural Slavery based in the philosophical principles of Natural Law. He views the slave as a human, but an incomplete human since the slave depends on a master. Those who are "slaves by nature" lack the key character that makes a human human. It is the master who thinks for the slave.[26] For Sepulveda, the slaves' incomplete humanity was reflected in the lack of reason and property ownership: "Neither do they have written laws, but barbaric institutions and customs ... they do not even have private property."[27]

The parameters of humanity are reason, freedom, and property ownership. Such notions were used both against and in defense of Indians' humanity and rights. Francisco de Vitoria, who is considered to be the father of international law, recognized Indians as "rightful owners of their property."[28] Vitoria evokes the Roman concept *dominium* in order to justify the Spanish dominion. *Dominium* carries the double meaning of jurisdiction and ownership. In light of it, the Spanish presence in the Americas can be interpreted as a legitimate exercise of freedom over one's property—which is the key sign of rationality.[29]

The modern-colonial worldview imposed on the Americas bears the banner of secular humanism. Yet even a cursory look at secular humanism's genealogy shows the extent to which it is informed by both Renaissance theology and Europe's colonial enterprises. More broadly, examining the anatomical composition of modernity through the lens of religion and coloniality unveils the ways in which the key terms constituting the foundational grammar of liberalism, such as reason, freedom, and the human, are, to a large degree, informed by the dominant theological logic of the time: at the crossroad of colonial enterprises and the rediscovery (invention) of the human (subject) and the advancement of reason. It was on such a theological premise that the erection of the post-theocratic human subject took place.

Wynter draws the connection between the invention of the secular-liberal subject of modern reason and the politico-theological transition that Europe was undergoing in the fifteenth and sixteenth centuries. She pays close attention to Renaissance humanism and its secularist agenda in which the reconfiguration of the human being's place in relation to theology and the state was at stake. Thus, Man was inaugurated as the rational and political subject of the state, a particular genre of the human that is universalized and overrepresented as the only mode of being.[30] The invention of Man, however, required its other. The colonial others of the Americas occupy the space of negativity as Man emerges as the normative universality. They become the "physical referents of its reinvention of medieval Europe's Untrue Christian other to its normative True Christian Self."[31] The invention of Man also required the transference of the old theological concepts into secular terms. The old theological notion of Original Sin was now displaced in the early modern imaginary by being transferred to the colonial other, the Native/Black, who became the repository of lack (sin), the lack of being.[32]

The question of the human, central to the European modern imaginary, emerges as a colonial-theological project. Wynter makes visible the enduring power of religion that cannot be easily disentangled from the secular. In doing so, she insists on the close link between the politico-theological problem and the problem of coloniality. She challenges the apolitical reading of modernity by exposing the racializing process of colonial politics that breeds the foundational edifice of the modern European imaginary. The problem of violence deriving from colonial governance and politics is inseparable from the metaphysical problems of epistemology and ontology—albeit irreducible to them. The allegedly secular metaphysics, Wynter points out, is inherently theological.[33] Coloniality is enacted in and through the secular ontological order. Wynter's work suggests that all political theology is, to a large extent, a (de)colonial theology.

Complicating Coloniality

When looking at the early conversations that shaped the study of modernity/coloniality, the "standard narrative" usually revolves around the axis of race as the central component of coloniality. However, such a narrative has faced challenges for its homogenizing account of the constitution of power. Critics point out that the multivalent manifestation of coloniality calls for attention to ways in which gender co-constitutes the colonial order. The invention of the racial/colonial order and being is gendered. The notion of Man, as Wynter has coined it, refers to the normative conception of the human who reflects the modern, Western, bourgeois ideal of being. Undoubtedly, Man also points at the patriarchal aspect of the normative universal. This important observation by Wynter, which remains underattended in her own work, finds various creative resonances across the different thinkers of the Americas who articulate the problem of gender as one of the key components of coloniality.

Two figures deserve particular attention as I sketch out a brief genealogy of decolonial critique and religion in the Americas: Gloria Anzaldúa and María Lugones. A pioneering visionary in Chicana feminism, Anzaldúa advanced a decolonial philosophical theory of multiplicity by honing the notion of *mestizaje*. Anzaldúa's mestizaje hosts a complex layer of multivalence. In her work, the in-between space of ambivalence oppressed by the colonial dualistic universals is transformed into a new site of possibilities for resisting the violent ontological order constructed by the racist heteropatriarchy. She locates the gendered and racialized body as the primary site in which coloniality takes a hold of being. Her queer, Indigenous, brown, and immigrant body is the battleground through which the ideological apparatus of coloniality sanctions its hierarchical order of being,

The mestiza disavows any dualistic and static sense of identity. It signifies a cosmopolitan consciousness capable of resignifying the symbolic grammar that predicates being as well as the normative social relations that condition it: "As a mestiza I have no country, my homeland cast me out; yet all countries are mine because I am every woman's sister or potential lover. (As a lesbian I have no race, my own people disclaim me; but I am all races because there is the queer of me in all races)."[34] This multiplicity, while innate to every person, is not to be taken for granted. The borderland is not only symbolic but also physical. Numerous people inhabit the US-Mexico borderland and cross it every day. The US-Mexico border is *una herida abierta* (an open wound). Its inhabitants embody all the values negated by the white Western subject: *Los atrovesados*, Anzaldúa writes, are "the squint-eyed, the perverse, the queer, the troublesome, the mongrel, the mulatto, the half-breed, the half dead; in short, those who cross over, pass over, or go through the confines of the 'normal.'"[35] For Anzaldúa, one can enter the new mestiza consciousness only by facing the deep painful moments of paralysis and fear that continuous acts of crossing entail. Departing from the old self, the self who is determined by the colonial dualistic worldview, requires the courage to walk into the terrifying territory of the unknown. The journey into the unknown and toward the new consciousness is an embodied experience that takes place through the body. This is why Anzaldúa relies on earthly, immanent imageries, particularly that of animals. For instance, her journey is described as a process of reconciling with the serpent, the symbol of prehuman creativity in her (Indigenous) tradition: "the symbol of the dark sexual drive, the chthonic (underworld), the feminine, the serpentine movement of sexuality, of creativity, the basis of all energy and life."[36] It is by "entering into the Serpent" that she comes to terms with her own flesh, her animality—realizing that she is a body.[37] For Anzaldúa, the body is the primary site through which coloniality is sanctioned and also resisted. The notion of coloniality of power, articulated by Quijano, Dussel, and Mignolo, largely points to its epistemic dimension. Their work commonly situates the axis of power in knowledge—albeit irreducible to it (especially for Quijano for whom material appropriation and exploitation is one of the main pillars of coloniality). Knowledge is derivative of knowledge production; knowledge production is derivative of the epistemic paradigm or framework. Coloniality of knowledge indicates that knowledge (the episteme) conditions and shapes our existence in the world. Often missing in these conversations is the place of the embodied self, the experience of flesh in which the materiality of coloniality is inscribed. The absence of the body is perhaps symptomatic of the patriarchal mechanism that has persistently denied the body and its desires. Anzaldúa demonstrates how the degradation of the body—which is often gendered, associated with the feminine—is a constitutive mechanism of coloniality. The invention of the racial/colonial other, Anzaldúa reminds us, is inseparable from the patriarchal machine whose order of being is always gendered. The serpent points at Anzaldúa's own struggle to affirm and celebrate her own corporeality/animality. More important, the serpent is the symbolic medium through which she channels and reconciles with her own spirituality.

Anzaldúa presents a compelling decolonial reading of religious symbols and practices when she employs the Aztec deity *Coatlicue*, the serpentlike female goddess figure who represents the dark, earthly energy of creativity and life. The Spanish colonization of the Indigenous people was followed by the domestication of the Indigenous religious symbol into the Christian ideal of the obedient figure of Guadalupe. In this sense, "entering into the serpent" carries twofold meanings: the reconciliation with her inner animality (and its creative, earthly, sexual desires) hints at the encounter with the divinity she locates within herself. The reclaimed vision of Indigenous religion plays a crucial role in her journey as it provides her with the creative inspiration and the political vision for her politics of becoming. Anzaldúa's mestiza ontology of multiplicity is rooted, in this sense, in the religious sensibility that accommodates the self of the multiple-in-one, the one-in-multiple, which lets her "transform herself into a tree, a coyote, into another person."[38]

Some scholars have expressed concerns about Anzaldúa's use of Indigenous religious narratives along with the term *mestiza*, a term that has a problematic history. Josefina Saldaña-Portillo argues that Anzaldúa's move can be problematic in that it may romanticize the Indigenous past while silencing their present reality. Here I agree with Mariana Ortega's argument that while it is important to emphasize vigilance against the appropriation of Indigenous identity—including the not-always-liberatory meaning of the term *mestiza*, mestiza may still offer "numerous possibilities of transformation."[39] Interestingly, Ortega partly agrees with Saldaña-Portillo's critique about the potential romanticization of Indigenous traditions in Anzaldúa's appeal to an Indigenous deity, as she cannot find a visible connection between the Indigenous goddess and the reality of the present-day Chicana and Indigenous people. I believe such a view reflects a narrow understanding of religion as it fails to attend to religion's crucial place in culture and history.[40]

Anzaldúa's important work has served as a guidepost for the advancement of Latinx feminism and decolonial thought in the United States. Her critique of the Western episteme, white supremacy, US immigration history, and heteropatriarchy has generated particularly strong resonances within the US Latinx community. Anzaldúa's widely popular status in the United States contrasts sharply—and perhaps ironically—with her relatively obscure status in Latin America. While her writing addresses the US audience, there is a much larger, hemispheric relevance to her thought and writing, which makes her an important interlocutor of decolonial thinking and politics in the global south. This is particularly more evident in her work on the gendered/sexed dimension of the body and animality—all of which are channeled toward her new vision of religion. In other words, perhaps some of the most crucial contributions that Anzaldúa makes are highlighted in her critique of the coloniality of gender and religion. Coloniality sanctions a gendered and racialized worldview through which power relations and social identities are constituted. Colonial religion plays a dominant role in the process. The new mestiza consciousness hints at Anzaldúa's journey of struggle across the matrix of coloniality through which she shapes new myths and re-creates herself.

For Wynter too, the creation of new myth has a pivotal place in decolonial thinking and struggle. She points out that the Word of Man dictating the present order is a deliberately invented story—a modern/colonial project. This particular story's everlasting influence is likely due to its cosmogonic nature. In other words, this story was given to us as a cosmogony, an origin narrative. The universalizing of a particular mode of being requires metaphysics and an origin story to house a worldview. Wynter finds the possibility of decolonial resistance in autopoiesis that is our ability to create and tell new origin stories and new myths. Understood this way, Anzaldúa's writings and work can be seen as a powerful model of counterpoetics: a visionary decolonial project that seeks to transform not only a particular form of episteme, concept, or theory, but also the foundational myth on which colonial modernity and its worldview are grounded.

Pointing out the absence of a rigorous analysis of gender in the ongoing conversations in decolonial thought, Lugones has highlighted the crucial place of gender in the constitution and installation of modernity/coloniality. Whereas Quijano views gender as constitutive of coloniality, Lugones finds Quijano's notion of coloniality of power insufficient for capturing the complex "construction of the scope of gender" as Quijano views sex/gender as being defined by the control of sexual production and resources.[41] In other words, the problem with Quijano's framework is its overly simplified and biologized understanding of gender/sex, which "presupposed sexual dimorphism, heterosexuality, patriarchal distribution of power, and so on."[42] Drawing on Oyeronke Oyewumi's work on the Yoruba and Paula Gunn Allen's work on Native American tribes, Lugones argues that gender, like race, was a category that was invented or introduced as the means of control.

The difference between the category of gender imposed on European women in the Americas and Indigenous women also demonstrates gender's critical role alongside race in social categorization and production of identities. The problem of gender correlates with the colonial-modern logic of conquest and genocide based in racial hierarchy as well as human superiority over nature and in which a certain normative set of attributes became the signifier of full humanity (Western, white, man, civilized, Christian).[43]

The notion of coloniality of gender advanced by Lugones lets us understand coloniality as an all-permeating modern system of signification and production of social relations. The production of social identities and the control of production (and resources) involve the biopolitical axis of gender and sex. While Lugones's work has been widely engaged and celebrated by many theorists working at the intersection of gender and decolonial thought, some critics argue that Lugones overgeneralizes and misrepresents gender relations in Yoruba and Indigenous communities.[44]

For decades, feminist scholarship has resisted the tendency to reduce gender/sex to private issues. One could say that a decolonial analysis of gender was already present in the works of feminist scholarship before the field of decolonial theory took shape in recent decades. The works of those who insist on intersectionality by pointing out the inseparable connection between race and gender were already hinting at important decolonial visions (examples of such works, to name a few, are by bell hooks, Gloria Anzaldúa, Chandra Mohanty, Audre Lorde, Angela Davis, and Jacqui Alexander). In light of such genealogy, both Anzaldúa and Lugones resist the narrow understanding of the mechanism of power that demarcates a dividing line between the intimate and the public, the personal and the political, sex and power.

Important to Anzaldúa and Lugones is the place of Indigenous communities and struggles in theorizing decolonial resistance. That it is often the decolonial feminist scholars—and not their male counterparts—who engage Indigenous voices (Indigenous women in particular) is indicative of the marginalization of both gender and Indigeneity in decolonial theory. For many, it is precisely the liminal status of Indigenous and women's voices that makes it imperative to turn to those sources for theorizing decoloniality. Sylvia Marcos, for instance, finds in Mesoamerican Indigenous women's religion an important decolonial philosophical vision that is grounded in the Mesoamerican cosmovision of duality. The Nahuatl notion of duality distinguishes from dualism as it points at the nonrigid/static relation of reality characterized by plasticity and dynamism.[45] Duality indicates a strong resistance to the modern Christian worldview imposed by Europe. The Mesoamerican cosmovision is rooted in a relational cosmology that affirms the immanence of the sacred in the world. It affirms the experience of the body and it views the originating force of the universe as feminine.[46] The encounter of Indigenous religion with Christianity gave birth to ecofeminist theology that bridges the Indigenous cosmovision and the Christian worldview.[47]

The question of Indigeneity is not a simple issue that can be easily disentangled from decolonial thought. Decolonial thought takes as its starting point the acknowledgment of the existence of decolonial intellectual movements preceding theorization by academic terms. The central figures in the archive of decolonial thinking—including the ones reviewed here—advance their ideas in direct conversation with Indigenous thinking (Quijano, Mignolo, Anzaldúa, Lugones, Mariátegui, Glissant, and Walcott). It would be far from possible to do justice to the wide-ranging diversity of Indigenous voices that intersect with the trajectory of decolonial thought in this short section. However, two figures are important to mention for the purpose of this chapter's main goals.

The Quechuan-Aymaran thinker Fausto Reinaga proposed *Indianismo*, based in a dialogue between Marxist ideas and revolutionary Indigenous ones. Often regarded as the prophet of the Bolivian Indigenous Revolution, Reinaga suggests Tawantinsuyu-Kollasuyu (the Inca state) as the archetype of communism that preceded Marx. He denounces all forms of Western thought as imperialist and genocidal, including religion (Christianity) and Marxism.[48] At the heart of his reading of Western thought and civilization lies the problem of race. At its very core, the West is founded on the idea of racial superiority. The Indigenous-Incan utopic vision he proposes is founded on an antiracist and anticolonial solidarity: it calls for those who are racially oppressed and persecuted to unite under the banner of Kollasuyu for an Indigenous-driven Third World revolution.[49] The utopic community that Reinaga describes attends to the fundamental religious orientation of the Quechua and Aymara people, a crucial component of full and total humanity. He ties the egalitarian orientation of this community (which stretches to all aspects of social life including racial identities) to religion. The ideal of "total humans" involves the participation in the ritual of "Padre Sol y la Madre Tierra" with the only leaders of the society being the Amautas, the teachers/bearers of wisdom of the Inca tradition whose job was to reveal the Truth at the festival of the Sun.[50] This utopic society, Reinaga calls it, is "the Kingdom of Life and Truth (El reino de la vida y la verdad)."[51] His vision of racial-class equality does not point to a social-political program divorced from fundamental philosophical principles that attend to both physical and spiritual needs of life. The Andean cosmovision is, for Reinaga, inherently decolonial.

In North America, Vine Deloria's work has made seminal contributions to Native American studies, especially in the areas of law, sovereignty, and religion. Deloria challenges the federal Indian law by pointing out the colonizing semantics that structure it.[52] He calls for imagining the Native American identity otherwise, beyond the confines set by the colonial-settler society.[53] Like Reinaga—and like many other Indigenous thinkers of the Americas—Deloria critiques Western civilization, and his view on the emancipation of Native American communities is not separable from religion. It is Indigenous people's relation to the sacred that informs their understanding of the self and the world, including time and space (land). Deloria contrasts Christianity's construction of religion based in (linear) temporality and the Native American communities' understanding of religion, which is grounded in space. The western/Christian view overlooks the centrality of space—and time's subservient nature to it—that characterizes Native American religions and worldviews, thus ultimately missing the ideas of kinship and the unity of life.[54] Federal-legal decisions regarding land issues in Native American communities evidence such logic. For Deloria, Native American resistance entails a challenge to the philosophical principles underpinning the law in the US West, which involves a theological-epistemological reconfiguration of the worldview driving the colonial politics against Native Americans.

The Indigenous intellectual traditions played a crucial role in shaping anticolonial struggles in the Americas. They have survived the long historical regime of colonial violence, informing and inspiring decolonial thought since before its theorization by academic discourses. At the same time, Indigenous thought suffers from appropriation and intellectual extractivism. Silvia Rivera Cusicanqui critiques the Indigenous discourses employed by the elite academic class, arguing that its projection of Indigeneity is often essentialist/orientalist; it reduces Indigenous people to an exoticized and fixed identity. Such discourses benefit the elite academics' own status while subjecting the Indigenous people to neoliberalism's "multiculturalist" ornament.[55] The persisting tension in conversations about decolonial thought rests on the distance or gap between decolonial thinking as a form of academic discourse and the historical reality of Indigenous communities.[56]

Academic Division of Labor

Against the Eurocentric accounts of capitalist modernity, Paul Gilroy demonstrated in the early 1990s the crucial place of the Black Atlantic in the formation of Western modernity.[57] A decade before Gilroy, Cedric Robinson had already pointed out the lack of the analytics of race in Marxist theory. Robinson observes that Marx and Marxist thinkers neglect the crucial significance of the racialized division of labor in the rise of early capitalism.[58] Equally problematic for Robinson is the fact that Marxism fails to consider the long history of liberation struggles that had been occurring already before Marx. Many such movements belong to the Black radical tradition, a tradition that often goes unregistered in the mainstream narratives of modernity.

The study of Black diaspora traditions is particularly important in the Americas in which the inception of the New World was inaugurated along with the birth of the largest African diaspora in history. The emergence of the modern European selfhood against its other (Americas) has taken place not on symbolic and philosophical register alone; it was also the material expropriation—which included slaves—that made the rise of Europe's hegemony possible. The historical experience of the African diaspora across the Americas is vital not only for properly articulating the problem of colonial modernity but also for thinking about the decolonial struggle and future. There seems to be, however, a contrasting hemispheric divide between the global north and the global south within the field of Black studies. The experiences and struggles of these two distinct contexts illustrate their important differences. It is precisely these differences, as well as similarities between the two, that begs a closer hemispheric conversation between them.

The African American experience is generally studied by a broad range of scholars in North America, including many in religious studies. The works of many African American political thinkers are commonly incorporated into the conversations within the study of religion, especially in the works of theologians, ethicists, philosophers, historians, and sociologists. What facilitates such flexibility is the proximity of their political thought to explicit theological ideas due to the relatively strong prevalence of Christianity among Afro-descendant communities in the United States. Contrastingly, Afro-religious communities of Latin America and the Caribbean are studied mainly through social scientific methods (anthropology and history). These studies are usually empirical and descriptive, while, in contrast, the intellectual traditions that emerge in parallel to these communities are rarely investigated by the same scholarly community. Scholars of religion, in other words, often analyze the local religious "communities" and their "practices" but not their theory, thus reinforcing the practitioner-scholar divide in religious studies as Aisha Beliso-De Jesús has pointed out.[59] Such a divide reproduces the academic division of labor between the West and the non-West or between the global north and the global south. The Christian West/north provides theory (text), whereas the global south is consigned to practice (ritual). The rigid categorical binary associates the white Christian West with secularism, critique, theory, text/thought, and the non-West with religion, tradition, practice, community, and bodies. In his recent book *The End of the Cognitive Empire*, the Portuguese legal scholar Boaventura de Sousa Santos discusses the problem of global knowledge production, a system structured by the overwhelming hegemony of epistemologies of the north. De Sousa Santos observes that the epistemologies of the north played a crucial role in the reproduction of the capitalist, colonialist, and patriarchal world order. In this geography of reason, the "Eurocentric epistemological North" is "the only source of valid knowledge whereas the South belongs to "the realm of ignorance." He adds: "The South is the problem; the North is the solution. On these terms, the only valid understanding of the world is the Western understanding of the world."[60] A similar problem structures global feminist scholarship. As Raewyn Connell observes, feminist writings from the global south that circulate internationally are usually empirical and descriptive whereas conceptual and methodological frameworks are reserved for the global north.[61]

This should not be reduced to the mere problem of representation and inclusion as we often find in the (neo)liberal rhetoric of multiculturalism and diversity. The problem of knowledge production is correlative with violence, a violence that denies other forms of knowing and being: a disguised violence that inculcates the same old structure of exclusionary hierarchy without coercion. Such asymmetrical structure of knowledge production and distribution equally conditions the study of religion in which Afro and Indigenous religions are sites of ethnographic data analyzed through theories imported from the global north. The extensive body of knowledge emerging from different parts of Afro and Indigenous communities in the Americas takes diverse forms and shapes. Many such forms of knowledge offer a rigorous, relevant, and creative array of analytic lenses, yet seldom are these ideas recognized as proper theory by academia, which constantly reinforces its own disciplinary boundaries and practice with its Eurocentric norms and parameters.

Following the insights already offered by numerous critics of the global south, I argue that the conceptual and methodological frameworks, epistemic assumptions, and theoretical categories used in the study of modern religion cannot be articulated outside the Black and transatlantic perspective. Conversely, it is when we theorize the Black Atlantic through both secular and religious optics that we can better understand the emergence of colonial modernity as a secularist imaginary and project of the West. In the following section, I briefly discuss two different ways Blackness and the transatlantic experience are theorized in their relation to colonial modernity.

The Martinican psychiatrist Frantz Fanon presents an intriguing set of phenomenological reflections on racialized (colonized) existence alongside an anticolonial revolutionary politics. Another Martinican-born poet and philosopher, Édouard Glissant, and the Saint-Lucian writer and poet Derek Walcott propose a poetic vision of a creolized ontology that conceives the Caribbean identity as the site for negotiating the possibility of transformation and of a decolonial future. These interventions let us identify the paths through which coloniality is materialized via racial relations, conditioning the prevailing structure of social order in the (post)colonial Americas. At the same time, they also reveal what modernity covers; they expose the codependency between the unmarked ideals of Western abstract universals and the colonial other as the site of the negation of such ideals. While only Walcott addresses religion explicitly in his work, their thoughts together hint at important challenges and insights for thinking about religion and power in the colonial Americas. Particularly interesting and important is the common place of the sacred as a philosophical foundation that fosters a constructive vision of a creolized pan-Antillean identity in their works. Exploring this connection, between decolonial thinking and the sacred, is a highly important task that needs attention.

Two Different Paths

Frantz Fanon is widely regarded as an indispensable thinker for theorizing the problems of race, colonial politics, and decolonial revolution. Fanon articulates poignantly the symbolic system of signification that shapes colonial social relations—a worldview based in a strict racial hierarchy. For Fanon, this worldview is not symptomatic of a particular philosophical norm reinforced by the modern West. Rather, this symbolic system is constitutive of the Western world and its metaphysics that is the foundation of what contemporary thinkers call the modern-colonial imaginary of the West.

Fanon observes that colonial governance cannot be administered by coercion alone. Its fundamental mechanism requires metaphysics: a theological worldview that makes the colonized accept the reality as it is. It also requires a theology that justifies the Manichean dualism dictating the colonial reality and its values, a theodicean order in which the white/colonizer embodies the Good and the Black/colonized represents absolute evil: "The colonist needs... more than physical control. He turns the colonized into a kind of quintessence of evil. The native is declared impervious to ethics, representing not only the absence of values but also the negation of values."[62] (Anti)Blackness and coloniality form the backbone of Western metaphysics in which the racialized/colonized other becomes the prerequisite (or antithesis) of ontology, making the being-there of the normative (that is white) Man possible. Fanon's work sheds light on what Blackness reveals. The emergence of the modern-rational human takes place alongside the invention of racialized beings in which the latter is the receptacle of all negative values that the former negates. It is Fanon's important observation that the colonial management of social relations is sustained by a Manichean theology, or, better, theodicy.[63]

Fanon's intervention offers important insights and challenges to the problem of the politico-theological and the secular. The transition from theology to the secular, from the church to the state, from faith to rationality cannot be fully explained without Europe's colonial enterprises that have informed the modern European imaginary. When devoid of the nexus of modernity/coloniality and the analytics of race, political theology's engagement with law, violence, and sovereignty leaves out any excluded others who operate outside the parameters of inclusion/exclusion that are the abject of political life.[64] Their exclusion does not indicate an exception (à la Agamben) but an ordinary aspect of the everyday life on which the universally assumed conceptualization of Western political life takes place. Fanon probes the ways in which the politico-theological manifests in the colony. Conversely, Fanon's work also reveals the ways in which the colonial problem haunts the politico-theological question. Reading Fanon as a critic of political theology might at first seem counterintuitive. The reference to religion in his work is scarce and subtle. It requires the careful work of unpacking and the creative work of identifying the unexplored sites and connections. For instance, his reference to Manichean theodicy ("a world of good and evil") as the metaphysical foundation of colonial worldview offers possibilities for reading the colonial order as a theological problem.[65] Fanon brings to light the ways in which the category of secular humanism often overshadows the theology (the colonial theology of whiteness) that constitutes European humanism and its colonial vision.

Wynter advances the Fanonian insight into a full-fledged critique of the colonial political theology. She views colonialism and secularism as mutually co-constitutive. The figure of Man reflects the project of the modern ideal of the secular-rational subject, whereas the invention of the inferior race required the transfer of the old theological notion of Original Sin onto them so that they materialize ontological (racial) lack. The invention of race and the governance of racialized beings necessitate theology:

> At the end of the eighteenth and during the nineteenth century the construct of an atavistic, genetically dysselected Lack of normal human nature took the now purely secular place both of Original Sin and of the earlier hybridly religio-secular construct of Sensory Nature. The new Lack was not conceptualized as that of lack of racial "normalcy" and was embodied in the recently freed Black/Africoid population, who now took the place of the prebaptismal Laity as conceptual Other, as the embodiment, that is, of the "dysgenic human subject" in place of the "fallen natural man" of the feudal-Christian schema.[66]

Decolonial critique and struggle consist of challenging the hegemonic conception of the normative human, "the secular liberal monohumanist conception of our being human, its overrepresentation as the being of being human itself."[67] For Wynter, the Caribbean intellectual tradition represents a revolt against the "order of discourse" dictated by the "Word of Man," which instituted the secularization of human existence as the normative modality of being.[68] Here she evokes Glissant as one of the key figures to partake in the intellectual revolt against such order. Glissant conceptualizes the historical site of the Middle Passage as a new ground of generative beginning (and becoming). In chapter 5, I read Glissant's decolonial vision alongside his recreation of the sacred in conversation with Walcott. Central to both thinkers is the project of theorizing Antilleanness, a project that employs creolization as a critical method and site for thinking about the future.

Glissant proposes creolization and the Caribbean as method by situating them in the Middle Passage. The generative power of creolized becoming emerges from the site of violent genesis, the birth of a people out of a traumatic rupture. A great extent of Glissant's thinking is devoted to working through the impasse that marks the (post)colonial self whose new beginning and self-determination is conditioned by the colonial difference. If Wynter turns to the symbolic signification of Blackness in relation to white European universality, both Glissant and Walcott are invested in exploring the generative creativity of Blackness (and Antilleanness) that has made survival possible through history. The haunting memory of the past speaks to the complex weight of history as well as the cultural-existential groundlessness the colonial self must reckon with. But the obstinate power of creative becoming and solidarity that ensured survival must also be reckoned with. This generative power, which is also a living testament to the horrifying memory of survival, guides the open wound into a site of transformation, of new beginning.

The colonial myth of origin and purity reinforces the status of the Antillean's otherness in its relation to Man. One of the abiding questions that concerns many Caribbean writers is the search for a new center of gravity, a new ground for people who trace their genealogy to discontinuity, rupture, death, and violence. Glissant is one among many thinkers who theorize creolization as an alternative ontological framework for rethinking traditional notions of essence and being with the end of redeeming the historical memory (and reality) of the Afro-Caribbean diaspora. Creolization indexes multiple registers of meanings, but for Glissant it indicates, at its core, an ontology of becoming in which the self and their world are the active sites of negotiating their ever-unfolding acts of self-creation. Such a process, for Glissant, is spiritual, "sacred."[69]

Creolization does not lend itself as a finalized solution to the problem of coloniality. Creolization defies teleological temporality. Rather, it beckons at the transformative temporality of self-creation. For Walcott, the work of self-creation or rebeginning in the archipelago resembles the work of the poet who must face the everyday task of "making his own tools like Crusoe, assembling nouns from necessity, from Felicity, even renaming himself."[70] For Walcott too, the re-creation of the world is sacred. Its process consists of "its remaking, the fragmented memory, the armature that frames the god, even the rite that surrenders it to a final pyre; the god assembled cane by cane, reed by weaving reed, line by plaited line."⁷¹ The process and politics of creolization are generated by the profound power of resilience witnessed in the history of survival: the surviving of the deadly voyage (the Middle Passage), the exploitation of labor and violence (slavery), and the ongoing subjugation of the archipelago within the global neocolonial design. Neither the name *Antilles* nor its vision of creolization is a utopic solution to the conditions of coloniality. Survival is an active and arduous struggle. Walcott writes, "I mean the Caribbean Sea, whose smell is the smell of refreshing possibility as well as survival. Survival is the triumph of stubbornness, and spiritual stubbornness, a sublime stupidity, is what makes the occupation of poetry endure."⁷²

Walcott's writings point at the intricate place of religion in the (post) colonial Caribbean. Religion cannot be disarticulated from the Caribbean social imagination and from the history of its survival. It is engraved at the heart of social and political life. Yet Walcott's articulation of religion does not easily translate to modern, West-centric categories that prescribe a much narrower definition of religion. Likewise, while explicit references to religion are scarce in Glissant's writings, he occasionally connects his vision of creolization to the figure of the sacred.⁷³ Segregating religion in the works of the Caribbean intellectual tradition betrays the very essence and orientation of their thoughts in which religion, as a key ingredient of culture, nurtures social life. Religion forms the vast mechanism of power that shapes social relations in (post)colonial Americas. As Sylvester Johnson writes in the context of African American religions, "Religion tends to be easily relegated exclusively to the realm of ideology or belief. This rendering obscures the overwhelming worldliness of religion and its profound role as a network of social institutions, materialities, technologies, and cultural practices."⁷⁴ Conversely, religion also informs the social imagination and political agencies that instigate movements of resistance against such a power mechanism.

The substantial place and significance of religion in Caribbean poeticism has not been properly explored by scholars of religion in the same way that the poetic works of William Blake, Walt Whitman, or Henry David Thoreau have been engaged. Unpacking the understated allusion to religion in Glissant, Walcott, or any other thinker of the Caribbean intellectual tradition is not a task without its challenges. Ignoring these important literary-aesthetic references that inform their political thought, however, leaves the archive of decolonial thinking incomplete.

Many of Glissant's writings resonate, for instance, with the apophatic tone of mystical texts, even when he never makes any explicit reference to religious language. This parallel indicates the possibility of a conversation between secular and religious mysticisms, which might suggest new ways of thinking about the very category of the secular and religion. It raises important questions as to what kinds of issues, questions, meanings, and possibilities are concealed or obliterated in the text under the nominal categories of the religious and the secular, thus possibly closing the gap between apolitical readings of the seemingly "universal experience" of the mystical and the question of power.[75]

Considering the mystical from the historical context conditioned by power adds important insights to the conversation about the construction of the category of the mystical. Many scholars have already interrogated the problematic assumption of the term *mystical* as a universalizing category. They have observed that the understanding of the mystical is historically and culturally conditioned.[76] In light of this, the prevalent apolitical readings of mystical texts can be bracketed by excavating the various registers of power and desire often veiled within the figures of speech and the obliterated historical context. The rigid line segregating mystical experience from power and history can be reconsidered as well as the dominant construction of the mystical as a privatized, apolitical notion. It will also open the door to diverse forms of poetics as new sites and sources for thinking about mysticism.

Glissant and Walcott point at the possibility of a different register of religion. Religion has functioned historically as an important channel of coloniality. But it has also inspired various world-making struggles under the rule of colonial power. Glissant and Walcott help us pay close attention to the ways in which religion (articulated as "the sacred") is repurposed, despite coloniality, and continues to nurture creative accounts of survival and resistance. They show that religion is never a distinctive category or reality in the Antilles but the center of gravity for social life and possibilities of a decolonial otherwise. Overlooking the profound tie between generative visions of decolonial thinking and the sacred (whichever form it may be) might be precisely symptomatic of the coloniality of knowledge that persistently reinforces the religion/secular binary. This is not to say that a clearly elaborated notion of the sacred molds the spirit and movement of decolonial resistance in the postcolonial Americas. The diverse registers of the sacred usually take murky shapes. At times, they are presented as antithesis to the sacred, that is, as a disavowal of the dominant notion of the sacred (and of religion more broadly), yet, even in negation, they are not renounced. The irreplaceable place of the sacred in Caribbean decolonial imagination remains yet to be fully explored. The rich and diverse body of writings emerging in the Caribbean has produced an essential current of theory that allows us to revisit the epistemic principle that laid the foundation of Western (colonial) modernity. These theories have started to have a more visible impact in recent years as they are being introduced to Western academic conversations. They provide vital theoretical and methodological frameworks for the study of religion, Caribbean or/and otherwise. In their critique and rejection of colonial modernity, these thinkers of the global south suggest the possible remaking of religion—as they reject the homogeneous imposition of the secular. Reversely, where their critique of religion is more evident, it reveals their broader critique of colonial modernity.

The prevailing hostility against the theorizing of the sacred in the field of religious studies instantly demarcates segregating boundaries across the discipline, quarantining any such attempt in the narrow "specialized subfield" of theology. The notion of the sacred as it was popularized by phenomenology of religion in the twentieth century was widely rejected toward the second half of the century due to its essentializing nature. According to Mircea Eliade, the key figure in twentieth-century phenomenology of religion, the sacred constitutes the defining element of religion. In Eliade's view, the sacred lays out the foundation of one's orientation and meaning-making in an otherwise homogeneous (or chaotic) world. With this, critics point out, Eliade carries on the problematic heritage of the nineteenth-century European study of religion, a tradition that has essentially propagated Protestant theology (or "crypto-theology" as Donald Wiebe calls it) under the name of the study of religion. Phenomenologists' understanding of the sacred has greatly reinforced the dominant notion of religion that was already informed by universalizing and essentializing categories that have their roots in the Western/Christian concept.[77] The critical conversations that emerged in reaction to phenomenology of religion and Eliade in turn have shaped profoundly the theories of religion that developed in recent decades.

These critics of the sacred are right in their rejection of the sui generis approach to religion. Such an understanding of the sacred is indeed ethnocentric and essentializing, as it defines religion as a category separate from history and power. It fails to account for the history of its formation, both as a lived religion and a concept. It attributes to religion an atemporal character that transcends history and power (ideology).[78] However, locating and theorizing the sacred in the archive of decolonial thinking is fundamentally different from phenomenologists' use of it. It does not signal a move toward depoliticizing and privatizing the sacred. Rather, the sacred in decolonial thinking mobilizes against the forces that seek to privatize it. The prevailing animosity against the sacred suffocates any attempt to theorize alternative forms of the sacred that emerge from subjugated forms of knowledge. Also problematic is that these critiques often operate under the assumption that secularist method/theory warrants a certain scientific objectivity.

Here I do not want to replicate the West-centric approach and (re)claim or prescribe religion solely based on a particular notion of the sacred. Religion cannot be reduced to the realm of mind and text (thinking or belief). Religion is entangled in every aspect of the social fabric. Its diverse forms and expressions are studied by scholars who examine various artifacts that reflect the complexity and diversity of culture and society. One of the key problems with the essentializing notion of religion is that it lifts up Christian categories of belief and text as primary sites for defining religion. But rejecting this epistemic and theoretical framework need not lead to the rejection of these categories altogether. Just as religion cannot be reduced to belief (thought) alone, Afro and Indigenous religions cannot be reduced exclusively to ritual and practice. Turning away from the realm of thought and belief (including theory and text) for theorizing religion in the Americas may end up reanimating the questionable binary that reproduces the academic division of labor between the global north and the global south. The former is the administrator and producer of theory; the latter, of artifacts. The method of academic inquiry is still largely structured by the worn-out Cartesian subject-object division. In this epistemic scheme, the West is still the sole subject of knowledge (production). To repeat de Sousa Santos's words again, the global south is the problem and the global north offers solutions. The asymmetric market of knowledge production begs the question about its role in the global matrix of coloniality when we consider that the current order of capitalist (neocolonial) globalization lies in continuity with the old Western/Christian imperial regime, and that the normative concept of the secular is, to a certain extent, a permutation of Christian hegemony.

The efforts made by contemporary theories of religion to dislocate West-centric norms that dominate the discipline made important contributions. Theorists' endeavor to reconsider the narrow notion of religion found refuge in the secularist-scientific inquiry as a method that warrants critical disciplinary norms dislodged from Christian theological categories. These critical conversations have been evolving (and so have been their definition of secularism) under the consistent goal of producing theories that can equitably account to the global reality/experience of religions. Such a turn, however, has not carefully reckoned with the unequal relation of power that structures the global knowledge production. The asymmetrical dynamic of this relation is intrinsic to the normative secularist principle that determines method and theory in the study of religion. Addressing secularism, Saba Mahmood notes, "to critique a particular normative regime is not to reject or condemn it; rather, by analyzing its regulatory and productive dimensions, one only deprives it of innocence and neutrality."[79] Following Mahmood, I seek to bring attention to the colonial innocence of the secular. As Mahmood explains, "Secularism is not something that can be done away any more than modernity can be."[80] Rather, I want to point at the undetachable tie between coloniality and the secular. Resorting to the secularist framework without carefully probing this link will drag us back to the endless loop of sameness that reproduces itself each time anew. Likewise, the dominance of the secularist framework in the study of religion without a critical scrutiny of secularism's place in the global neocolonial cartography of power will not help us distance ourselves from normative West-centric narratives but will reproduce yet a different permutation of the same homogenizing narrative.

Looking Ahead: Connections and Possibilities

The problem of coloniality in the United States has been articulated widely by scholars, many of them Latin American descendants, who work with a transnational framework. Their work usually reflects on the transatlantic colonial experience and the more recent American imperialist enterprises overseas. Extending this hemispheric perspective to study the American internal experience from a decolonial perspective may also open important conversations. Recent scholarship in the broader field of American studies (including Black studies, Indigenous studies, and Asian studies) demonstrates a fluid engagement with the transnational framework of coloniality to read the North American experience of racial relations.

Sylvester Johnson's recent suggestion that we view the history of American racial relations as a form of an "internal colonialism" also provides a useful bridge for reading the North American historical reality from a hemispheric or transnational viewpoint. Johnson rightly points at the inseparable nexus of race-colonialism by viewing race itself as a form of "colonial governance administered through the frame of essential differences among human populations."[81] African American studies, he argues, following Charles Long, must be done in conversation with transatlantic studies. Johnson argues for the need to approach the historical experience of the African diaspora in the United States from the viewpoint of the modern global imperial design. The colonial articulation of power in the Americas must be examined through the transatlantic framework so that North American race relations can be situated vis-à-vis the colonial-modern configuration of the world. This way, African American religious thought would gain a much more ample theoretical platform for exploring its broader political and theoretical significance within the global configuration of power. The analytics of modernity/coloniality and its transnational/transatlantic lens allow scholars of religion to relocate the contributions of African American religious thought within the broader global cartography of decolonial struggle and critical studies of modernity. Seen through a transnational perspective, the significance of African American thought is conceived as a critique not only of US racial relations but also of the broader problem of coloniality conditioning the global relations of power and knowledge (production).

Recent conversations in Black studies have gained much traction across a broad circle of scholars who are invested in theory. Perhaps the most influential of these conversations is what is often dubbed as the Afropessimism debate, which suggests intriguing questions and challenges to the study of religion and decolonial theory in the United States. The interlocutors of Afropessimism trace the root cause of the ubiquitous anti-Blackness and the reality of Black suffering to the symbolic—albeit irreducible to it. Anti-Blackness, they argue, is constitutive of Western metaphysics.[82] Borrowing insight from Orlando Patterson's seminal work, they claim that Blackness signifies social death. Black social life is impossible in a world "sutured by anti-black solidarity" in which life is structured as life-in-death.[83] The debate is often presented as (Afro)pessimism versus (Black) optimism with the intervention of those who insist on hope—despite anti-Blackness. Insisting on hope, Fred Moten attempts to rescue Blackness from the zone of nothingness by reconsidering the affective registers of failure and unattainability as a source of resistance. Agreeing with pessimists' diagnosis of anti-Blackness, Moten calls for the resignation of ontology as he finds it incompatible with Blackness. Blackness for Moten exceeds the phenomenological field conditioned by anti-Blackness (ontology). It precedes and exceeds ontology, "ontology's anti- and ante-foundation, ontology's underground, the irreparable disturbance of ontology's time and space."[84] Moten's constructive reading draws on a wide range of literary, political, aesthetic, and performative sources with the end of gauging the political possibilities foreclosed by the regulative logic that dictates ontology. As the other of ontology, Blackness signals possibility: "If pessimism allows us to discern that we are nothing, then optimism is the condition of possibility of the study of nothing as well as what derives from that study."[85]

Exploring the unlived possibilities includes the task of undoing the religious/secular binary as Moten alludes to mysticism as a medium or placeholder for Blackness—an alternative to ontology.[86] Commenting on Nishida Kitaro's reading of the East Asian concept of *Mu* (nothingness)—a mystico-philosophical term recently explored by African American theorists and artists—Moten posits (the nothingness of) Blackness as an antithesis to sovereignty. Moten observes that Nishida's mystical rendering of *Mu* is capable of putting sovereignty on hold, but not in the hold, as he postulates the absolute as the opposite, "the inverse polarity" of the individual. He rightly points out the ontotheological sovereignty being recast in Nishida's mystical philosophy in which sovereignty is reified through its "brutally material imposition."[87] Contrastingly, Blackness signals a rupture of the sovereign imaginary in which transcendental subjectivity is substantiated by its relation to nothingness.[88]

Moten's evocation of mysticism to reconstruct Blackness (as a countersovereign figure) and to ground his politics of refusal/fugitivity has yet to take concrete form. But even in its scattered articulation, it deserves attention from scholars of religion as he reconsiders mysticism not as a mere alternative to the rationalist inquiry of Western metaphysics but as a disavowal of the theologico-political injunction that sanctions ontological foreclosure against nothingness/Blackness. There are important registers of possibilities for reconfiguring the relation between mysticism and power (or the problem of race), which I have discussed above. Of particular importance is his critique of the sovereign figure that is often suspended yet subsists in the writings of mystical thinkers. Articulating Blackness as the other of sovereignty raises crucial questions for thinking about political theology, Blackness, and coloniality as articulated by Fanon and Wynter. The parasitic link between sovereignty and Blackness becomes the axial foundation for the constitution of colonial modernity; if anti-Blackness is constitutive of the politico-theological machine, unpacking its implication becomes a pressing issue. Such inquiry displaces the secular and the putatively secular foundation of the political, thus possibly reaffirming Achille Mbembe's claim that sovereignty is determined by "the right to kill" and "the capacity to define who matters and who does not, who is disposable and who is not."[89]

The Afropessimist/Black optimism debate re-illuminates the central place of race and the mechanism of racist governance in the constitution of the West and its metaphysics. Their argument helps us tap into the problem of political theology left somewhat dormant in the writings of Fanon while reaffirming the critique advanced by Wynter: that the current order of knowing/being is grounded in a secular theology conditioned by coloniality. It is, however, important to point out the place of a transnational perspective (or lack thereof) in these conversations. The primary proponents of this conversation, who happen to be mostly based in North America, tend to uplift anti-Blackness as an exceptional category over other forms of colonial violence while framing the discourse largely in the American-bred conversations about slavery—a tendency that is more conspicuous in the writings of pessimists. For critics, the problem is that the long tradition of Black radical struggles in the global south has relentlessly insisted on an otherwise. The voices of these Black anticolonial thinkers and their revolutionary politics often yield place to claims about the equation of Blackness with social death and the exceptionality of anti-Blackness.[90] My intention is far from weighing in on the pessimism versus optimism debate in favor of one position over the other. The North American field of Black studies stretches far beyond the pessimism/optimism debate. The voices that emerge in the field are diverse and they often cross numerous boundaries and categories—beyond the particular debates and positions that I lay out here. Rather, I am pointing at the critical place of the transnational (and hemispheric) framework in these conversations. Anti-Blackness and coloniality are mutually co-constitutive, despite a clear distinction between the two. Articulating anti-Blackness without coloniality may result in a narrow hemispheric confine that alienates North American theory from the political struggles and the intellectual traditions of the global south. The problem of anti-Blackness theorized by North American Black studies allows us to tap into the problem of coloniality through the lens of religion (political theology). It also adds critical questions that complicate homogenizing narratives of coloniality. What are the ways in which anti-Blackness constitutes coloniality, and vice versa? What are the differences in the way that coloniality manifests in the global south compared to the global north? What do such differences (as well as commonalities) indicate about the constitution and the mechanism of power in each context? What kinds of sites, experiences, and questions does the notion of anti-Blackness suggest might be missing in the analytics of coloniality/modernity? In what ways do they complicate or complement each other? If Western metaphysics is inseparable from Western religion and its theology, and if anti-Blackness is constitutive of Western metaphysics, what is religion's relationship to anti-Blackness? What are the ways in which theology—both religious and secular—has reinforced and reenacted anti-Blackness? And what kind of decolonial imagination and movement does it take to undo the coloniality of anti-Blackness?

To free the human whose being is predicated upon the nonbeing of Blackness, Calvin Warren writes, the ground (the foundation of metaphysics) must be destroyed and deconstructed: "Black freedom then would constitute a form of world destruction."[91] This apocalyptic orientation, common to Afropessimism, can also be glimpsed in Césaire's and Fanon's writings, both of whom viewed the end of the world (colonial and racist) as fundamental to their own poetic and political visions. But what concerned Césaire and Fanon even more than the end of the world was the question of beginning, that is, the creation of a new world after the apocalypse or catastrophe. Caribbean poeticism has always situated Antilleanity in groundlessness. The colonial abyss out of which Antillean history is born deprives the ground. The Caribbean poet is always between shorelines, writing from the depth of the ocean, planting its constantly evolving underwater roots, seeking ever new centers of gravity. Colonial violence devastates the ground. But the lack of ground does not foreclose life itself. Colonial ruins leave not only deaths (in their many forms) but also forms of existence that persist and insist—on life. Writing about the "wake work" in the aftermath of slavery, Christina Sharpe writes, "We, Black people everywhere and anywhere we are, still produce in, into, and through the wake an insistence on existing; we insist Black being into the wake."[92] The ocean and the archipelago bears witness to the water grave, the site of apocalypse and burial that, nonetheless, does not cease to unfold new realities, new beginnings. Glissant writes, "The Indies are imaginary, but their revelation is not."[93] Caribbean decolonial poetics is a testament to the oceanic groundlessness that bears new realities in the aftermath of slavery that is the aftermath of the Middle Passage and plantation life.

2

CRISIS AND REVOLUTIONARY PRAXIS
Philosophy and Theology of Liberation

The problem of modernity, coloniality, and religion (secularism) finds a distinct political and intellectual platform in twentieth-century Latin America through a movement known as liberation theology (LALT). Liberation theology emerged during the 1960s and 1970s in Latin America in the wake of the growing social unrest caused by economic inequality and political instability. The movement took both intellectual and grassroots form as it was driven by theologians and clergy as well as the *comunidades eclesiales de base* (basic ecclesial communities, or CEB). The movement has had a massive impact well beyond the boundaries of the church across the continent, playing a major role in conscientizing communities and organizing dissent movements that confronted violent military regimes during the second half of the last century. Many social-political movements that emerged during this time were significantly influenced by and were in conversation with liberation theology.

The key agenda advanced by LALT centered around the critique of the political-economic structure and the social conditions created by it, that is, underdevelopment, poverty, and social inequality. In dialogue with Marxist social analysis and dependency theory, early proponents of LALT offered a comprehensive theological critique of the politico-economic system that relies on the exploitation and the alienation of the poor majority. Theologically, the significance of LALT rests on its inversion of method for doing theology. Theological methods were traditionally based in deductive epistemology. Theology was the study of the human situation in light of the universal truth—the knowledge about God. LALT calls for a methodological shift, a theological method that is based in the human context. Traditional theological dogmas are now open for reinterpretation in light of the changing or revolutionary human situation.[1] Theological hermeneutics—from which the knowledge about God is derived—is born in the everyday life experience of the poor and the marginalized rather than the dogmatic formulae geared toward justifying universal knowledge about God. Another key theological contribution of LALT lies in its rejection of the dogma/praxis binary. Proposing a theological method centered around the concept of praxis, LALT challenges the traditional epistemic framework that relegates praxis to secondary status.[2]

Underlying LALT's social analyses is the problem of Euro-American imperialism. Dependency theory, a key social scientific foundation of LALT, approaches political economy through a transnational framework. According to dependency theory, the economic development of the core (Europe and the United States) is closely linked to the underdevelopment of the periphery (Asia, Africa, Latin America) from which both natural and human (labor) resources are extracted at low cost. The unequal structure of economic development is sustained by the North Atlantic imperialist policies sanctioned in the periphery. The socioeconomic landscape of mid- to late twentieth-century Latin America was strongly shaped by such global imperial design. Factors included the growing political influence and intervention of the United States in Latin American states; the economic dominion of American and European corporations over local economies; the growing rate of poverty, particularly among rural peasants and Indigenous communities; and the widespread wave of US-sponsored military regimes that repressed dissent movements with terror and violence. This is why, from its early days, LALT was always driven by a strong critique of Euro-American imperialism.

LALT's commitment to anti-imperialist politics, however, has not always successfully translated into an apt critique of the larger problem underlying the Euro-American imperialist presence in modern Latin America, namely, the problem of coloniality. The question about LALT's contribution to decoloniality and its possibility as a viable decolonial critique is one that is marked with ambiguity, a topic that I address later. Suffice it to say for now that LALT falls short overall—at least in its early and most popularly circulated form—as a compelling form of decolonial thought. Yet I also question the omission of LALT in contemporary conversations about decoloniality, as I show that a nuanced reading of its complex trajectory and intersection with early Latin American decolonial thinkers sheds light on its potential and possible contribution to ongoing conversations about decoloniality.

This chapter takes a close look at LALT with the end of probing its contributions and limits and thus carefully reconsidering LALT as a potential resource for theorizing decoloniality in the Americas. The primary goal is to show that, despite its visible limitations, LALT has produced an important political and intellectual movement that contributed to the protodecolonial conversations in important ways. This allows us to reflect further on some of LALT's important claims and ideas that will let us revisit the orientation and character of decolonial thought, particularly in areas that are often considered to be lacking: the problem of class, political economy, and religion. Situating LALT within the genealogy of decolonial thinking is important because of the central place LALT takes within the intellectual landscape of Latin America in the second half of the twentieth century. This juxtaposition allows us to gain a broader perspective on LALT's relationship with its contemporary decolonial scholarship in the Americas, a relationship often marked by missed opportunities. Despite the proximity between LALT and the early generation of philosophers of liberation, the exchange between these two has left much to be desired, without leading to a substantial conversation, at least from the perspective of LALT.

My goal is to reflect on the insights offered by LALT as a potential resource for reconsidering the place and possibilities of decolonial thought for understanding the problem of power in the Americas. This endeavor leads eventually to a double plea: it calls for those invested in liberation theology to engage with the study of coloniality of power/knowledge and take the problem of race as a key concept for studying power and religion; it also calls for decolonial theorists to consider LALT as an important source for thinking about colonial modernity in Latin America. While acknowledging the historical significance of LALT as an authentic Latin American intellectual intervention, decolonial theorists have seldom engaged with LALT, partly due to LALT's Eurocentric theoretical (and theological) orientation. The omission of LALT, I argue, is also likely due to the dominant secularist framework operative in the field of decolonial theory. Leaving out this important religious-political movement means an oversight of the comprehensive character of power that constitutes colonial modernity in Latin America.

The problem of the secular plays differently in this chapter because I am engaging with an explicitly theological movement and mode of thinking. Many figures I review in this chapter write unambiguously in theological fashion; but the nontheologians I examine in the chapter also equally diagnose secularism as an ideological platform that accommodates colonial epistemology (coloniality of knowledge). These voices unequivocally reject the secularist binary. In their view, the link between religion and power stretches beyond the modern secularist binary that privatizes religion. We find in their work a rich and insightful body of critique that gets to the heart of the problem, namely, the secular as a problem of coloniality. At the same time, these nonreligious writings provide us with insights that allow us to reflect on the underexplored dimensions of LALT and revisit its potential as a decolonial critique.

This chapter starts by taking a close look at the philosopher of liberation Enrique Dussel. Philosophy of liberation was born adjacent to LALT. It was an intellectual movement initiated by South American (Argentine) philosophers in the early 1970s. The conversation involved contributions by philosophers such as Enrique Dussel, Arturo Roig, Rodolfo Kusch, Juan Carlos Scannone, and Horacio Cerruti Guldberg, among many others. These thinkers reflect the different methods and approaches within the movement, such as historicist (Roig), ontologist (Kusch), and analectics (Dussel and Scannone).[3] Another way to classify the methodological diversity within the conversation is suggested by Juan Carlos Scannone in which we can identify those who turn to "people" in order to reflect from their cultural and popular knowledge (Kusch, Scannone), those who turn to exteriority (Dussel), or those whose critiques are grounded in a Marxist conception of class oppression (Cerruti).[4] The fundamental principle that binds these diverse voices is the premise that the "praxis of liberation is the 'first act,' the point of departure and the hermeneutical locus of a radical human reflection."[5]

The priority of praxis constitutes the central axis of both philosophy and theology of liberation. These two movements share an important common orientation. Both movements were born as a reaction to the shared problem that is the political and economic situation of Latin America in the mid- to late twentieth century. They equally rely on the same analytics developed by dependency theory to understand the Latin American problem. While they have mutually influenced each other, philosophy of liberation and theology of liberation have not been active conversation partners, save in their early stages of formation. Here I focus mainly on Dussel not only because he is the most influential and widely known figure among philosophers of liberation, but also because of his contribution to the recently emerging conversation about decolonial thinking. Dussel is also important for exploring the connection between liberation theology and philosophy of liberation because he was one of the few philosophers of liberation who was actively engaged in conversation with liberation theologians in the early days.

As a philosopher partly influenced by different streams of religious intellectual traditions (Latin American Catholicism, Paul Ricoeur's Catholicism-inflected hermeneutics, and the Jewish thought of Franz Rosenzweig and Immanuel Levinas), Dussel acknowledges the broad sociopolitical implication of LALT without reducing it to a privatized category of religion. He finds in LALT an authentically Latin American form of thinking that is deeply committed to those who are excluded from the totality of Western modernity. In contrast, secularism for Dussel parallels the totality of Western modernity, often accommodating its colonial epistemology. Latin American thinkers writing in the wake of postcolonial modernity did not always subscribe to the modern secularist category of religion. They believed that religion, disarticulated from its Western colonial conception, serves as a critical reserve of possibilities for inspiring and empowering decolonial modes of thinking and action.

After reflecting on LALT via Dussel, I turn to the early twentieth-century Peruvian philosopher José Carlos Mariátegui. Mariátegui is regarded as a highly original thinker whose contribution is crucial for thinking about the problem of power, class, and race in the (post)colonial Americas. I situate Mariátegui at the juncture of the genesis of both modern decolonial thought and LALT. As I will discuss, Mariátegui's philosophy influenced both Aníbal Quijano (a key figure of Latin American decolonial thought) and Gustavo Gutiérrez (a key figure of LALT) in significant ways. Mariátegui allows me to zero into the intersection as well as the missing connection between decolonial thought and LALT. My intention in probing the rather loose and unclear link between these two movements is not simply to re-illuminate LALT's potential as a form of decolonial thought. The overall absence of LALT in contemporary discussions of decolonial theory is not unrelated to decolonial theorists' reductive view of religion. I want to interrogate the simplistic narrative that often dismisses LALT by bringing to light the rather complex shared trajectory of these two intellectual threads. Overall, LALT displays visible limitations as a decolonial critique. However, considering the mutual influence between LALT and decolonial Latin American philosophies in their early days, it is important that we reflect on the existing connection as well as the missed connections between the two, and to explore its implication for thinking about the nexus of race, religion, and coloniality. LALT offers important insights that resonate with many of the crucial questions many key twentieth-century decolonial thinkers were wrestling with, such as the problem of religion, race, political economy, and epistemic coloniality.

Decolonizing Thinking: Philosophy of Liberation

The intellectual climate out of which philosophy of liberation emerges is marked by an important conversation involving two influential Latin American philosophers of the time. The conversation was driven by questions about Latin American cultural identity and the possibility of a Latin American philosophy. In his book *Existe una filosofía de nuestra américa?* (1968), the Peruvian philosopher Augusto Salazar Bondy presents a pessimistic view on the possibility of an authentic Latin American philosophy. Broadly speaking, two points led Salazar Bondy to this claim. First, his own understanding of philosophy was largely informed by Euro-American standards. He was particularly inclined to the Anglo-American brand of analytic philosophy and had a clear vision of what constitutes philosophy. He insisted on a particular method and form of philosophical thinking and writing. Second, and more important, however, was the political and cultural circumstance in which Latin America was situated. For him, philosophy was the expression of the cultural life of the community, which seemed impossible for Latin America, a continent that was held hostage by cultural and political domination caused by Euro-American imperialism. An authentic Latin American philosophy presupposes originality, authenticity, and peculiarity, all of which signal the creation of new ideas.[6] Such intellectual endeavor is absent in the Third World due to underdevelopment and imperial/colonial domination. As Salazar Bondy writes, "Our social existence has been and continues to be alienated. This means that the true subject of history, oppressed and laid aside, split and alienated, has not found itself yet as a living community."[7] In this sense, the absence of method for doing philosophy is not just a disciplinary issue confined to scholarly orientations, but a cultural and historical problem in which the dominant philosophical thinking fails to reflect the true cultural conditions of the community due to its "transplanted and installed" nature.[8] Important to note here is that the emphasis is not on the inability of the Third World but on the global imperial condition that produces such unequal order. His provocative position was a plea for a revolutionary change of the global epistemic, cultural, and political order.[9]

In a sharp contrast, the Mexican philosopher Leopoldo Zea insisted on the possibility of an authentic Latin American thought. Responding to Salazar Bondy's provocative thesis, he asserts that it is precisely the particularity of the Latin American circumstance that gives it a universal meaning as an authentic philosophy. Philosophy is the expression of the human struggle to solve problems, in their particular circumstances.[10] For Zea, the recognition of Latin American philosophy as an authentic and universal form of thinking bears a liberatory implication in itself. The inauthenticity of Latin American philosophy is certainly due to its subordinate place, due to it being a bad copy (*mala copia*) of European philosophy. However, it is precisely this inauthenticity that gives Latin American philosophy its authenticity, for it does not signal inferiority but difference and particularity. Latin American philosophy signifies an original philosophy in this sense.[11] Lying at the heart of the debate is the question about the possibility of a genuine philosophy. At its core, the question is oriented toward the problem of power in the (post) colonial Americas. It raises, in essence, the question about the possibility of a genuine Latin American identity and a form of thought disarticulated from coloniality. Against this intellectual backdrop, Dussel seeks out a genuine Latin American philosophy capable of divesting from colonial and Eurocentric forms of thinking/being. To do this, philosophy must be situated in the geopolitical context. For Dussel, thinking takes place in the specificity of one's sociopolitical location. Dussel inherits Zea's intellectual desire to rediscover a Latin American brand of thought, while also taking seriously Salazar Bondy's admonition against colonial forms of knowing.

As I already discussed in chapter 1, Dussel's philosophical trajectory takes a decisive turn in his encounter with Levinas's thought. Inspired by Levinas's concept of alterity as the opposing alternative to totalitarian metaphysics, Dussel situates Latin America as the other of European modernity, which he views as a totalitarian myth. Situating thinking in the concrete context means for Dussel to reflect on Levinas's exteriority from the global geographical context. The geopolitical context from which Levinas's thought sets out is Europe, the ambiguous place of Jewishness as the internal exteriority of Europe. Dussel challenges Levinas's fixation on Europe by calling for the need of a hemispheric vision: Europe and its internal fissures cannot be articulated without the geopolitics (of knowledge) that shapes the modern-colonial world. To think about Europe, in this sense, requires thinking from the periphery. To think from the periphery, however, does not need to mean mirroring Europe and its ways of thinking. For Dussel, the critique of Europe and its modernity must turn away from its endless preoccupation with Europe and start thinking from its exteriority. The endeavor to break from within rests on dialectics, and this explains, for Dussel, Hegel's problematic view of world history. Dussel accuses dialectics of being responsible for the totalitarian metaphysics that leaves no room for exteriority. Contrarily, he proposes the notion of analectics. Analectics indicates exteriority. Unlike dialectics, which subsumes difference under its totalitarian trajectory, analectics hints at radical exteriority beyond the reach of totality. Analectics indicates the alterity of the other that the totalitarian movement of dialectics fails to enclose.[12] In this sense, Latin America is the alterity of Europe. Its marginalized and oppressed people have always existed and survived the violence of Western modernity from outside. Dussel therefore suggests the notion of transmodernity, which indicates the radical exteriority of the Americas. That which has persisted outside/beyond Western modernity might serve as the reserve of possibilities for resisting the system of totality.[13]

The place of exteriority is crucial for the totalitarian center. The Americas' exteriority is constitutive of Europe in that Europe can establish itself as such only because of its other. In conversation with social scientists Aníbal Quijano and Immanuel Wallerstein, Dussel traces the shift in material conditions that made the emergence of Europe as the center of the modern world possible. The place of the Americas as the exteriority of Europe (and European modernity) is facilitated by these shifts in material conditions. The birth of modernity, often regarded as an inner European phenomenon, needs to be viewed with colonialism or, rather, coloniality. The rise of Western hegemony is the result of colonial expansion and accumulation, which relied on the racist management of labor and resources. Wallerstein's world-system theory is useful for understanding the operative mechanism of Western capitalist accumulation that necessitated the Atlantic commercial circuit. However, as already discussed in chapter 1, Wallerstein still locates the inception of modernity within Europe, namely, the Enlightenment. For Dussel, the colonial Americas was not a mere contributing factor to the rise of the hegemonic Western modernity. Rather, coloniality is both the material and the epistemic foundation that makes the emergence of Europe as the universal axis of world history possible. He writes, "Europe's centrality reflects no internal superiority accumulated in the Middle Ages but it is the outcome of its discovery, conquest, colonization, and integration of Amerindia all of which give it an advantage over the Arab world, India, and China."[14] In this sense, philosophy cannot be separated from the violent geopolitical space in which it was conceived.[15] So is the case with ontology. Ontology, as articulated and advanced by Europe, was conceived from a worldview that was inaugurated with violence and domination. The central philosophical ethos of the modern West, *ego cogito* is predicated upon the question about the humanity of the other (the new world): "Before the *ego cogito* there is an *ego conquiro*; 'I conquer' is the practical foundation of 'I think.'"[16] Such an ontology, Dussel notes, is "the foundation of imperial ideology."[17] Its status as the "rational thinking that expresses Being" is enforced by the existence of nonbeings or less-than beings. The new form of thinking that defies epistemic/ontological violence cannot, therefore, be located within the grammar of traditional ontology. Rather, philosophy of liberation sets out its trajectory in the space of exteriority; "the reality beyond Being," and otherness "anterior to all anteriority."[18] Transmodernity points at the struggle against the violence of Western modernity, the reality and the struggle of those who have always persisted outside of modernity.

Similarly, Dussel's reading of Marx is also inflected by his understanding of Levinasian exteriority as well as Friedrich Wilhelm Joseph von Schelling's *urgrund*. For Schelling, urgrund points at that which exists as an a priori of Being. As an anterior of Being, urgrund indicates the nothing that precedes the totality of Being. It can also be viewed as the creative source of life that precedes Being since becoming something takes the (creative) labor of negating the nothing that lies before oneself.[19] Within the Marxist notion of the production of value, value is understood as the foundation of capital. Marx's notion of surplus value raises the problem of measure that is the uncompensated human labor that facilitates capital accumulation at the expense of workers' labor (exploitation). The inequivalence of measure, however, means that the value the worker creates out of surplus labor is not founded in capital. Dussel names this "living labor" in his reading of Marx's *Economic Manuscript of 1861–1863*. Living labor is indicative of the labor that lies outside the rule of capital: "not-capital, not-objectified labour."[20] While for Marx, human labor is the object of exploitation, it is also, Dussel comments, the source of an otherwise. He cites Marx: "The worker... has the possibility of beginning it again from the beginning, because his life is the source in which his own use value constantly confronts capital again in order to begin the same exchange anew."[21] Dussel's notion of living labor points to the exteriority of human life and labor. It indicates that life and labor are not fully appropriable by the totalitarian system of capital. Like Schelling's urgrund, the otherness prior to Being, living labor hints at the possibility of an alterity in the face of the all-enclosing rule of capital. This way, the value that the worker creates is not a re-creation from capital. Rather, it is a new creation, a creation from nothing, from the outside of the totality of capital. Since it always exists beyond the totalitarian regime of capital, living labor holds the capacity or the possibility of constructing an alternative mode of production and exchange.

We find in these readings how the notion of totality (as well as its constitutive other, alterity) takes a central place in Dussel's work. The notion of totality itself represents a certain form of violence as it operates on the logic of exclusion. Totality negates the existence of otherness inscribed within, the indelible traces of exteriority engraved in the fabric of being/reality. At the same time, it is the existence of this negated otherness that makes the being-there of the presumptive totality possible in the first place. In this sense, totality is a myth that must be deconstructed. European modernity as an all-encompassing totality is made possible only by the negation of its inner otherness, that is, the Americas. Similarly, capital is constituted by that which cannot be registered in its index of value and measure. Living labor points at capital's exteriority. Capital can buy labor capacity but not the totality of life—the "living" labor in its corporeality:

> The price of the labour capacity in the wages, covers an essential fallacy: it is thought that the value of labour is paid when in reality only the value of the labour capacity is paid. The "labor capacity" has value because the corporeality of the labourer has assumed, consumed and incorporated commodities (means of subsistence) which have value.... In a certain way, as the incorporation of wages, the "labor capacity" is now the fruit of objectified labour also—and thus it shall be commensurable, interchangeable, sellable for money: both shall be objectified, past labour. But "living labour" shall never have value; thus, its non-value could not

be determined; it shall not have a price nor shall it be able to receive wages... because it is the "creating source of value."[22]

As Eduardo Mendieta comments, the Marx we find in Dussel's reading is a humanist, an ethicist who offers a metaphysical interpretation of Marx. In it, one finds a critique of the totalitarian system of thinking inherent in Western metaphysics.[23]

An important aspect of Dussel's work that remains perhaps under-recognized is the place of religion in his thought. Early in his career, Dussel wrote several books that deal with religion in Latin America. More specifically, his continuing interest in religion lies in the Christian church's (and its theology's) role in mobilizing mass anti-imperialist social movements in Latin America. The European thinkers from whom he learned were also influenced by the tradition of religious thought yet very few of them engage religion explicitly. Contrastingly, Dussel does not reduce religion's place to private and speculative realms. His engagement with religion, particularly LALT, is significant in numerous ways for thinking about religion and colonial modernity. Dussel's attention to religion aligns with his critical reading of secularism in Western thought. Religion's role in shaping the historical formation of colonial modernity (both within and outside of Europe) was crucial, and its undying influence in today's global order is evident. However, Dussel observes, Western modernity claims its identity as secular. The emergence of the modern *cogito*, which is a derivative of *ego conquiro* (I conquer), means that the Western ego presents itself as the materialization of the divine. In this sense, the modern secularist proclamation of the death of God signifies that the West has deified itself.[24] He rightly points out that the process of secularization in the post-Enlightenment West was a transmutation of religion into a different form rather than the demise of religion in the public sphere altogether. The centralized political system (the state) now takes its place so that the ideology of the nation-state and its political apparatuses of governance symbolize the divine.[25]

Dussel's incisive commentary on the politico-theological problem is linked to his even-more piercing diagnosis of secularism as a symptom of coloniality. He is one of the pioneering critics of the twentieth-century Americas who diagnosed secularism as co-constitutive of coloniality. These thinkers' critical assessment of secularism predates the (post)secular debate that has been taking place in Western academia over the last three decades. More important, they diagnose one of the central problems of secularism that is largely missing in contemporary conversations: secularism's link to coloniality. For Dussel, the secular-philosophical articulation of being and of the world in Western post-theistic intellectual environment is nothing but an articulation of sameness that is the ideology of the hegemonic class: "What are phenomenology and existentialism if not the description of an 'I' or a Dasein from which opens a world, always one's own?"[26] Dussel's critique is directed at the heart of the problem of the secular. His intervention takes us to a distinct genealogy of political theology that distinguishes itself from the European iteration. Whereas the latter tends to probe the mechanism of absolutization in the nexus of law and sovereignty often within the framework of the state, Dussel extends his analysis to a much broader scope via Marx and Latin American philosophy. He borrows Marx's critique of commodity fetishism to amplify the implication that the ideology of the secular bears on political economy. In politics, fetishism refers to the absolutization of the will of the representative over the community it represents. In economy, it indicates the process in which the productive, living social labor is appropriated by capital. The thing (capital) becomes a person while the workers become a thing (that is an instrument that serves capital).[27] This inversion (fetishization) demands divinization. Or, better, the inversion is itself a deification. The philosophers' claim of the death of God (Hegel and Nietzsche), therefore, begs the question "Which God has died? The fetish? Europe as divinized?"[28] Dussel shows us how the advocates of the secular (and secularism) are eager to scrutinize religion, yet largely fail to turn their critical perspectives to the deified entity of the state, the political-economic system driven by fetishizing capitalism, and the colonialist modern order that absolutizes the West. A genuine form of secularism in this geography of power (and of knowledge) is having "the courage of being atheistic vis-á vis an empire of the center, thus incurring the risk of suffering from its power, its economic boycotts, its armies, and its agents who are experts at corruption, violence, and assassination."[29] A genuine secularism involves a critique of the empire, the state and the various forms of violence it sanctions against the poor and the marginalized. It rejects the religion and the god of the fetishistic order dictated by global capitalism. It calls for a disenchantment, not from religion, but from the system that sustains itself at the expense of the sacrifice of the other. Without this critical edge, secularism is a tool that accommodates the colonial worldview and the bourgeois ideology. Dussel cites Marx's famous claim: "the beginning of all criticism is the criticism of religion."

On the altar of the fetishistic religion of the bourgeois modern West are the Amerindians, the Black slaves, colonial Asians, and women who constitute the sacrificial offering required for worship.[30] The operative mechanism of the secular power is informed by religious imaginary and symbols. Constructing and mobilizing of political values and operations are, in a way, secular transcriptions of theological transactions. Thus understood, religion (Christianity to be more specific) cannot be constrained to an affirmation of a metaphysical idea just as atheism is not the negation of the metaphysical concept of a transcendent deity. Rather, atheism for Dussel is the fight for justice that denounces the deified system as unjust, as no longer divine. He writes:

> If the system is divine, it is immutable. If it is not divine, one must be atheistic about it. But one can hardly deny the divinity of a system, present or future, if one does not affirm that the divine is other than all systems. Only this affirmation—first practical and then theoretical—is the condition that makes revolution possible—liberating mobilization against a fetishized system. The practical affirmation of atheism is the struggle for justice. That is, whoever fights for the liberation of the poor affirms in practical manner that the system is unjust, that it is not divine.[31]

With this reversal, the atheist who is uncritical of the divinized (fetishized) order is rendered a worshipper of the fetishistic religion whereas the religious person dedicated to the fight for justice can be viewed as a true atheist. Similarly, enchantment points at the divinized colonial order of knowing/being while the commitment to liberative religion can be viewed as a true form of atheism. It is against this backdrop that Dussel expresses his unreserved endorsement of LALT. He views LALT as an authentically decolonial, transmodern critique of the imperialist/colonial West. In his early years, Dussel was deeply involved in conversations with the leading figures of LALT. He founded and convened CEHILA (Comisión para el Estudio de la Historia de las Iglesias en America Latina y el Caribe / Commission for Historical Studies of the Church in Latin America and the Caribbean), which included many of the major liberation theologians of the time.

Nevertheless, Dussel's philosophy has been challenged by many critics. Expanding on all these points of criticism is certainly beyond the scope of this chapter. But it is important to highlight some key points that raise relevant questions. Perhaps one of the most controversial aspects of Dussel's philosophy is his notion of exteriority/alterity—which is also often viewed as his original contribution. The problem lies, critics observe, in adopting the Levinasian notion of exteriority in its "unpredictable and differential quality" that evades totalitarianism, Dussel takes an absolutist position by "dictating the terms under which alternatives" to the present totalitarian system can be measured.[32] In other words, as Ofelia Schutte points out, Dussel's alterity reifies a new absolute on the name of the poor and the oppressed. Dussel's appropriation of Levinas is a double-edged sword in that while its geopolitical application opens new possibilities for a critique of Eurocentric episteme (and the following political ramifications), such application indicates, as Nelson Maldonado-Torres observes, a mistranslation of a metaphysical category (that points to transontological difference) to a concrete reality (that points to subontological difference).[33] As a result, the notion of radical exteriority becomes a generalized concept, an undifferentiated whole articulated from above, while the particular others of history may be obliterated.[34] Philosophically, the radicalness and the originality of Levinasian alterity lie in its unlocatability. Levinas's other, even as it manifests as the face of the other, always escapes one's grasp. It always indicates an elsewhere, an otherwise. It also disavows the very distinction of inside/outside. The radical nature of the exteriority of the other lies in its immanent transcendence, which does not indicate a unilateral outward movement but a transcendence engraved at the deepest inner dimension of the self. In Dussel, however, this exteriority seems to hint at a unilateral direction. Dussel acknowledges the double dimension of exteriority. The Americas is inseparable from European modernity and vice versa. Europe is constituted by the radical exclusion/exteriority of the Americas. Nevertheless, the complexity of exteriority's multiple locality is later lost as Dussel puts a heavy emphasis on the outer dimension of exteriority. This results in a transcendence perhaps too radically placed outside. In his effort to disavow the absolute of totality, Dussel creates another absolute, an absolute that is all too clearly in a vantage point of purity lying above and beyond. In the same vein, Dussel's notion of analectics carries the risk of reproducing the absolute in its resort to radical exteriority. Analectics offers an important critique of the problems of dialectics represented by Hegel's understanding of world history. Dialectics operates on the mechanism predicated upon sublation. Its "proper category," Dussel adds, is totality.[35] While its complexity and ambiguity cannot be reduced to the simple notion of synthesis, dialectics is often understood as absorbing difference into the coherent synthesis of totality—as it is shown in Hegel's philosophy of history.[36] While dialectics operates from the center, analectics, Dussel asserts, emerges from the periphery, from the place of exteriority. He writes:

> Es superación de la totalidad pero no solo como actualidad de lo que está en potencia en el sistema. Es superación de la totalidad desde la transcendentalidad interna o la exterioridad, el que nunca ha estado dentro. Afirmar la exterioridad es realizar lo imposible para el sistema (no había potencia para ello); es realizar lo nuevo, lo imprevisible para la totalidad, lo que surge desde la libertad incondicionada, revolucionaria, innovadora.[37]

> [It is the overcoming of totality but not only as the actuality of what is in potency in the system. It is the overcoming of totality from internal transcendentality—from exteriority that has never been within. To affirm exteriority is to realize what is impossible for the system (there being no potency for it); it is to realize the *new*, what has not been foreseen by the totality, that which arises from freedom that is unconditioned, revolutionary, innovative.]

Here we find Dussel acknowledging the spatial ambivalence of exteriority. Exteriority is an internal transcendentality that was never subsumed to totality. But its paradoxic opacity gets lost instantly as he pushes its transcendent aspect perhaps too far. He adds that this transcendence is a nonreality, something that has never been a part of the reality. The opaque and distant other, now infused with a sense of messianic purity, becomes the segue into the absolute: an unconditional and invariable reference of liberation. Purity evacuates ambiguity. It can suffocate the opacity of the colonial space marked with the intense and complex reality of power. In the same way, Dussel's project of transmodernity posits Latin America as the timeless signifier of absolute transcendentality.[38]

Despite these limitations, Dussel's work makes a crucial contribution to the study of religion, power, and (de)coloniality in Latin America. The study of religion and the study of coloniality have seldom crossed paths in academic conversations until recent times. For Dussel, the critical study of philosophy (or production of knowledge) requires a critical scrutiny of coloniality. And the study of coloniality cannot be set apart from religion. Likewise, a critical study of religion begins, for Dussel, from interrogating the system of coloniality and its powerful currency, that is, race. While a popular reference in contemporary archive of decolonial theory, Dussel's original critique of religion remains rather underexplored. I have not offered in this section a comprehensive outline of Dussel's theory of religion, but I want to bring attention to a clearly original insight that his articulation of the problem of religion, secularism, and coloniality offers. Like many of his contemporary philosophers of liberation, Dussel pays careful attention to the vital place of religion in a way that draws a sharp contrast with contemporary theorists who often seem to subscribe to a secularist method and relegate religion to a reductive category. Dussel provides us with an amplified perspective on the politico-theological character of colonial modernity. He rightly traces the ontological implication involved in the formation of colonial modernity and he uncovers the theological register that lies underneath it. That the concept of the political is built on the edifice of race and coloniality bears instant implications for the critique of secularism. Dussel highlights the colonial function of the secular with clarity. Colonial modernity deifies the West. The process of secularization the West has imposed globally is, for Dussel, a permutation of religion that sacralizes the legitimized system of violence (the state), and its symbol (Western Man and his values), all of which are materialized in the all-powerful rule of market (neoimperial) capitalism.

Mariátegui and Quijano: Liberation Theology at the Dawn of (De)coloniality

From the standpoint of modern Latin America, religion was never viewed as the opposite of rationality. Those who grappled with the question of Latin American modernity, such as José Enrique Rodó, Juan B. Justo, Alfonso Reyes, and José Carlos Mariátegui, were all critical of organized religion, but they never proposed disenchantment as a solution. Rather, they saw rationalism as compatible with the values that were excluded by the Enlightenment such as aesthetics, subjectivity, and spirituality.[39]

The Peruvian Marxist journalist and philosopher José Carlos Mariátegui offers a unique perspective into the complex relationship between colonialism and secularism in early twentieth-century Latin America. Despite his canonical status in Latin American Marxist intellectual history, the pioneering insight his reading of religion offers remains partly unexplored. Whereas his take on religion and its link to revolutionary politics is widely discussed, his elaborate articulation of secularism's place in the establishment of neocolonial, modern-liberal order in Latin America has been largely overlooked. Mariátegui is a crucial reference in modern Latin American political thought; he made critical contributions to the critique of the problem of race, power, and religion in (post)colonial Latin America, yet he remains an obscure figure in the North American (or North Atlantic more broadly) circle of the study of religion.

Mariátegui noted the inaptitude of traditional Marxist analytics for addressing the class issue in Latin America. Socialist revolution for Mariátegui must incorporate peasants into its struggle. Traditional socialist theory does not view peasants as agents of revolution. But in Latin America, particularly in the case of the Andean Peru, the majority of peasants are of Indigenous origin, and they constitute the lowest (most alienated and exploited) social class. This renders the category of land and race indispensable for analyzing Latin American political economy as they are inseparable from the problem of class. In other words, revolution cannot simply amount to replacement of one ruling system by another in the colonial Andes. Rather, it must aim at the broader problem that is the colonial articulation of power through the broad web of social and material relations. In Mariátegui's observation, the modern-liberal order imposed on Latin America including its secularist installation of religion institutes coloniality of power, and vice versa. The link between religion and coloniality (of power and knowledge) is evidenced in the history of colonial missionaries. For Mariátegui, the missionary activities were not confined to the narrow boundary of religion. Their work covered the much broader realm of life, sociocultural and political—including local economic activities and exchange of knowledge.[40]

An important insight Mariátegui offers for reading the politico-economic situation of the (post)colonial Latin America rests on his analysis of the problem of land and race. The peculiar history of modern Latin America made land a complex knot of connection between class and race. He was one of the first Latin American thinkers to point out that the colonial structure of domination survives colonialism. The nineteenth-century wave of decolonization did not dismantle the colonial feudal system after the revolution, leaving the problem of land (unequal distribution) intact.[41] In much of South America, revolution was led by ruling elites (who were mostly of European ancestry) who never let go of their control of land after complete decolonization took place. The further reinforcement of labor division based on skin color perpetuated the marginalization of Indigenous communities. The key insight Mariátegui offers, according to Quijano, is that the democratic-bourgeois revolution is not capable of addressing the class problem in Latin America since the feudal structure is deeply inscribed in social systems.⁴² Thus, Mariátegui concludes, Latin America is controlled by the coloniality of power that survives decolonization.

As a theorist of revolutionary politics, Mariátegui believed that insurrectionist politics in the (post)colonial Andes required the reconfiguration of religion beyond the Western-liberal (secular) conception. The church and its colonial theology played a critical role in the colonial process. But the problem for Mariátegui is not so much about religion itself but its colonial permutation. The transfer of colonial religion was, in a way, a process of secularization. The conversion to colonial religion involved the training of natives for new (modern) systems of production, a process that was accompanied by acculturation, which included the diverse elements constitutive of social life. In this sense, the colonial order was a total call for the reinvention of life, one that is compatible with the rational/secular character of the Christian Europe.

Devoid of the transformative spiritual power, colonial religion was a clerical apparatus that functioned in the interests of the state.⁴³ This was also the case with Indigenous religions that often became the ideological apparatus of the empire (e.g., the Inca). That the imperial religion surrendered to colonialism (or colonial religion) was, for Mariátegui, symptomatic of the problem of political theology that ossified the spiritual potential of Indigenous religion and cosmology.⁴⁴ Nevertheless, Mariátegui did not reject religion altogether. Against the traditional Marxist view, he saw in religion a profound potential for driving revolution and social change. The problem was not so much in religion itself, but the modern ideal of secular rationality that displaces religion from local (Indigenous) metaphysics and truncates the political possibilities cultivated by spiritual, ethical, and aesthetic sensibilities. The Christian evangelization of the Americas was less a religious enterprise than an ecclesiastical one.⁴⁵ Its process was a bureaucratic installation of the state-sponsored clerical apparatus that was in fact aiming at secularizing the natives. Religion, including in its secularist iteration, was always an important channel of colonial control.

Mariátegui further advances his theory of revolution and social change by adopting the French philosopher George Sorel's language of myth. Sorel's notion of myth provides, for Mariátegui, a deeper theoretical ground for addressing the broader philosophical problem symptomatic of the modern bourgeoise world. Secular rationality is incapable of directing profound social changes. Only religion (myth) can do: "Bourgeoise civilization suffers from a lack of myth, of faith, of hope ... gods."⁴⁶ Colonialism as a secularist project devastates our inner understanding of ourselves as human, spiritually and intellectually. The spiritual and philosophical void is an important question for Mariátegui because political desire is inseparable from human being's innermost metaphysical visions: "The strength of revolutionaries is not in their science; it is in the faith, their passion, in their will. It is a religious, mystical, spiritual force."[47]

Perhaps Mariátegui's most substantial and constructive reflection on religion lies around his works on revolutionary politics in which he mainly attempts to mediate religion with Marxist notions of class conflict and revolution. Most contemporary scholarly discussions on Mariátegui and religion seem to focus on this intersection too. Mariátegui's creative reading of religion is associated mostly with issues of class and political economy. However, an important part of his critique of colonialism is directed at the role of religion and its modern-liberal agenda of secularization. Mariátegui did not develop a systematic and constructive theory of religion for an anticolonial project as he did with his Marxist account of revolutionary politics. But he managed to reconcile Marxism with religion through the mediation of Sorel. Sorel's notion of myth becomes a crucial tool for Mariátegui's reading of Marxism and religion. Sorel saw in religion an indispensable element that gives life to politics, which he called myth. In S. P. Rouanet's words, the Sorelian notion of myth refers to "a social force, a system of images, whose function is to galvanize the masses ... to facilitate action by simplifying the problems at stake."[48] Interpreting the spread of Christianity as the result of proliferation of its myth (the coming of Christ), Sorel suggests myth as the critical power that drives revolution. His concern for myth is motivated by pragmatic reasons. Myth liberates revolutionary impulse from the facticity of the event that drives the masses. In Marxist revolutionary terms, the question is not whether general strike is possible or whether capitalism will actually collapse. What myth does when it is spread efficiently is to move the masses and lead them to revolution.[49] Behind such understanding lies Sorel's anti-intellectualist or antipositivist views. He viewed intellectuals and parliamentary socialists as obstacles to revolution, as problematic examples of moral cowardice.[50]

In the same vein, he viewed theory not as a tool but as a hindrance to action. Rouanet writes, "Sorel, thus, believed that concepts are completely inadequate as a motivating force for action and that history reveals the tremendous fecundity of myths."[51] Myth moves people to action, justifying sacrifice, defying reason, and restoring heroism. In this sense, Michael Tager writes, "Only myths could move men across the threshold between speech and action by transcending politics based on rational calculations."⁵² This is a highly unorthodox idea that conflicts directly with Marxist dialectical materialism as it is the *idea* and *will* that become the driving force of revolution, over against material force and condition. Sorel's heterodox reinvention of Marxism has been constantly subject to contestation. His voluntarism and functionalist view of myth along with his radical rejection of science and intellectualism made Sorel a controversial figure among Marxist thinkers. He would often be accused of distorting Marxism and providing the theoretical framework for neo-fascist ideals.⁵³

While Mariátegui was significantly influenced by Sorel, he did not adopt Sorel's entire system uncritically. Rather, Mariátegui found some key Sorelian insights useful for recalibrating the colonial mechanism of power in the Andes in which religion is divorced from the human and conjugated with the state. His visionary analysis of the Eurocentric reason and its role in the hegemonic enactment of coloniality led Mariátegui to Sorel as the latter's antipositivism offers a useful theoretical platform for separating Marxist analytic tools from deterministic conceptions of Marxism. Sorel's incorporation of religious concepts such as belief, sacrifice, and virtue highly appealed to Mariátegui, who was critical of the mechanistic determinism that the mainstream (European) socialism was advocating.⁵⁴ Determinism, he declares, contradicts the fundamental spirit of Marxism: "Marxism, where it has shown itself to be revolutionary—that is, where it has been Marxist—has never obeyed a passive and rigid determinism."⁵⁵ Despite his emphasis on political economy, Mariátegui adds, Marx "always understood the spiritual and intellectual capacity of the proletariat to create a new order through class struggle as a necessary condition."⁵⁶ The voluntarist nature of Marxism marks the entire trajectory of its development in history. In Mariátegui's own words:

> The voluntarist character of socialism is, in truth, no less evident—even if less understood by its critics—than its determinist foundation. To give it its true value, though, it is nevertheless enough to follow the development of the proletarian movement from the actions of Marx and Engels in London at the beginning of the First International to the present, dominated by the first experience of a socialist state: the USSR. In this process, every word, every Marxist act, resounds with faith, will, heroic and creative conviction, whose impulse it would be absurd to seek in a mediocre and passive determinist sentiment.⁵⁷

Most important, determinism fails to cater to the postcolonial Andean context in which revolution is entwined with complex issues of knowledge, culture, race, and land. Knowledge is grounded in metaphysics or/and religion, which is rejected by positivism/determinism. In this sense, it is no accident that Mariátegui turned to Sorel. As Quijano notes, what makes Mariátegui intriguing and relevant is not so much the clarity of his thoughts or his reading of Sorel. Rather, his greatest contribution lies in reinventing Marxism by way of contextualizing it to the Latin American situation of his time.[58] Such relevance, I submit, is still highly valid in the Latin American context of our time.

In this sense, Mariátegui's use of the Sorelian notion of myth should not be understood in functionalist terms; myth is not a mere political tool that serves pragmatic purposes of mobilizing the masses, as is the case with Sorel. Rather, it fills the void created by the hegemonic installation of the secular. The secularist agenda creeping underneath colonialism has deprived Indigenous people of their religious and philosophical ground. Science and reason, the ultimate beacon of Western liberalism, cannot attend to the depth and fullness of the human, the sacred that makes us human. He writes, "Bourgeoise civilization suffers from a lack of myth, of faith, of hope.... Western man for some time has placed Reason and Science at the altar of dead gods."[59] Yet the secular, with its banner of liberal reason, has proved itself misleading: incapable of testifying to the reality of public life in which religion and politics are inseparably entangled with each other; insufficient to attend to the deepest reality of the human whose political reality and desire cannot be separated from her/his innermost metaphysical desires. Mariátegui writes, "But neither Reason nor Science can meet the need of the infinite that exists in man. Reason itself has been challenged, demonstrating to humanity that it is not enough. Only myth possesses the precious virtue of satisfying its deepest self."[60] Myth grounds human beings. What makes us human is the capacity to believe otherwise, to hope for the impossible yet to come, that the deepest aspiration of our ideals might find materialization on the horizon of history. Revolution is inseparable from myth since they both play the same function of attending to fundamental metaphysical needs of the human: "As Sorel has noted, the last five years have proved that revolutionary myths can take up the profound consciousness of men with the same plenitude as the ancient religious myths."[61]

Nevertheless, just as Sorel was criticized by the French Marxists, Mariátegui was also widely criticized by Latin American Marxists for misunderstanding, distorting, and spiritualizing Marxism. The Peruvian thinker, in their eyes, was paying too much attention to metaphysics and theory over political economy, which is the key substance of Marxism.[62] On a different note, while Mariátegui was aware of the danger lingering in the Sorelian notion of myth—the possible fascist abuse of it for the manipulation of masses— he did not elaborate further on it. This is because he found problems not in myth itself but the political ideologies that manipulate it.[63] It is important to clarify that there is a clear distinction between Sorel's notion of myth and Mariátegui's use of it. Whereas Sorelian notion of myth indicates general strike, Mariátegui's points at the broader social revolution. As Schutte observes, Sorelian myth is meant to rule out perspectives; Mariátegui's myth is linked to the inauguration of a new consciousness.[64] What makes Mariátegui one of the most original and important Latin American Marxist intellectuals of the twentieth century is arguably his reinvention of Marxism by situating it in the Latin American context. In doing so, Mariátegui opened the possibility of mediating Marxism with the (post)colonial articulation of power engraved in various issues such as land, racial politics, knowledge, and religion—beyond the constraints of dogmatic determinism. He understood that colonial power survives the historical manifestation of colonialism and conditions the present. However, Mariátegui's critique of the colonial Andes/Americas has not always been read in tandem with his creative reading of Marxism. The connection between these two important areas of Mariátegui's contribution was lucidly theorized by Quijano who articulated the notion of the coloniality of power, which provided an important theoretical framework for later generation of scholars in decolonial thinking. Schutte's reading of Mariátegui in *Cultural Identity and Social Liberation in Latin American Thought* expands Mariátegui's broader relevance for questions of cultural identity that are central to the post/decolonial inquiry. I argue that Mariátegui's work as a form of political theology suggests the rethinking of the modern-liberal notion of religion that conditions the discourse of politics, revolution, and the human.

Mariátegui's political theology sought to disarticulate the colonial matrix of power. Revolution in the postcolonial Andes cannot be conceived without undoing the intricate knot of liberal-secular coloniality. In his analysis of myth and class struggle, Mariátegui shows how the liberal-secular understanding of religion becomes the defining element of the proletariat, which distinguishes it from the bourgeoisie: "the bourgeoisie no longer has any myths. It has become incredulous, skeptical, nihilistic. The reborn liberal myth has aged too much. The proletariat has a myth: the social revolution. It moves toward that myth with a passionate and active faith."⁶⁵ The truly revolutionary social force emerges out of faith, religious passion. Politics becomes a matter of theology: political theology. Revolution deconstructs the division between the sacred and the secular: "The strength of revolutionaries is not in their science; it is in their faith, their passion, in their will. It is a religious, mystical, spiritual force. The revolutionary excitement as I wrote in an article on Ghandi, is a religious emotion. Religious motives have been displaced from the heavens to earth. They are not divine. They are human, social."⁶⁶ The deep imbrication of colonialism and religion makes the project of delinking from coloniality a theological project. Revolution and decoloniality become a theological task.

As I mentioned already, Mariátegui's analysis of colonial power served as the foundation for Quijano's notion of coloniality of power. However, it is not Quijano who further advanced a theory of religion in conversation with revolutionary politics, but a group of Christian theologians identified with the movement known as liberation theology. Mariátegui's charge against liberalism and the subsequent turn to religion suggests religion as a potential resource for decolonial thinking and struggle. The liberationist project taken up by Latin American theologians has demonstrated its clear historical contributions as well as its limitations. Despite its anti-imperialist orientation, the limits of liberation theology as a post/decolonial method rests on its heavy reliance on European social theory and theological framework. Perhaps this is why, despite their sympathetic reception, decolonial theorists rarely consider Latin American liberation theology a serious interlocutor. Or perhaps the omission of LALT in the study of (de)coloniality can be attributed to the dominant secularist framework that informs the ongoing conversations.

Against the postmodern and postcolonial skeptics, there have been in recent years various attempts to reconsider liberation theology from the post/decolonial viewpoint.⁶⁷ These critics generally view liberation theology as a critical interlocutor in reconstructing a viable theological alternative capable of addressing the problem of violence and inequality sustaining the neocolonial global order. Some seek to repurpose the potentially limiting orientation of liberation theology with the end of suggesting new directions in the postcolonial age (Luis Rivera-Pagan, Ivone Gebara, Marcella Althaus-Reid, Nancy Bedford, Nelson Maldonado-Torres, Mayra Rivera, Jonathan Pimentel) whereas others recast liberation theology as a viable decolonial option despite the limits presented in the works of first- and second-generation liberation theologians (Juan José Tamayo, Nestor Miguez, Joerg Rieger and Jung Mo Sung, Andrew Irvine, Claudio Carvalhaes, Joseph Drexler-Dreis, Nicolas Panotto, Filipe Maia). Both groups acknowledge liberation theology's commitment to anti-imperial struggle and theory. They are also wary of the suggestion that innovative theological works done by liberation theologians should not be dispensed with altogether as theology recalibrates its post/decolonial orientation.[68]

Since its inception, liberation theology has been firmly grounded in the anti-imperial political vision informed by Marxist social theory and grassroot social movements. LALT's anti-imperial vision shares its roots with contemporary decolonial theory. Dependency theory, the primary theoretical source informing both decolonial theory and LALT, offers a strong critique of the West's neocolonial economic (and political) hegemony that operates on an exploitative mechanism. In this sense, it is safe to say that the trajectory of LALT has partially intersected with decolonial thought, even though such crossings have not resulted in substantial conversations. It is not my intention to re-illuminate the decolonial potential dormant in LALT for the sake of refashioning LALT as a compelling resource for a decolonial critique. The point is not so much about rescuing LALT but revisiting the misconstrued place of religion within the trajectory of twentieth-century decolonial thinking. Wrestling with the insights advanced by LALT might help us recalibrate the place and possibility of decolonial thought for a more relevant and comprehensive analysis of the problem of power (and religion) in Latin America. Reversely, reflecting on what is left undeveloped by LALT will help us rethink LALT's place within the twenty-first-century cartography of power in Latin America. That the contributions of LALT are unacknowledged (and undertheorized) in the conversations about decolonial thought points at an important methodological problem that I repeatedly raise in this book, namely, the secularist framework that prescribes (the study of) religion. The far-reaching impact that LALT had across the Latin American social and political landscape is unique and profound. Omitting an intellectual and political movement of such scale by segregating it to the narrow realm of religion fails to attend to the historical complexity that configures religion and coloniality in the Americas.

When we take into account that the key ideas Mariátegui proposed are essentially a decolonial rendition of Marxism, it is not difficult to see the shared theoretical root between Latin American decolonial thought and LALT. Mariátegui's writings on revolution, land, and religion had a strong and lasting influence on the Latin American intellectual scene, and the leading figures of LALT were also informed by his thinking. One of the most important early proponents of liberation theology, Gustavo Gutiérrez, finds in Mariátegui an inspiration for contextualizing revolutionary social thought from the Latin American perspective. What Gutiérrez found inspiring in Mariátegui was his ability to creatively deviate from the dogmatic orthodoxy of theory (traditional Marxism)—despite his strong commitment to Marxist critique and praxis—in search of a paradigm that is more relevant to problems specific to the Latin American context. Mariátegui privileges praxis against the traditional Western binary that separates knowledge from praxis, and this, for Gutiérrez, is deeply useful for rethinking the relationship between belief and praxis.[69] Mariátegui's vision of the human was not one that was determined by a static modality of knowing. Rather, the human being is driven by faith, a faith that inspires one to act, feel, and struggle.[70]

Also testifying to the decolonial potential of LALT is the fact that a decolonial reading of Exodus informs the central hermeneutical principle of LALT.[71] Based on this, some commentators have recently started to claim LALT as an original form of (proto)decolonial thought.[72] I resist the temptation to make strong claims about the decolonial potential and contribution of LALT, while at the same time interrogating the rather simplistic dismissal of LALT in contemporary conversations about Latin American decolonial thought. The theoretical foundation of the main figures of early LALT is mostly based in European theology, philosophy, and social theory. Despite their clear stance on economic-political imperialism, the analysis of the broader impact of coloniality is largely absent in these works. However, these limitations do not necessarily suggest that LALT's potential and contribution be easily dispensed with. Walter Mignolo's dismissal of liberation theology as "Western theory" both echoes and perpetuates the liberal-secularist framework that prescribes religion's role to a narrow social function.[73]

Mignolo's assessment of LALT draws a historical parallel with the German political theologian Jürgen Moltmann who made a similar accusation in his now-famous correspondence with the Argentine protestant liberation theologian José Miguez Bonino in the mid-1970s. Responding to Miguez Bonino's charge against European political theology of the absence of sociopolitical analysis and concrete identification with the poor, Moltmann writes that LALT lacks originality as it is built on the foundation of Western social theory (Marxism). Moltmann's accusation—which he later drops by admitting his own misunderstanding—is misplaced for two different reasons. First, the use of Marxism by LALT is not a unilateral, defining character of LALT. Their adoption and use of Marxist analytics is neither uncritical nor passive. As I mentioned already, LALT is informed by a social analysis built on a contextualized use of Marxist theory. This results in the original reconfiguration of analytic frameworks and conceptual ideas, such as orthopraxis (and faith as a twin mirror of praxis), the affiliation of religion with revolution, and anti-imperialist politics as well as the emphasis on the peripheral perspective or locus of enunciation (à la Mignolo) via dependency theory. LALT's Marxism was more akin to a Marxist humanism with an emphasis on ethics rather than a dogmatic formula for revolution. Second, similarly, LALT's use of European political theology does not indicate LALT's complete dependence on it. LALT drew many of its theoretical foundations and insights in conversation with European political theology, but they were also critical of its limitations as a theology that was produced from the first world (center). Resonating with Miguez Bonino's critique, Gutiérrez comments that European-American progressive theology's interlocutor is the liberal ideology with the bourgeois class being its historical subject.[74] In contrast, the agents of LALT are those "without a history."[75] Juan Luis Segundo has also pointed out the danger of diluting the absolute character of historical intervention presented in LALT. Commenting on Johann Metz's and Jurgen Moltmann's eschatology, Segundo observes a relativist view on the commitment to action in their work, a position derivate of the power-class differential between Europe and Latin America.[76]

Reflecting on the historical trajectory of LALT, Dussel locates Hugo Assmann's work *Teología de la liberación* (1969) as the founding text that offers the first methodological definition of liberation theology.[77] But before Assmann offered his systematic work on liberation theology, it was Segundo whose visionary early works laid out the theoretical foundation of liberation theology. Segundo draws on social scientific analyses in his theological work already in 1961. Adjacent to this growing early movement of protoliberation theology headed by Segundo (a circle that included both Gutiérrez and Assmann), there was the grassroot movement initiated in Brazil, later widely spread through Latin America, called CEB. Influenced by Paulo Freire's important work on liberation pedagogy, CEB was organized by rural laity with the aim of studying the Bible, building solidarity, and providing material and educational resources to the local masses. In the aforementioned 1969 work, Assmann clarifies LALT's relationship to European political theology by highlighting LALT's difference in its method, goal, and orientation in relation to the former.[78]

Whereas Mignolo overlooks the contribution of religion in anticolonial struggle, Dussel finds in religion (and in liberation theology) "a truth" that exceeds the colonial fabulation of secular rationality. Dussel diagnoses the shortfalls of progressive political theologies born in Europe by pointing toward their failure to address the imperialist dimension of the West and its theology. Political theology rightly questions the problem of class struggle from the perspective of religion but it limits its analysis to the boundaries set by national Marxism.[79] Dussel rightly situates theological knowledge in the geopolitical context by pointing out the limits of thinking that fails to address the situation of the periphery (Latin America), which suffers from the violent domination by the center.[80] He provincializes European political theology by clarifying that its audience is Europe. These theologies speak to their own problem despite their continuous appeal to universality. North Atlantic theologies, he adds, are theologies of the center. They are "I" centered.[81]

The same decolonial principle that constitutes philosophy of liberation applies to liberation theology. Challenging the totality of European modernity requires that one think from its exteriority, the periphery. Being in Latin America, Dussel adds, indicates a different reality: a reality that cannot be addressed by the theologians of the Northern Hemisphere who lack a genuine interest in (hence, a compelling diagnosis of) the reality of the periphery. LALT hints at a decolonial alternative, a theology "de lo nuestro."[82] It overcomes the limits of European political theology built on the ontological foundation of the "I conquer," which reduces the other to an abstract idea. Liberation theology emerges from a radical methodological shift in which the central method of doing theology is born out of the praxis for liberation and the experience of "the periphery, coming from outsiders, from the lumpen of the world."[83] It is important to note that Dussel is not a mere interlocutor who supported LALT from the outside. He was actively involved in the conversations about LALT from its early days, and his contributions are formative of the trajectory of the development of LALT just as his own philosophy was informed by it.

The idea of liberation was a central topic in philosophy circles in the late 1960s and early 1970s of Latin America. These philosophy gatherings included not only philosophers (among whom Dussel was a part) but also theologians such as Hugo Assmann and Juan Carlos Scannone.[84] Dussel was one of the cofounders of CEHILA, an organization that produced some of the most important scholarly works of LALT. In his early years, he dedicated as much time writing about theology and the work of the progressive church (LALT) as producing philosophical works. For Dussel, as for many philosophers and theologians of his time in Latin America, both theology and philosophy of liberation were born in the same womb and they addressed similar concerns. Liberationist movements emerging in the 1960s and 1970s Latin America, in which LALT was a part, had a broader social impact beyond the boundaries of the church. Diverse forms of social, intellectual, and political movements with liberationist orientation spread across Latin America during this time.[85] Dussel was one of the first and most original voices who insistingly articulated the need for a decolonial form of thinking not only among Latin American philosophers of his generation but also among liberation theologians. In many of his theological writings written in direct conversation with theologians, Dussel consistently and unreservedly argued for the need to break from Eurocentric modes of thinking. Unfortunately, his contemporary theological interlocutors did not go as far as to break from European theological and epistemic methods. While LALT already carries a strong decolonial orientation in its geohistoric commitment and its political engagement, its potential is often eclipsed by the limitations evident in the methods and theoretical frameworks that the early generation of liberation theologians have adopted. Considering Mariátegui's influence on LALT and Dussel's involvement in its early phase, the absence of a more visible decolonial perspective in early LALT is truly a missed opportunity. It is, however, an oversimplification and mischaracterization to ignore LALT's contribution altogether and exclude it from the critical theorizing of a decolonial otherwise. Since its inception, LALT was never a homogeneous movement with a single theoretical axis or a homogeneous methodological framework. The diverse voices and perspectives that represent LALT point at multiple diverging trajectories that signal new possibilities and orientations.

Decolonial Liberation Theologies I: The Market,
Commodity Fetishism, and Utopic Reason

As LALT undergoes a methodological shift toward the late 1980s due to the transition in the political landscape of Latin America, the Costa Rica–based DEI (Departamento Ecuménico de Investigación), headed by Franz Hinkelammert, Pablo Richard, and Hugo Assmann, advanced a distinctive brand of liberation theology (a work they already started in the mid-1970s) by centering their focus on the analysis of economy (market capitalism) and its relationship to theology. Particularly influential is the work of Hinkelammert whose critique of the ideology of the market and utopic reason has generated a significant repercussion across Latin American social theorists. Hinkelammert views capitalism and its utopic reason as constitutive of modernity. Utopic reason is the ideological principle of Western capitalist modernity that strives for the idea of an infinite and seamlessly linear progress. This system takes a theological character in Hinkelammert's observation. His observation creates a strong resonance with Walter Benjamin's critique of secularism, capitalism, and Western modernity. His critique also parallels (and precedes) Dussel's critique of the fetishizing force of capitalism as a politico-theological machine. Following Marx's critique of commodity fetishism, Hinkelammert argues that the capitalist market, with its force that institutionalizes (and abstracts) human relations, is a system that brings about death. The fetishizing and abstracting power of death is reinforced by the absolutization of the market, the consecration of its institution and logic.[86] The secular order advanced by the modern West has championed disenchantment with transcendental deities yet its absolutization of the utopic reason (based in infinite progress) and market capitalism illustrates the theological apparatus that sacralizes a transcendental world produced by abstraction. Hinkelammert re-illuminates Marx's critique of commodity fetishism as an important critique of the political theology of capitalism. For Marx, true religious images are found in the system that turns commodities into subjects. It sacralizes commodity relations between human beings, a relation that administers life and death.[87] The theological aspect of Marx's critique intensifies as he calls the world of commodity subjects a world of polytheism. The multiple gods that represent various commodities are sustained by the unifying (hence, monotheistic) axis of capital.[88] The problem of sacralized capital is not restricted to modern capitalism. Since Columbus and early colonial settlers in America, true religion has always been the religion of gold (*religion del oro*).[89] The deified capital as a historical continuum that stretches through colonial modernity sacralizes, for Hinkelammert, the myth of secularization: "No hay secularización, sino divinización del mercado. Es a la vez fetichización del mundo que sustituye la Entzauberung (desmagización, desencantamiento) del mundo, que Max Weber constataba. Sin embargo, el fetiche, del cual ya hablaba Marx, sustituye la magia. En el fetiche la omnipresencia del mercado está dada" (There is no secularization but divinization of the market. It is at the same time the fetishization of the world that replaces the *Entzauberung* (disenchantment) of the world that Max Weber noted. Nevertheless, the fetish, which Marx had already indicated, replaces magic. The omnipresence of the market is given in the fetish).[90] Hinkelammert amplifies Marx's critique of religion and market to develop his own critique of the secular world that constitutes itself through sacrifice (death of the marginalized). This secular order is theological in its character. It absolutizes its values, currency, and transactions that commodify life and relations. Its driving force is the theological promise of infinite progress and gain. Along with Dussel, Hinkelammert has advanced a theological critique of Western secular modernity that sacralizes the capitalist market and its operating mechanism. While the decolonial aspect of Hinkelammert's analysis might not seem explicit at first, it is important to note that his work has developed in the specific geopolitical context of Latin America in reaction to the neocolonial reconfiguration of the global political economy in which Latin America was the frontline of its political-economic experiment. His early academic career in 1960s and 1970s Chile let him be the firsthand witness to this process in which he had to flee the country after the US-backed coup led to Pinochet's dictatorship and turned Chile into one of the earliest living experiments of the global neoliberal agenda. In this sense, Hinkelammert's critique of the theological ideology of Western secular modernity and its deified market capitalism presupposes Latin America as the colonial site of primitive accumulation constitutive of the former. Reading Hinkelammert alongside Dussel allows us to re-illuminate the distinctive contribution that Latin American philosophies and theologies of liberation offer for a decolonial critique and theory of religion. Particularly, their critique of the theological character of the secular and its affiliation with the Western modern capitalist order unveils the intricate ways in which religion and economy constitute colonial modernity. The myth of modernity materialized through colonial capitalism demands sacrifice as an offering. For Hinkelammert and Dussel, capitalism is a religion, with the market placed on its highest altar of worship whose rule relies on both the utopic promise of progress and the blood of the disposable. The coloniality enacted in the secular carries both theological and material characters. Its theological and material characters are in fact two sides of the same coin. The secular accommodates the absolutist theology of the powerful market in the colony seamlessly. The sweeping presence of fetishized religion in the modern West and Latin America calls for a broad response from religious communities that have, against the tyranny of the deified colonial capitalist machine, relentlessly built networks of solidarity that disrupt abstracted social relations.

Both Dussel and Hinkelammert demonstrate the central place of religion as a critical analytic lens for a decolonial critique of capitalist modernity. Their reading indicates the theological axis that undergirds the secular system of political economy. The fetishizing power of market capitalism and its metaphysics is mobilized by the theology that is internal to its mechanism. In fact, the commodifying abstraction is itself a theological power, an act of divination. The Americas (and the global south more broadly) is the colonial market essential to the system, that is, capitalist modernity. Whereas traditional Marxist accounts view primitive accumulation as a prehistoric form of capitalist expansion, Dussel and Hinkelammert view primitive accumulation, following Rosa Luxemburg, as central to the modern capitalist system. The capitalist system of production and exchange in core regions (mature accumulation) necessitates a continuous sanction of imperialist expansionism in colonial periphery (primitive accumulation).[91] LALT's critique of colonial modernity consists of a vigilant rejection of the mythical (theological) violence that legitimizes colonial capitalism as an absolute system of transcendence. LALT as a broader social movement signifies in this sense a counter politico-theological struggle against the political theology of colonial capitalist modernity.

Decolonial Liberation Theologies II: Sex, Desire, and Economy

Along with the works of the DEI school, various voices that challenge the homogeneity of the category of the poor—one of the major problems for which the early liberation theologians have been often critiqued—started to emerge. Important works dealing with the oppression of women by feminist theologians such as Elsa Tamez, Ivone Gebara, and Maria Clara Bingemer have started to locate gender as a key hermeneutical axis for thinking about liberation and theology.[92] Along with gender, the question of race has been pushed by Black and Indigenous theologians of Latin America. The works of Afro-Latin American theologians such as Antônio Aparecido da Silva and the works of Indigenous theologians such as Eleazar Lopez Hernandez and Aiban Wagua, among many others, place the problem of race and Indigeneity at the center of liberation theology.[93]

A compelling account of liberation theology with a decolonial and feminist orientation can be found in the work of the queer theologian Marcella Althaus-Reid who has rigorously challenged the homogenizing construction of the poor in liberation theology. In conversation with various Latin American thinkers and postmodern philosophies and theories, she approaches the issue of oppression and violence in Latin America as a problem not only of economic exploitation, but also of sexual and (neo)colonial oppression. A narrow understanding of the mechanism of power results in segregating the problem of economy and class from the intersectional issues of race, colonialism, gender, and sex. Consequently, LALT (particularly its early proponents) has constructed the victims of history by employing the simplistic notion of "the poor," which many critics have been pointing out since the 1980s.

One of the central axes of Althaus-Reid's work lies in breaking down the binary that subjugates sex and body to the private. Breaking down this binary and re-illuminating the relevance of sex/body in political (and social) life has always been the shared goal of feminist thinking and movement. The originality and significance of Althaus-Reid's contribution rest on her creative excavation of the intimate connection between normative discourse about sex, economy, and theological imaginations. She observes how this complex intersectionality of power is both derivative and generative of the colonial logic, or, better, coloniality.[94]

The question of gender and sex is central for thinking about the oppression and the liberation of the poor in postcolonial Latin America. The story of colonization, Althaus-Reid observes, is a story of patriarchal exploitation of women.[95] The oppression of women has always carried economic implications. Women's bodies and their labor were objects of appropriation and exchange (often for survival from the perspective of the women). An explicit link between sex, economy, and religion is already present in early colonial times when Christianity "imposed a sexual economic order of usury, of usage of people in relationships."[96] Women were rated by their reproductive work/capacity while a significant part of land property belonged to the church. This was not merely a system affecting a particular population in the colonial Americas, but a total reconfiguration of relationships—the invention of a new existence and identity propelled by Christian ideals and institutional practices, more specifically, Christianity's alliance with an economic system that runs on the exploitation of labor and women. This intimate connection holding together the operative mechanism of the colonial order continues to inform the current system of neocolonial order. To understand the ongoing rule of the triple axis (sex, economy, God) of coloniality, Althaus-Reid closely examines the intricate connection between the dominant sexual politics lurking in the theological language (symbol) of God and the economy. Particularly important are her provocative use of sexual imageries and metaphors for reading theological concepts. The decoupling of sex from theological languages is indicative of the problematic binary that privatizes and depoliticizes sex.

Read through the lens of (hetero)sexuality, countless theological images and concepts project a (hetero)sexist norm predicated on the subjugation of women, diverse forms of nonheterosexualities, and more important, desire. Althaus-Reid's book *Indecent Theology* offers a plethora of readings and analyses that point at such nuanced connections. In her readings, the figure of divinity is conceived as a patriarchal, heterosexist authority who constantly demands passivity and obedience. Undoing these loaded knots of ideology calls for "perver/tive" reading practices that radically challenge the normative order. The segregation of sex and body in theological languages sets powerful social and epistemic norms that have historically degraded values/symbols/practices associated with the non-Christian/Western other. Such ideals also inform and drive dominant economic models and systems. Althaus-Reid's work sheds light on the correlation between economic models and relationship models by tracing how both economic desire and erotic desire are channeled and reflect each other. The models that regulate the exchange of intimacy concern the economy of bodies. Althaus-Reid writes, "Economic desires walk hand in hand with erotic desires and theological needs. An economic model is a relationship model based on erotic considerations concerning the economy of bodies in society, their intimacy and distance and the patterns of accepted and unaccepted needs in the market and the making of the politics of satisfaction."[97] Sex organizes categories of economy. Normative (hetero)sexuality and theology support normative economy models: "The economy of bodies considers the basics of what we need, while intimacy and distance are to be seen in the way society is organised and how the mechanisms of production for meeting those needs are regulated."[98] Theology, as the foundational reserve of Western cultural and epistemological norms, is implicated in the production and maintenance of this order. Every theology, Althaus-Reid adds, "implies a conscious or unconscious sexual and political praxis."[99] The triple implication of sex, theology, and economy indicates that "the dislocation of sexual constructions goes hand in hand" with the dislocation of both normative theology and the hegemonic politico-economic system.¹⁰⁰ Through *Indecent Theology* and *The Queer God*, Althaus-Reid offers numerous examples of theological symbols, narratives, and doctrines instrumental to the construction of sexual norms and economic models.

The complexity and the interdisciplinary breadth of Althaus-Reid's method go well beyond the traditional models of LALT. She was trained in the tradition of LALT and she clearly situates her own work within the discourse of LALT. Her own project begins at the very site in which LALT is rooted, which is solidarity with the poor and the struggle for their liberation. However, the homogeneous category of the poor displaces the complex reality of the marginalized subjects. The stories of women (particularly poor women), immigrants, Indigenous people, and queer people can be violently erased by the vague category of the poor. This not only fails to undo Christian theology's own implication in the production of subjects dictated by the patriarchal construction of sexuality but also forecloses the subversive potential of sexuality: "What happens then is that if the shanty townspeople go in procession carrying a statue of the Virgin Mary and demanding jobs, they seem to become God's option for the poor. However, when the same shanty townspeople mount a carnival centered on a transvestite Christ accompanied by a Drag Queen Mary Magdalene kissing his wounds, signing songs of political criticism, they are not anymore God's option for the poor."¹⁰¹ Her critique of the asexuality of LALT is followed by her critique of the Eurocentric method and theory with which LALT has organized its scholarship. Despite its important contribution, LALT was not critical of the traditional epistemological framework of Western theology. While dislocating the traditional theological method with its analysis of class, Althaus-Reid observes, "Christianity as a totality was left wanting."¹⁰² How LALT articulated its revolutionary theological ideas did not break from the dominant Western theological pattern, thus domesticating various subversive elements lurking in theology.¹⁰³ At the same time, the popularization of LALT in North Atlantic academia boosted what could be called a theological voyeur-tourism, which fetishized the authentic "native" and "poor" of Latin America. LALT, this way, became a "theological theme park (Disneyland)."¹⁰⁴

Althaus-Reid offers an important analytic for understanding the complex mechanism of power through which coloniality operates via theological symbols and practices. Theology as the knowledge about God enforces regulative principles of normative sexuality. The collusive installation of hegemonic discourses of theology and sexuality conditions the sociopolitical imaginary that structures the economic system. Her proposal for revisiting LALT is marked with "indecency," that is, an "indecent theology." The cardinal methodological principle of her theology is the understanding and acknowledging of the centrality of intersectionality. Liberation of the oppressed must speak to/with the marginalized class in the global neoliberal economy, but those most affected are often women, the Indigenous population, immigrants, and anyone deviating from normative sexualities. Traditional theology has colluded not only with ideas and principles of the ruling economic class, but also with hegemonic sexual norms and discourses. An indecent theology is a critique and refusal of these intersectional norms that are implicated with each other. Althaus-Reid's provocative reading and queering of traditional theological concepts and symbols is geared toward reconstructing the values, practices, and orientations that were colonized by traditional theology. One such site is the materiality of the body. Both the messiness and the possibility of the flesh and its desire reveal the complex entanglement of power (and religion) inscribed in social relations. Such complexity demands a multidisciplinary approach that goes beyond the parameters of traditional scholarly methods. Althaus-Reid's indecent proposal, therefore, calls for decolonizing method and theory. The multiple loci in which power is inscribed must be identified and disentangled through stories, objects, practices, symbols, and exchanges of the ordinary people who are struggling for survival. Her own writing navigates a wide spectrum of sources, including academic ones such as French philosophy and theory; post/decolonial thought; vernacular arts and poetry; nonnormative sexual practices; material objects; and stories. Particularly notable is her use of stories as she extends her sources not only to traditional stories of struggle and survival, but also to stories of sex and "illegitimate" sexual exchanges, stories of everyday practices of ordinary people who, despite suffering from the violence sanctioned against them, reveal the possibilities of their agency and creative desires, which are often written off by academic theories and discourses. Althaus-Reid's work indicates important signals for both LALT and decolonial theory. Her work extends the breadth and the scope of LALT to important sites of intersectionality that had been largely missing in the field. She points toward the complex crossroads and sites in which the coloniality of power, in its religious iteration, externalizes across Latin America. Her work allows us to identify and reflect on numerous sites and possibilities of a decolonial otherwise that have been looming in unexpected sites, encounters, and exchanges all along Latin America.

Conclusion

Both the contribution and the ongoing relevance of LALT have been underappreciated in recent North Atlantic academic conversations that often tend to quickly jump into a dismissal or mischaracterization of LALT. Such premature diagnoses are produced by many different factors, one being the general contraction of interest on the problem of political economy and class within the historical climate of the post-Soviet expansion of the global neoliberal regime. The new global order aggravated the already asymmetrical share of the global south in the market of knowledge production, thus accelerating the monopoly of English publications (followed by German and French), mostly produced by scholars based in the global north. LALT's access to the global market of knowledge has dwindled significantly as its circulation outside the Hispanophone world is strictly reliant on mediation by select European and American scholars. Where some of the new voices in LALT are introduced to the global academic community, they are measured by conceptual methods and categories formulated by theories of the global north, which often misconceptualize religion and LALT within the broader intellectual and social cartography of the Americas. Just as the proper place and impact of religion in Latin America are misconceived, so are the broader transnational conversation and solidarity LALT has established across cultural and religious boundaries. For decades, LALT has established an expansive network of dialogue and solidarity with various social and religious movements of the global south, playing a crucial role in the formation of various liberationist movements that often took anti/decolonial forms. These include diverse forms of Christian contextual theologies across cultures as well as Jewish, Buddhist, Islamic, and other forms of liberation theologies. The scope of these broader exchanges is vast and its significance has yet to be fully articulated.

My goal in this chapter was far from recasting LALT as an innovative source of decolonial theory by putting it into a dialogue with newly emerging theories and concepts. What I hope to rescue LALT from, however, is the overall absence of LALT in contemporary academic conversations, including in religious studies (theology) and decolonial theory. Such absence is rooted in an oversimplifying view of religion within the social-cultural texture of the Latin American context. Historically, LALT has presented visible limitations. But it is important to remember that the often-recurring critique leveled against LALT is usually based in the reading of a few early figures well known to the West. LALT cannot be reduced to a few thinkers. Its trajectory is heterogeneous; its scope and influence are much broader than what is often known to readers in the West. Exploring these diverse trajectories may open various possibilities of dialogue and critique of (neo)colonial power relations that keep shaping the dominant understanding of knowing and being in the twenty-first century. The brief review I presented offers nothing but a mere glimpse, a partial perspective on the ever-expanding field.

LALT cannot be reduced to the narrow subfield of theology. Tracing its historical development, it is far from difficult to notice its overlapping trajectory with the Latin American currents of decolonial thought. Both LALT and decolonial thought share their roots with the progressive branch of early to mid-twentieth-century Latin American social philosophy. Many of the seemingly secular iterations of decolonial thought in Latin America are significantly informed by religion. Reducing religion to a particular realm, in this sense, belies the foundational figures of Latin American decolonial thought who commonly viewed religion as constitutive of (coloniality of) power. Exploring the missed connection between decolonial thought and LALT also brings to light the insights and visions LALT offers to decolonial theory. LALT revolted against the traditional Western theological method by situating theological knowledge in geopolitics and by breaking from the hierarchical binary of knowledge (dogma) and praxis. LALT rightly diagnosed the social-political problem of the postcolonial Americas as a theological problem. Many LALT critics (Enrique Dussel, Franz Hinkelammert, Hugo Assmann, Jung Mo Sung) view market capitalism as the ideological foundation of the neoliberal/colonial West, which overtook the theological function of religion. Their critique of the colonial secular or secular coloniality brings political economy to the central stage of decoloniality. Rejecting the colonial order, LALT reminds us, requires subverting its powerful mode of the control of production. The colonial capitalist mode of control is not a mere economic tool or mechanism. Rather, it is a cosmology, a worldview. Despite the secular terms with which it is articulated, capitalism and its neoliberal market operates theologically. In this sense, thinking about a decolonial future invites a theological-materialist critique of the colonial capitalist mode of production and exchange. Just as religion structures the presumably secular system of power, it also serves as modes of organizing new worlds, new movements, and new economies. Imagining and organizing a different order, a decolonial otherwise requires re-articulating a different mode of desire and relations. Such endeavor, LALT signals, is a politico-theological project.

PART II

Poetics

3

PHENOMENOLOGY OF THE POLITICAL
Fanon's Religion

The emergence of colonial modernity as a secular imaginary and project of the West begs a careful investigation of both religious and secular sites. The origin narrative of Enlightenment modernity recounts the story of an epochal transition characterized by the progressive movement of the secular Spirit. Represented by Max Weber's thesis of disenchantment, the secular and the process of secularization are associated with the transition from superstitious beliefs to scientific rationality. According to this narrative, the formation of Western modernity is understood as a process of disenchantment.

There have been various interventions in recent times that complicate the dominant narrative of the secularization thesis. Against the simplistic narrative of secularization as the total displacement of religion from the public, these voices suggest the transition to an "immanent framework," "public religion," reenchantment, or/and postsecularity.[1] Alongside the critical study of secularism, another critical line of inquiry (dubbed as political theology) has emerged, further complicating the oversimplifying religion/secular binary. Whereas the former focuses on the historical process of secularism (secularization), the latter interrogates the secular as the conceptual apparatus that organizes political life. Political theology traces the genealogical trajectory of the political back to religion, thus demystifying the supposedly apolitical (and nonreligious) nature of the secular. The traditional narrative of the modern liberal West presents the secular as a neutral (thus normative) platform organized by contract (law). Political theology argues that it is not contract but decision, or violence, rather than law that constitutes and sustains the liberal secular order. Decisions, sanctioned through violence, organize the political. Traditional Christian theological concepts significantly inform these processes.

The modern liberal concept of political life based on the notion of social contract lifts the secular as the guarantor of rational judgment and governance. Political theology refutes the purported impartiality of the secular. The dominant stream of political theology grapples with the intimate correlation between Christian theological ideas and secular political concepts that constitute the backbone of modern liberalism. The secular's normative and purportedly apolitical (hence universal) position covers over the inseparable loop of violence that feeds itself. In this sense, the study of political theology—at least in its dominant stream—often unfolds along the various ramifications of Carl Schmitt's famous dictum that "all significant concepts of the modern theory of the state are secularized theological concepts."[2] The important insights offered by political theology regarding the constitution of Western modernity raise important questions for the critical study of colonial modernity.

Christianity's place in the colonization of the Americas refuses the simplistic binary of religion and the secular in which the early stage of colonization is associated with religion and the later stage of (post)colonial governance, with the secular. If Europe's modern secular order is significantly informed by Christian theological ideas, the understated place of the colonial other (as the double of Europe's modernity) in the arena of European political theology becomes an interesting and important question. We might then start looking at colonial modernity as a problem of political theology. What are the complex processes in which coloniality became the axial pillar of modernity along with "the theological"? What are the ways in which coloniality (the colonial other) informs the politico-theological imagination of the West and vice versa?

The Coloniality of the Secular largely seeks to answer the above questions. This chapter focuses on a thinker who offers indispensable insights for thinking about the complex connection between modernity, coloniality, and secularity. The Martinican psychiatrist, philosopher, and revolutionary Frantz Fanon poignantly denounces the deep-seated philosophical foundations that give rise to the racist imaginary of the West. Racism for Fanon is not a mere anomaly or perversity of the modern society but a problem that pertains to the larger symbolic system of signification, which constitutes the foundation of the Western world. The inherently racist/colonial worldview of the West is principally articulated in its particular notion of the human that represents the universal and normative mode of being, while the colonial other is the imperative double of the normative human. Through my reading, I show that, for Fanon, the invention of this human and the management of the order that breeds it requires a theological process, namely, political theology. Modernity is co-constitutive not only of coloniality but also of the theological that haunts the political. The theologico-colonial is constitutive of modernity.

Coloniality as a Politico-theological Problem

Fanon can be situated in the genealogy of thinkers who viewed secularism as symptomatic of colonial modernity. Turning to Fanon for insights about religion might sound counterintuitive. After all, he was not very much invested in the question of religion. He did not write much about it and when he did, his take is often closer to derisive dismissal than a well-informed examination. However, there are many original ideas lurking in his writings, often overlooked by scholars of religion, which deserve closer attention. Fanon's writings are filled with important insights that help us resituate the problem of political theology in the global context of power that is conditioned by modernity/coloniality.

Fanon offers an important analytic for the study of coloniality. This analytic calls for resituating the locus of our critical study of being in the geopolitical site contested by power and violence. The formation of the modern capitalist world-system and imaginary took place upon the political and economic foundation provided by slavery and the plantation economy. The Atlantic, particularly the Caribbean, is the womb of colonial modernity that, as Antonio Benítez-Rojo puts it, was "inseminat[ed] ... with the blood of Africa."[3] The political and cultural formation of transatlantic Black diaspora communities offers an account of countermodernity (Gilroy) that helps us read the dominant (Eurocentric) narrative of the West/capitalism-led modernity with a critical eye on the complex entanglement between modernity and coloniality. The popular narrative of Western modernity and liberal democracy eclipses the dark history of the entanglement between Europe and the transatlantic world, between democracy and the plantation. In Achille Mbembe's parlance, the colony is (Western) democracy's double, its "nocturnal face" without which it cannot exist.[4]

Blackness serves for Fanon as the central signifier for repurposing the post-plantation racial other. But it is not an ontological category that is displaced from historical and material reality. The main site of his reflection and struggle is the lived experience of colonized/racialized beings, as both his own involvement in the Algerian Revolution and his clinical work in psychiatry bear witness to. Blackness signifies the ontological condition of the being who is perpetually exposed to symbolic and material violence. This unlivable condition is amplified by Fanon's vivid phenomenological reflection. His approach to the problem of race and coloniality points at its complex methodological and theoretical layers, an inquiry that refuses a simple (and single) account. One of his most original and influential contributions to the critical study of race and colonialism is perhaps his phenomenological analysis of racialized existence in *Black Skin, White Masks*. I offer a close reading of Fanon's phenomenology of race and reflect on its significance in chapter 4.

On a broader note, Fanon offers a phenomenological account of the political, that is, how the political constitutes and manifests itself in the colony. Unlike the phenomenology of race he presents in *Black Skin*, which is a direct engagement with phenomenological concepts and ideas, his essay "Concerning Violence" in *The Wretched of the Earth* is not an explicitly philosophical treatise that deals with the grammar of phenomenology. In my reading, however, "Concerning Violence" offers an insightful phenomenological analysis of the political by tracing the trajectory through which political life is constituted by the violent sanction of normative universals and the distribution of regulative identities in the colony. A paramount insight Fanon offers here, which has been largely overlooked by Fanonian scholarship, regards religion's function as the metaphysical foundation of the political. Both the full extent of his sharp critique of religion and his gesture to repurpose it remain underexplored in any contemporary study of Fanon. But religion also remains unthematized and underacknowledged in Fanon's own thinking. His own secular epistemic framework hindered him from recognizing the full depth of his own critical insight about religion and coloniality. A similar secularist epistemic framework informs significantly the contemporary study of Fanon and decoloniality.

Throughout the entire oeuvre of his work, Fanon constantly insinuates that the colonial imaginary and order are linked to concepts and logics drawn from Christian theology. Political theology constitutes coloniality. Conversely, this means that coloniality informs the politico-theological. If the emergence of the modern Western imaginary correlates with the invention of the colonial other, the eclipse of the theological and the subsequent rise of the political in modern Europe cannot be properly understood without a deep analysis of this linkage. Political life is a theological problem as well as a colonial problem.

One of the key premises of *The Coloniality of the Secular* is that secularity (the secular) hinges the two ends of modernity/coloniality. The diverse thinkers I read in the book commonly allude to the significant role that the secular has played in the hegemonic installation of Western modernity. The conversations about the connection between secularism and colonialism/race in the discipline of religious studies did not start until the late twentieth century. Numerous anticolonial thinkers have argued for a long time that secularism is an ideological framework that fosters colonialism. Many such voices come from thinkers who were working with "secular" ideas and sources. Studying the secular intellectual traditions that contest colonial modernity is crucial for revisiting current conversations about religion and power in the (post) colonial Americas. These conversations are generally informed by a narrowly prescribed concept of religion that forecloses a much-needed analysis of religion's constitutive role in coloniality.

This chapter reflects on the somewhat subtle yet complex link between religion and coloniality by probing the problem of political theology through the analytic of modernity/coloniality. In conversation with Frantz Fanon, I seek to excavate the theological root of the political in the colony. While Fanon's relationship to religion is complicated—and while he was neither invested in the question of religion nor favorable to it—political theology provides a useful lens through which we can identify the relevance as well as the contribution that his secular humanism bears for the study of religion and vice versa. If, as Paul Kahn remarks, "political theology recognizes multiplicity in the forms of the sacred," reading Fanon alongside political theology might illuminate the various forms of the sacred that constitute the colonial reality while, at the same time, shedding light on the many forms of the sacred carved into various shapes of countercolonial thoughts and movements.[5]

Fanon's thoughts add indispensable insights to the study of coloniality. If the contribution of South American thinkers (Aníbal Quijano, Enrique Dussel, Walter Mignolo) rests on unpacking the epistemic dimension of coloniality that shapes the global order of knowledge and knowledge production, Fanon's work probes the ontological conditions that enforce the colonial order of being. His work points at Blackness as the site of production (as well as the reinforcement) of the symbolic that sustains the colonial-racist metaphysics. My reading suggests that Fanon does not simply dismiss or turn away from religion in search of a decolonial future. Rather, his relationship to religion is much more complex and ambiguous.

Through my reading, I attempt to demonstrate how, on the one hand, Fanon's phenomenology of the political unmasks the (Manichean) theology that feeds the colonial worldview and its order of being. On the other hand, I demonstrate in chapter 4 how his phenomenological reflection on race offers the possibility of rethinking the sacred, one that is reconceived through his faith in new humanism, that is, the capacity to question and re-create reality. My goal through the following two chapters is far from sacralizing Fanon or emphasizing the centrality of religion in Fanon's anticolonial thought. I must also acknowledge the difficulty of using Fanon for theorizing religion as he does not seem too invested in religion and his position is consistently ambivalent. Nevertheless, I submit that his sporadic engagement with religion offers invaluable insights for thinking about the connection between the politico-theological problem, race, and coloniality.

Phenomenology of the Political

Fanon holds an ambiguous view on religion overall. He seems mostly critical of the role religion plays within the colonial order. He expresses repugnance against Indigenous religions by calling them myth, superstition, and magic. At the same time, as Federico Settler observes, Fanon "recognized the significance of the sacred in cohering social collectivities and in the recovery of the black self."[6] Fanon recognized that national culture should provide the spiritual resources to cohere the nation. This is because the sacred occupies a substantial place in the social fabric of the colonized. Settler adds, "Colonialism is fortified by the sacred but also colonialism mutilates the sacred traditions."[7]

While acknowledging religion's place in culture as a vital ingredient that fosters national identity, Fanon constantly displayed a rather unfavorable view of religion. The ambivalent understanding of religion that fluctuates between two contrasting views reflects perhaps his own ongoing personal anxiety that often overwhelms the man who inhabits the crossroad of conflicting desires. This is a man who is constantly negotiating the negative colonial affects of denial, refusal, shame, and the desire to restore to wholeness a self split between the two radically contrasting worlds. Religions, particularly native religions, are constant sources of anxiety for Fanon. At times he is critical of the problematic association of native religions with irrationality made by Western critics; but, simultaneously, he reproduced the same problematic associations. We can see this in his different treatments of institutional religions (such as Catholicism and Islam) and Indigenous religions. The latter is often an object of shame and abhorrence for Fanon.[8] His understanding of religion largely reflects the dominant Western categorization of tribal religions at the time. The collective consciousness in these societies, Fanon observes, is conditioned by "magic" and "myth," and this presents a distracting obstacle that tames the colonized's motivation for anticolonial struggle: "Zombies, believe me, are more terrifying than colonists.... [T]here is no reason to fight them because what really matters is that the mythical structures contain far more terrifying adversaries. It is evident that everything is reduced to a permanent confrontation at the level of phantasy."[9]

Fanon's complicated relationship with religion captures the dilemma and the burden of decolonial critique. The very critical terms the decolonial thinker uses to grapple with the colonized's condition already belong to the colonizer's language. The epistemic framework and category that inform critical discourses are already conditioned by Western categories of secular rationality—and Fanon was not fully free from these influences. In particular, his understanding of religion echoes the modern category of religion that was established by nineteenth-century European anthropologists and comparativists of religion. He was wary of secularism's complicit connection with the colonial ideology of the West, yet his critical sight falls short where he constantly employs the dominant secularist category of religion—to which I will come back soon.

An important lesson here is that it is far from difficult to identify the same oversight we find in Fanon across numerous examples in contemporary discourses of critical theory. As I already expounded in chapter 1, many interlocutors in contemporary decolonial theory are critical of the secularist discourse, yet they often overlook the secularist categories that reduce religion to a narrow notion. The compound interaction between religion and power is eclipsed by the reductive concept of religion in their works. The critical study of the formation of race and (de)coloniality in the Americas is overshadowed by the erasure of religion, an important constitutive element of (de)coloniality. The same problem can also be found in the field of religious studies where many scholars speak about the problem of the secular but are not as critical of the deeply embedded secularist epistemic framework that informs various critical theories. The secularist epistemic framework at play here consigns knowledge and knowledge production to particular forms and locations. Like the normative ideal of the human (Man), this unmarked epistemic framework universalizes a particular mode of knowing (Europe/West) as the sole arbiter of knowledge. Forms of knowing that emerge from non-Western locales are measured and classified according to these normative principles. These unmarked principles are in fact heavily *marked* with a Western secularist inflection (rooted in Euro-Christian history), and they underlie the study of religion, particularly of non-Western religions. Religions of the global south are studied by scholars who are drawn by exotic symbols and rituals of these communities yet who are often not as invested in the intellectual production by the same communities. The theories and methods used to study these religions are usually reserved for works produced by European (and Euro-American) authors. The unequal global division of intellectual labor is reproduced in the academic field in which the West is the reservoir of theory while the non-West is the reservoir of data.

Coming back to Fanon, his treatment of Islam was different from Christianity as Islam played a significant role in the Algerian Revolution. He acknowledged Islam's contribution to revolution despite his lack of a deep understanding of Islam and the full extent of its connection to the revolution. His limited understanding of the intricate interaction between religion and culture, particularly regarding Islam, partly overshadows his views. He did not fully understand the degree to which the tradition of anticolonial struggle in the modern history of Algeria was deeply Islamic in nature.[10] Fanon praised the self-organization of Algerian peasants in their involvement in the anticolonial resistance but failed to understand that the origin of such movements was Islam.[11] Fouzi Slisli unpacks the numerous cultural and historical references that Fanon makes about Algeria without acknowledging their connection to Islam. Slisli wonders, "Was he ignorant of this Islamic tradition or did he choose to ignore it?"[12] Whatever the case may be, Fanon's harsh stance toward Christianity and African (and Afro-diasporic) Indigenous religions did not extend to Islam. Yet his ambivalent attitude toward religion also informed his view of Islam. He refers to the mystical Islamic worship of holy men in Algeria as maraboutism and lists it among the list of "old superstitions," alongside witchcraft and djinn (Arabic spirits).[13] Such a view of religion is not surprising when considering Fanon's professionalization in Western medical practice. A great part of Fanon's deep immersion in the worldview of North African Muslims came through his clinical observation and study as a psychiatrist. During his time at the Blida-Joinville Psychiatric Hospital in Algeria, he treated a large group of Muslim patients. There, he observed that many of his clinical tools (from Western science) did not work efficiently on his Muslim male patients. The main reason for this discrepancy was cultural difference. The local population adhered to a completely different worldview informed by religion, which made the seamless application of Western methods difficult. The patients' religion-based worldview conflicted often with the scientific method of the psychiatric approach. The traditional worldview grounded in religion did not help with the procedures as there is a widespread tendency among locals to ascribe mental illness to a spiritual problem.[14] Yet Fanon did not let go of his ambivalent position toward religion. Even in his characterization of Islam as rather primitive and traditional, he would not set an immediately strict binary of values that stigmatizes Islam in its entirety while uplifting the secular worldview. Discussing the traditional tribal structure of the local Muslim society, Fanon discusses the transformation of landownership implemented by the French. The process of land (wealth) redistribution aggravated the economic condition of the poor. Prior to the privatization of property, there were poors, but not proletarians.[15] What Fanon implies is that, even when certain Western innovations are more beneficial since they reflect the advance (and the potential benefit) of technology, not all such customs and implementations always signify a true sense of progress.

Fanon's ambivalent position toward religion, especially Islam, is widely reflected in his extensive clinical notes from his Blida-Joinville years. He continuously signals his intention behind the report being not a value judgment, but a better understanding of the Muslim society and culture for a more efficient treatment of the mental ailments. Judging certain conducts and beliefs that appear as "primitive" to us, Fanon notes, "is only a value judgement, one that is both questionable and bears on poorly defined characteristics, which scarcely helps us progress in our knowledge of the

Algerian Muslim man."[16] In one of his notes, entitled "Daily Life in the Douars," Fanon offers a comprehensive report on the general sociocultural constitution of the Muslim community bound by a unifying religious identity. The general tone of his report is neutral and even favorable at times. He gives one of his most sympathetic accounts of religion, sketching out the constructive function that religion plays by providing the foundation for community, security, and order. Religion offers a coherent worldview, making possible the creation of a community founded on a seamless order.[17] Yet, even in this sympathetic articulation, it is not difficult to notice Fanon's subtle display of secularist prejudices against religion. Religion still appears as the binary opposite of the technologically advanced present. It is depicted as outdated and simple, associated with nature, tradition, and the past.[18] Overall, Fanon seems to oscillate between two conflicting views of religion, reproducing at times the West-centric understanding of religion, and then rejecting it at others. The anxiety that overwrites his view of culture and identity as he faces the endless burden of having to define Blackness in opposition to whiteness, Africana identity in opposition to European norms, seems to shape his view of religion.

Reading Fanon through the lens of religion lends important insights that might help us analyze the complex nexus that constitutes the Western secular Man and his colonial/racialized other, that is, the colonial abject. Despite the lack of reference to explicit religious languages, Fanon attributes the primary characteristics of colonial violence to theology. As Michael Lackey observes, instead of suggesting that theology benefits from colonization, "Fanon argues colonization is at the service of theology, that theology is the parent and original."[19] Lackey's reading of Fanon raises important questions for contemporary conversations in political theology. Fanon points toward the underattended problem of coloniality in political theology. He invites us to critically examine the subtle yet inextricable ways in which the politico-theological problem carries over into the colony and vice versa. Political theology helps us probe the power mechanism that constitutes coloniality whereas coloniality offers a useful lens through which we can study the close link between the construction of the colonial other and constitution of political theology in Europe. If decolonial thinking sheds light on the colonial root of modernity, political theology investigates the theological edifice of modernity. The colonial and the theological are both constitutive pillars of Western modernity. These tripartite elements (or pillars) are mutually co-constitutive. However, the concept of the secular often obscures the multifaceted formation of modernity. The secularist discourse often dilutes the theological edifice of both modernity and coloniality, thus fostering a notion of modernity that distinguishes itself from normative values, sectarian positions, and power struggles. The violence of its theology and the theology of its violence are obscured by the nominal framework of the secular. The secular hinges the two ends of modernity/coloniality. To understand the compound organizing mechanism of religion in the (post) colony, it is imperative to scrutinize the secular from the decolonial angle.

(De)coloniality and the Sacred

Preceding Fanon and Wynter, Aimé Césaire made a compelling observation on the problem of the politico-theological from the standpoint of the colonial Antilles. Césaire diagnosed colonialism as symptomatic of political theology by drawing on various theological metaphors to describe the violent reality of colonialism. For instance, he famously compares the French prime minister Georges Bidault to "a communion wafer dipped in shit."[20] Bidault was reporting to the French National Assembly on the French army's involvement in the anticolonial revolts in Madagascar. As J. Kameron Carter observes, the French colonial ideology and activity was, for Césaire, nothing other than a secular reenactment of the Christian ritual of the Eucharist in which the bodies of colonial others are consumed and transubstantiated in the creation of the Christian Western world order.[21] A colonial political theology par excellence.

The most notable reference for thinking about the nexus of modernity-coloniality-secularity is offered by Sylvia Wynter. Wynter argues extensively that the modern Western order is the product of a political theology in which the colonial other serves as the negation that constitutes the modern Western subject. The dehumanization of the colonial other reinforces the universality of Man, an ideal that projects the Western, bourgeois, white, secular mode of being. Wynter insists that the formation of this order is a theological transaction in nature, and she offers numerous examples showing how these various political and philosophical ideas embody theological concepts. The key axis that sustains this order is violence, that is, the sacrifice of the less-than-human. Her view of the modern/colonial order and its link to the secularist permutation of theology echoes many of the insights latent in Césaire's and Fanon's works. And while many key ideas remain partly dormant, I suggest that the phenomenology of the political Fanon presents in "Concerning

Violence" offers an insightful perspective on the trajectory through which the political manifests in the colony. Political life, Fanon tells us, is constituted by violence in the colony. And while he does not attribute all of it to religion, he makes important insinuations showing that he regards religion's place in the colonial order (and worldview) as fundamental.

Fanon understood that colonial politics requires more than coercion. Coloniality is a metaphysical problem. Colonial management necessitates a worldview, a theology beyond material conditions. He calls the colonial order a "Manichean world," a world of good and evil in which the colonist represents goodness and the colonized signifies absolute evil.[22] The divided world between good and evil, the two different species, is enforced through violence.[23] Following Lewis Gordon, I call this a Manichean theodicy. The dualistic world of good and evil is sustained by theological justification: "a reference to divine right is needed to justify [the ontological] difference."[24] The theodicean worldview justifies the unjust colonial reality with a punishment and reward scheme: "fatalism relieves the oppressor of all responsibility since the cause of wrong-doing, poverty, and the inevitable can be attributed to God. The individual thus accepts the devastation decreed by God, grovels in front of the colonist, bows to the hand of fate."[25] Colonial violence is derivative of theological violence.

In a world structured by a fundamentally dualistic theology, the endlessly miserable reality of the everyday life is a predestined fate for those who inhabit the lower stratum of the ontological pole. Fanon's reading of the colonial world through the lens of political theology—even when he does not thematize it as such—culminates as he gets to the logic (or politics) of redemption that underlies the colonial worldview. The economy of redemption relies on the currency of sacrifice (exclusion). In this sense, redemption is not for all: "many are called but few are chosen."[26] Redemption requires sacrifice. Fanon denounces theodicy and the theological concept of redemption and sacrifice as the organizing principle of the colonial order. The theological politics of redemption requires violence. Put differently, sacralized violence organizes political life. I read "Concerning Violence" as Fanon's critique and uncovering of this politico-theological problem in the colony. The phenomenology of the political he offers here breaks down the undetachable nexus of the sacred violence that constitutes the political in the colonial world. Fanon's critique of (theological-colonial) violence is followed by his reverse attempt to resignify decolonial violence as sacred that is "absolute violence"—as I will address in chapter 4.

Paul Kahn, an important contemporary commentator of the Schmittian political theology, recently made a notable intervention on the politico-theological problem, sovereignty, and violence. Kahn's approach to political theology draws a significant contrast from Fanon's trajectory, but it also offers important parallels. Commenting on the centrality of the sacred in the organization of political life, Kahn writes, "Neither the quest for justice nor the calculation of costs and benefits will bring us to sacrifice. Only the sacred can do that."[27] In his important study of the problem of political theology, Kahn claims that decision or the power to decide—and its violent grammar of sacrifice/exception—constitutes politics. Probing the Schmittian variations of political theology, Kahn reads the political as an expression of theological concepts in which "politics as an organization of everyday life [is a] life founded on an imagination of the sacred."[28] Schmitt's dictum that "the sovereign is he who decides on the exception" defies liberalism's conception of the political: "not law, but exception; not judge but sovereign; not reason, but decision."[29] Kahn's observation suggests that the political is conditioned by the sacred (the sovereign) whose very role is constituted by violence (decision). Kahn's analysis is useful for thinking about the problem Fanon is addressing because there is an important resonance between the two. However, Kahn situates the sacred exclusively in the Schmittian, state-centric conception of the sovereign. As critics point out, Kahn's account does not leave room for the various communities of struggle that speak to different experiences of the sacred.[30] It thus fails to capture the experience of the abjects who are not considered part of political life in the first place.[31]

The various iterations of the Schmittian political theology that dominate conversations in political theology do not adequately attend to the experience of political abjects whose existences do not register in the index of modern political life. In contrast to Kahn, Fanon articulates a similar problem but from the viewpoint of the excluded. The Fanonian critique of the economy of redemption and sacrifice is powerfully captured and developed by Achille Mbembe, who redefines the sovereign as "the power and the capacity to decide who may live and who must die."[32] The extrajudicial decision operates on the base of "the racial denial of any common bond between the conqueror and the native."[33] Mbembe insists that the biopolitical does not break from the politico-theological. In the colony, the biopolitical is also the politico-theological. The Foucauldian critique of biopower and the production of modern subjects through discipline and surveillance is not enough for understanding the lives that are predicated on death: people whose very existences are determined by the sovereign (sacred) injunction that distributes life and death.[34] In this sense, Mbembe resonates with Giorgio Agamben's line of thought, who, contra Foucault, argues that biopower and sovereign power converge to the point that we can view "the production of the biopolitical body [as] the original activity of sovereign power."[35] But more important, biopower alone does not account for the deaths and the many lives-as-deaths that are deemed disposable, those whose (in)existence do not find register in the lexicon of political life. It is to the reality of these political abjects that Fanon's critique of violence and the political is directed.

Reading Fanon's and Kahn's work on political theology side by side, we draw the important insight that the sacred and violence are co-constitutive of each other and of political life. The violence of the sacred and the sacredness of violence continuously feed each other, forming a Möbius strip. Kahn holds the Schimittian view that political life is organized on the grounds of a theological imagination. Sovereignty is the theological decision that sanctions violence, which is constitutive of political life. For Fanon, what is at stake in the political is the reality of the excluded whose sacrifice *dispenses* the foundational conditions of political life for the Western subject, yet whose existence is *dispensed with* in the narrative of modern Western political thought. Here, Agamben's analysis also falls short in that it does not account for the complex structure of racialization that constitutes the human.[36] What both Fanon and Mbembe demonstrate is the ways in which the sovereign sanctions death outside the normative parameters of political life—even when they are conditioned by biopower and sovereign power—and how this process produces the Western, white subject.

Fanon turns to the colonial reality in which the politico-theological operates in an order ruled by a starkly dualistic (theodicicean) worldview. A world in which the everyday reality operates through extreme measures of violence, a war paradigm, where life means avoiding the omnipresent death, a world in which "you are born anywhere, anyhow. You die from anywhere, from anything."[37] In chapter 4, I discuss how Fanon's sharp critique of violence and the sacred from the colonial perspective meets a powerful critique of ontology in his famous chapter "The Lived Experience of the Black Man" in *Black Skin, White Masks*. My reading here follows an achronological order as "The Lived Experience of the Black" was published almost a decade before "Concerning Violence." For my purposes here, discussing his critique of violence and political theology sets the stage for my reading of Fanon's intervention on the problem of phenomenology and race. Whereas Kahn's

Schmittian model situates the political (and the sacred) in the sovereign's (be that state or popular) capacity to sanction exception (violence), for Fanon, the axis of the political (and the sacred) lies in disavowal, the revolting gesture of refusal. As Mbembe writes, "The subject of the political is born to the world and to itself through this inaugural gesture, namely, the capacity to say no."[38] It is this revolutionary capacity to say no that constitutes the condition of the human. That is to say, the capacity to say no is the defining element of the political and the sacred. Decolonial critique and struggle consist in challenging the hegemonic conception of the normative human, "the secular liberal monohumanist conception of our being human, its overrepresentation as the being of being human itself."[39] In this sense, Wynter claims, the Caribbean intellectual tradition represents a revolt against the "order of discourse" dictated by the "Word of Man," which instituted the secularization of human existence as the normative mode of being.[40]

If the phenomenological method suggested by Maurice Merleau-Ponty urges bracketing of our unquestioned belief in the objective world, the decolonial phenomenology suggested by Fanon and Wynter also turns us away from the spell of the unquestioned faith in the world. Such a break, for Wynter, differs from the notion of disenchantment advocated by the narrative of Western secular rationality. Decolonial phenomenology calls for bracketing our unquestioned belief in the order of Man, the enchantment with a world dictated by a particular order of being, the only "order of discourse which it is our task to disenchant."[41] By calling for a break not from religion but from the order of being/knowing that is informed by the Western-patriarchal-secular-rationality, Wynter leaves open the possibility of linking the sacred with alternative oppressed modes of knowing and being. Such a disenchantment is not oriented toward reenchantment but leaves room for the possibility of an otherwise that might yet emerge.

The order of Man is founded on a worldview that normativizes a particular form of knowledge and existence. Decolonial phenomenology calls for interrogating one's belief in the order of things and recovers the faith in the possibility of a radically different reality: "To perceive reality in a new way: from a loss of trust in physical nature to a loss of trust in our modes of subjectivity."[42] Decolonial disenchantment signals an epiphany, a refusal of the world, the closure of its metaphysics and the opening of awe.[43] Decolonial disenchantment involves the reconfiguration of the sacred, which troubles the boundary dividing the sacred and the secular. The reconfiguration of the sacred implies the capacity to identify the sacred in the fabric of the ordinary reality that constitutes social relations. Such capacity, I argue, is indispensable in decolonial thinking, as demonstrated by many thinkers I examine throughout the book. Many generative ideas and constructive visions, these thinkers suggest, involve some form of intervention with/in the sacred, whichever murky shape they may be. I attend to this blurry site and ask what kinds of questions such a possible connection raises for rethinking the modern concept and categories of religion from the transatlantic standpoint.

Coloniality censors sacrality.[44] That secularism has consistently provided an efficient platform for the articulation of coloniality raises important questions about the relation between decoloniality and the need to interrogate the boundaries that segregate the sacred. When the sacred is isolated from the fabric of social relations, it obscures the enduring power of the sacred that is carved deep in the fabric of political life. It makes us lose sight of the symbolic power that sustains the colonial order that functions as a theological commandment.[45]

4

PHENOMENOLOGY OF RACE

Poetics of Blackness

Fanon's use of the phenomenological method deserves careful attention. In *Black Skin, White Masks*, his now-famous study of Blackness as a lived experience of being, is a powerful reading of the dynamic process through which racialized beings come to existence. Phenomenology probes the intimate connection between intentionality and object. Perception is intentionality and intentionality indicates one's orientation to the object. In other words, phenomenology clarifies that the object is an effect of orientation.[1] Racialized bodies are not "merely" (and accidentally) there. They result from concrete intentionality, that is, orientation.

I pay close attention to Fanonian phenomenology in this chapter not only because it offers an acute observation of the way objects (bodies) are registered in space (and time). His phenomenological reflection also allows us to think about the possibility of life, revolt, and world-making in the face of immeasurable violence. Fanonian phenomenology paints a bleak picture of the dire reality that the Black being faces every day in the white world. Fanon equates this reality with hell: "the zone of non-being," the total rejection of being, of humanity, nothingness.[2] However, Fanon also insists that Blackness is not merely relegated to nothingness. The lived experience of the Black being (existence) cannot be equated to being, and further, to the humanity of the Black person. He tenaciously refuses to resign the possibility of an otherwise. Against the common assumptions, my reading shows that religion in a way serves as a reservoir of such possibility for Fanon. As I will show later, the phenomenological method that Fanon employs allows us to build on the connection between his repurposing of Blackness and religion. His lengthy, pessimistic account concludes with a religious rhetoric that signals hope in which he re-creates Blackness as the embodied signifier of the sacred. Put differently, what takes place in Fanon's phenomenological reflection on his racialized body, I submit, is a reconstruction of the sacred. The secular humanist's staunch rejection of Western religion and metaphysics unfolds, paradoxically, alongside the unnamed figure or moment that evokes a certain sense of the sacred, a sacred presented as antithesis to the sacred.

In order to examine Fanon's reinvention of the sacred, I turn to his poetics. The philosophical depth and significance of Fanonian poetics cannot be properly explored without situating it within the twentieth-century Caribbean tradition of anticolonial poetics. Like many other aspects of his political thoughts, Fanon's poetics is born in conversation with the Antillean decolonial wave that unfolds amid the ruins of colonial modernity. Particularly important is the work of fellow Martinican Aimé Césaire, who deeply influenced Fanon. With his poetic writings, Césaire struggled to come to terms with the wounds of colonial violence carved into the identity of the colonized and racialized beings. In this sense, Césaire's primary concern was in reinventing the Black identity against the violent universals imposed by the Eurocentric order of being. Césaire's struggle to resignify the colonial identity (Blackness) oscillates relentlessly between hope and despair. Religion, particularly Christian theological imageries, plays a significant role in this drama of dialectical oscillation. Césaire's writings portray the epic drama of the genesis of the modern/colonial world. The rich texts filled with symbols and imageries pay particular attention to the tight link between whiteness and Blackness, that is, the white Europe as the subject of history and the Black colonial Other as its shadow. Césaire's reading of the dialectical relation between Europe and its colonial Other is characterized by metaphors and imageries of violent sublation. In this portrayal, the colonial Other is crushed, killed, eaten, and defecated by Europe (whiteness). This way, Césaire's work can be read as a prelude to the inauguration of Caribbean political theology.

In many ways, Fanonian poetics is a response and reaction to Césaire's anticolonial poetics. He picks up many ideas and questions Césaire has evoked. Fanonian poetics also inherits the critique of the problem of political theology that Césaire's poetics has inaugurated. The Jamaican philosopher and theorist Sylvia Wynter develops a full-fledged account of political theology by honing the questions and problems that are dormant in Césaire and Fanon. Wynter insists that the storytelling function of the human is fundamentally vital for resisting Man's reductionist definition of the human as bios—given, static, and predetermined. Poetics in the Caribbean has always signaled an attempt to dismantle the narrative imposed by Europe. Caribbean poetics proposes a new mode of revolt against "the order of discourse and of its Word of Man."[3] For Wynter, this is what the tradition of Caribbean poeticism testifies to, a tradition that includes Aimé Césaire, Frantz Fanon, Édouard Glissant, George Lamming, and Maryse Condeé, among others. Engaging with the works of Césaire, Wynter, and the tradition of Caribbean poeticism will allow me to grasp the broader significance and depth of Fanon's poetics. Poetics disrupts the normative narrative. It seeks to (re)create the world by reconceptualizing symbols and meanings. I read the decolonial refusal in Fanon as a moment of decolonial poetics. By reconceptualizing theological symbols ingrained in secular registers, Fanon gestures at the possibility of a decolonial otherwise.

Phenomenology of Race and Blackness

Fanon's reflection on Blackness and embodiment in "The Lived Experience of the Black Man" is one of the most widely read and discussed texts among all his writings. There he offers a profound reflection on the multifaceted mechanism of racialization. Fanon's reflection plunges its readers into the viewpoint of the abject, the man who is thrown into a world already fixed with signification, a world premised on the absolute rejection of his being: "I was indignant, I demanded an explanation. Nothing happened. I burst apart."[4] The encounter with the world or the moment one becomes aware of their encounter with the world is also the moment of realizing that such awareness comes too late. There is a temporality that precedes its coming into being: "There will always be a world—a white world—between you and us."[5]

One of the unique contributions of Fanon's reflection rests in his use of phenomenology as a method for thinking about racial embodiment. Borrowing insights from existential phenomenology, Fanon tackles racialization as a problem of signification that is mediated by the process of embodiment, a process that determines one's perception of the self and the world, which eventually conditions its relation as well as its motricity (action) in the world. Particularly, he is in conversation with Maurice Merleau-Ponty and his corporeal schema, which offers an account of the way that the subject is constituted and the way it moves—extending its body—in and through the world. The corporeal schema refers to the body's ability or agency to relate to the world, that is, the body's intention and orientation toward the world.

Merleau-Ponty's critical take on phenomenological reduction points at the critique of transcendental idealism that fails to situate the self in the world and presumes a unity of the world (and of the perceiving self). In laying out the foundations of phenomenology, Edmund Husserl insisted on turning to things themselves with *epoche* (bracketing), through which the "being" of the world is put aside so that our academic inquiry can focus on the givenness that is the appearance of reality. The primacy of phenomenological analysis for Husserl lies in the transcendental subject who makes the appearance of the world possible. Such a transcendental phenomenology is misleading for Heidegger, for whom phenomenological reflection takes place not beyond or outside the world but *within* the world. Merleau-Ponty advances further Heidegger's insight (he also got this insight from Gestaltists) by turning to bodily perceptions and sensations as the primary medium for reflecting on a being's belongingness and orientation *in the world*. The phenomenological subject becomes in Merleau-Ponty a corporeal subject, a body that constitutes itself always in relation to the world. By turning to body and perception, Merleau-Ponty taps into various topics first raised by his predecessors in the tradition of phenomenology, such as belongingness in the world (Heidegger) and the notion of the other (Sartre).

For Merleau-Ponty, the body is a mediating agent. Neither a mere object of reflection nor an empty vessel, the body and its senses are the foundations of phenomenological reflection that resist the "illusions of objective thought."[6] Seen through the body, openness to the world is an inherent structure of being: "The world is not what I think, but what I live; I am open to the world."[7] The relationship between the body and the world is also enigmatically intricate. Our body is not merely existing passively in space. Rather, Merleau-Ponty writes, "it inhabits or haunts space."[8] The very distinction between body and space is blurred here. The body does not belong *in* the world as a separate entity. Rather, it is *of* the world: "I am not in space and in time, nor do I think space and time; rather, I am of space and of time [*je sui a l'espace et au temps*]; my body fits itself to them and embraces them."[9]

Merleau-Ponty's turn to body is, in this sense, a turn to the world. As he writes, "There is no inner man, man is in and toward the world, and it is in the world that he knows himself."[10] Truth is mediated by the body, which reveals being's orientation in and to the world. Having a body differently marked (racialized) thus signifies a disorientation. Being loses its way in/to the world. Its body turns into the site where the subject faces negation, a break from the world that gives it meaning. Loss of orientation in/to the world is loss of being's meaning in the world, that is, loss of the world. And loss of the world means that being's inherent openness is suspended. Fanon finds his body "suddenly abraded into nonbeing" as he faces the racializing gazes, the hail of the little boy on the train, "look, a negro!": this interpellation he cannot flee from, for it is only through the structure of the dialectical recognition that he comes to *be*.[11] Whether you define yourself for or against it, you cannot escape from it as you are yourself always in relation to it, that is, the white world and its gazes.

The racializing gaze carries multiple implications for the being whose bodily perception is the central agent that mediates its meaning (orientation) in the world. Fanon's encounter with the gaze reveals a crucial phenomenological insight on the constitution of the subject in relation to its world. For Husserl, intentionality (orientation) constitutes *noema* (intentional object) without being altered by it in return whereas for Merleau-Ponty the opposite is the case: "But because somehow he who sees is of it and is in it."[12] The gaze as the somatic projection of intentionality goes both ways. The I sees the other and is seen by it at the same time. Fanon's description of his encounter with the other's gaze hints at the excruciating shock this encounter provokes in him. The gaze of the other fixes him in objecthood. Speaking of the other's gaze, Merleau-Ponty writes, "I do not simply feel myself frozen, I am frozen by a look. . . . I am wholly implicated, being and nothingness, in this perception that takes possession of me and that the other perceive me soul and body."[13] Being's openness to the world and the other's gaze indicates mutual recognition. Merleau-Ponty's ontology suggests that to be in the world means to be mutually implicated with the other. One's becoming is predicated on both the other who solicits reciprocity and the generosity of the world. The problem, for Fanon, is that reciprocity and generosity are denied to those who embody Blackness. Ontology fails to explain "the being of the black man."[14]

Juxtaposing the phenomenology of whiteness with Blackness, Sara Ahmed observes that Fanon's work exposes the privilege of whiteness, the easiness "with which the white body extends itself in the world through how it is oriented toward objects and others."[15] If the orientation to the object (the world) is indissociable from the constitution of consciousness in the tradition of phenomenology, Ahmed observes that Fanon reveals the stark contrast between white bodies who can "move through the world without losing one's way" and racialized bodies that are stopped and interrogated.[16] If intentionality is a required condition for consciousness's perception of the self and the world, such orientation and openness to the world is negated for the nonwhite body who is met not with reciprocity but with the objectifying gaze that dissects and amputates its body. Fanon writes, "I came into the world imbued with the will to find a meaning in things ... and then I found that I was an object in the midst of other objects."[17] As he desperately turns to the other amid the feeling of "crushing objecthood," the other seems to hint at the promise of alterity at first: a fresh breath of restoration and liberation. But soon he realizes that the other's attention is not a gesture of reciprocity but a gaze that fixes him there. His body is given back to him, not in an intersubjective way as suggested by Merleau-Ponty, but "sprawled out, distorted, recolored, clad in mourning."[18] The body schema inevitably fails for the Black person. Merleau-Ponty shows being's towardness to the world/other through what he calls the "body schema," which expresses body's spatiality. It is through the body schema (*un schema corporel*) that I am aware of my body's situatedness in space.[19] Here is a detailed description of Merleau-Ponty's account of the body schema:

> If I stand in front of my desk and lean on it with both hands, only my hands are accentuated and my whole body trails behind them like a comet's tail. I'm not unaware of the location of my shoulders or my waist; rather, this awareness is enveloped in my awareness of my hands and my entire stance is read, so to speak, in how my hands lean upon the desk. If I am standing and if I hold my pipe in a closed hand, the position of my hand is not determined discursively by the angle that it makes with my forearm, my forearm with my arm, my arm with my torso and, finally, my torso with the ground. I have an absolute knowledge of where my pipe is, and from this I know where my hand is and where my body is.[20]

The body schema indicates our implicit knowledge of the positionality of the different bodily parts in space. The Black body, Fanon claims, puts the body schema into question. The racialized body is unable to develop such schema since for the Black body "consciousness of the body is solely a negating activity."[21] The body schema fails and it is replaced by racial epidermal schema. Fetishized, his body no longer belongs to the world: "I existed triply; I occupied space."[22] The gazes directed at Fanon radically compromise his relation to space. Reduced to thingness, he now *occupies* space rather than being *of* it. Body's coordination with space fails as his consciousness and his awareness of his own body is split in three. The body schema presumes a certain hospitality of space. The body's mediation of its consciousness and space operates upon a presumed generativity of the world. Fanon's racial epidermal schema indicates that space yields hostility to Black bodies. Space is racialized. Perceiving the self's awareness of its own body and the world involves navigating through the spaces densely woven with power.

The body does not transcend enacted social norms. Our modes of existence are preconditioned by social relations. Fanon replaces ontogeny with sociogeny. Ontogeny is a biocentric understanding of life. Contrarily, sociogeny indicates that our existence is conditioned by symbolic registers that are im*press*ed on our bodies. The body and our mode of organizing (assembling) it in the world are socially instituted.[23] Existence is an invention. Sylvia Wynter picks up the insight that Fanon put forth (sociogeny) and refines it further. The invention of this particular ideal of the human as a universalizing mode of being occupies the central place of her intellectual project. Undoing this Man, for Wynter, involves turning our attention to the autopoietic function of the human, to which I will return in the next section.

Perception is mediated not by the body alone. For Merleau-Ponty, it also requires faith, a "perceptual faith." Perceptual faith is in a way the precondition of what phenomenology refers to as the prereflective, "natural attitude." Perceptual faith enables the naive conviction that we have full access to the given. It "assure[s] us that we have access to the things themselves through the intermediary of the body."[24] Perceptual faith guides our actions. The general mode in which we mediate the world and ourselves is through faith, which is an "unreserved commitment." He adds, "Each of our perceptions is an act of faith in that it affirms more than we strictly know, since objects are inexhaustible and our information limited."[25] By calling the uncritical commitment to phenomena faith, Merleau-Ponty elucidates the ambiguous nature of "the deep-seated set of mute opinions implicated in our lives."[26]

Faith plays a paradoxical function in phenomenological reflection. The goal of the phenomenological reflection is to suspend perceptual faith, the originary prejudice that is an integral element of our being in the world. However, stripping the subject of faith does not indicate that phenomenological reflection transcends or fully suspends all forms of faith or convictions (rationalizations). Faith for Merleau-Ponty also signals possibilities. In fact, philosophy as a mode of phenomenological reflection is itself a form of faith. Merleau-Ponty writes, "Philosophy is the perceptual faith questioning itself about itself. One can say of it, as of every faith, that it is a faith because it is the possibility of doubt."[27] Despite his critical take on faith, Merleau-Ponty does not reject it all together. Rather, he goes on to propose philosophy's task as a reconstruction of critical faith. In this sense, Edgar Orion is right when he claims that "if philosophy's historical dualism led gradually but inevitably to the disenchantment of the world... then Merleau-Ponty's philosophy might be read as the movement of the *Vorzauberung der Welt*, the (re-)enchantment of the world."[28] With a strong influence from Catholicism, Merleau-Ponty's phenomenology finds many resonating ideas with Christian theological concepts.[29] In his posthumously published work, *The Visible and the Invisible*, Merleau-Ponty develops an ontology of flesh in conversation with explicit theological ideas.

Articulating the body's co-constitutive relation with the world, Merleau-Ponty invokes the language of faith and wonder when he refers to the sense of porosity that opens up in being. He echoes Husserl who encapsulates phenomenological reduction as an experience of "stand[ing] in wonder before the world."[30] He refers to phenomenological reduction as wonder before the unknown and uncertainty of the world, as "transcendences that spring forth" show "the world as strange and paradoxical."[31] Faith is constitutive of who we are as beings who exist in a world filled with things that precede and exceed our sensory perceptions: "we do not see, do not hear the ideas, and not even with the mind's eye or the third ear: and yet they are there behind the sounds or between them, behind the lights or between them."[32] Reckoning with the invisible that permeates the phenomenological field is wonder-inducing. Phenomenological reflection (critical phenomenology) is inextricably an experience of faith and wonder. Mary-Jane Rubenstein defines wonder as a double movement comprising shock and awe. Wonder devastates but it also indicates transformation. Shock displaces us. In awe, we rediscover the world in being, being in the world, strange and paradoxical.[33] The world reveals itself in absurdity. Merleau-Ponty suggests that the goal of phenomenology consists of rediscovering faith in the world—a process that demands "attention and wonder," which will reveal the mystery of the world.[34]

If perception signals an act of faith, the failure of the body schema that Fanon experiences indicates a failure or loss of faith. A clear contrast exists between Fanon's loss of faith and Merleau-Ponty's suspension of faith. The precondition of the phenomenological reflection that Merleau-Ponty talks about is the unshakable awareness of one's body and its presence in the world (space). The failure of the body schema indicates that such awareness is foreclosed to Black bodies. Considering the centrality of body, this failure implies that Black bodies are denied the possibility of phenomenological reflection. For this reason, Fanon's critical-phenomenological reflection begins from a different place. It begins from the place that precedes (and exceeds) the ontological edifice of the modern West, whose founding myth is predicated on the negation of Blackness. It begins as a critique of the world constituted by racialized (and gendered) time and space in which the subject's becoming presupposes free movement (expanding, touching, exploring, settling, possessing) of unmarked bodies. Fanon's critique emerges as the rejection of the theological economy of being in which Blackness is the ontological marker that classifies the (sub)human.

The loss of faith in the world that Fanon experiences forces him to question his own body and sensation. The body, the key site for critical reflection that signals an openness to the mystery and generosity of the world in Merleau-Ponty's account, becomes an asphyxiating prison, a living hell for Fanon. The openness and the mystery of the world offers Merleau-Ponty a rich source of theological imagination. His late ontology of flesh articulates explicit connections with Christian concepts, particularly, the notion of incarnation. The mystery of the world testifies to God's incarnation in the world, God becoming flesh, the world being saturated with God. God's presence in the world as flesh invites the self to an ongoing life of reflection on its mystery, a mystery that conditions one's experience in the world.[35] From Fanon's viewpoint, God's presence in the world is known by the sovereign sanction that dictates (or distributes) life and death. The phenomenological truth that the Black body reveals points not to the generous outpouring of the divine into the world but to the overwhelming (divine) violence that saturates the world. The loss of faith in the world correlates with the loss of faith in the self: loss of faith in his own humanity, his own sacred dignity as a human being who is capable of loving and being loved by the other—"I moved toward the other . . . and the evanescent other, hostile but not opaque, transparent, not there, disappeared, nausea."³⁶ Objectified and thingified, Fanon's understanding of himself as a body is shattered; self-consciousness is displaced from his amputated bodily presence. He objectifies his own dismembered corporeal schema. He becomes a thing to himself. He moves slowly. He slips into corners and hopes to seek refuge in invisibility. Willing to accept (no)thingness, life as death, he says, "I slip into corners, I remain silent. I strive for anonymity, for invisibility. Look, I will accept the lot, as long as not one notices me!"³⁷ There is no way out, for Blackness is not invisibility. The problem is not unrecognition but the recognition of Blackness as nothingness. It is neither an existence as a human being nor a nonexistence, rather, an existence as nothing. This double-bind traps the self in a rigid binary, a binary Fanon refuses to accept. The ontological abyss demands a different type of response, a flight not away from nothingness but into it. Might nothingness, perhaps, instigate a different mode of political subjectivity and movement? What is the life and the possibility of nothing? Fanon concludes "The Lived Experience of Black Man" by drawing back to the tension or cycle of hope and despair, possibility and impossibility: "Yesterday, awakening to the world, I saw the sky turn upon itself utterly and wholly. I wanted to rise, but the disemboweled silence fell back upon me, its wings paralyzed. Without responsibility, straddling Nothingness and Infinity, I began to weep."³⁸ What lies in this in-between, in the middle of nothingness and infinity?

Between Nothingness and Infinity

Faced with absolute negation that reduces him to nothing, Fanon's hopes seem crushed. But the disemboweled self is not reduced to silence. The man relegated to a thing is not simply fixed to nothing or absence. What we see in the middle space is a movement, a shuttling movement between nothingness and infinity, between acceptance and refusal. There is crying, tears that are being shed, the act of weeping that defies the dualistic binary of speech and silence, being and nonbeing, action and nonaction. In his observation of Pierre Janet's patient who sobs in the middle of confessing her emotional obsessions, Jean-Paul Sartre wonders whether she sobs because she is unable to say anything or perhaps because she refuses to say anything.³⁹ Might Fanon's silent tears be viewed as a refusal, a hold that displaces its readers' expectation of an action or positionality? We may view the tears as a hopeless defeat, a pessimistic surrender, a passive moment of nonaction. But we may also read the sobbing subject as revealing itself by way of concealment, that is, circumventing confession: positioning itself as what it is not.

Following Sartre, Eugenie Brinkema suggests that we read tears as a concealment rather than a revelation. She writes, "The tear demands interpretation, but that reading does not point inward toward the depths of the soul—it remains a surface reading always, a tracing of the bodily production of the sign that signifies only its refusal to reveal itself."[40] Attending to the foreclosed sites and temporalities presents a fundamental threat to the ontological foundation of the colonial/racist world. Fred Moten writes, "What if the thing whose meaning or value has never been found finds things, founds things?"[41] Reflecting on the political possibility of Blackness and nothingness, Moten attempts to rescue failure and unattainability by transforming them into the source of hope and resistance. Agreeing with Afropessimists' diagnosis that anti-Blackness is the metaphysical foundation of the modern West, Moten turns to the world-making struggle Black communities have borne. Unlike the pessimists who claim that Blackness signifies social death (or life-in-death), he adds:

> What if the thing sustains itself in that absence or eclipse of meaning that withholds from the thing the horrific honorific of "object"? At the same time, what if the value of that absence or excess is given to us only in and by way of a kind of failure or inadequacy—or, perhaps more precisely, by way of a history of exclusion, serial expulsion, presence's ongoing taking of leave—so that the non-attainment of meaning or ontology, of source or origin, is the only way to approach the thing in its informal (enformed/enforming, as opposed to formless), material totality?[42]

Isn't nothingness, asks the physicist and critical theorist Karen Barad, a constitutive part of everything?[43] Nothingness does not signify lack or absence. Barad tells us that "the void is a lively tension, a desiring orientation toward being/becoming." A quantum vacuum is "an ongoing questioning of the nature of emptiness," meaning that it is the constant questioning of itself that creates nothingness.[44] The fugitive movement of the extra-ontological that Moten suggests hints at the refusal of choices as offered, an active questioning of ontology: a dynamic site of negotiating its subject's a/position within the map of movements structured by the dialectics of life/death, being/nonbeing, or position/opposition. When we subscribe to the binary dialectic of life/death, Grace Kyungwon Hong writes, "We see [the dead] only as those we must bring into the realm of the living, rather than those who, in and through their very condition of vulnerability to death (their deadly existence) produce their own forms of meaning(lessness) and new definitions of (non)existence that expand our own narrow sense."[45] Affirming death as a social form and meaning renders nothingness not as absence, but as presence—a form of social signification. Failure to do so "merely advances the validation of life that legislates their deaths. In so doing, we replicate the conditions that create these deathworlds by making life the only site of meaning or political possibility."[46]

I have attempted to highlight Fanon's piercing analysis of the modern/colonial world as a critique of the theological edifice that grounds the necropolitical management of the anti-Black world. I read his critique of violence and racialization as a nuanced commentary on the politico-theological problem in the colony. Much attention has been paid in Fanonian scholarship on the effects of the damage that dehumanization and violence enact on racialized beings, sociopolitical and otherwise. Some of these voices also suggest that we pay a close attention to the generative ideas that Fanon's works hint at. They find important constructive visions in Fanon's ideas, such as care, love (Maldonado-Torres, Bouteldja), fugitivity (Moten), poetics (Wynter, Mbembe), and rehumanization (Gordon), among many others. The bleak outlook we glimpse in *Black Skin* does not signal a retreat to resignation that is political pessimism. Fanon's writings and commitment to political struggle consistently demonstrate that the essence of being a human is in the possibility of praxis that is born out of love and solidarity with others. Building on these insights, I want to take a moment and bring attention to some of the generative vision that Fanon gestures at. Despite his dislike for religion, or rather, his ambiguous and complicated relationship with religion, there are moments in which his appeal to generative concepts and alterity seems to beckon at a certain sense of the sacred. My intention is far from jumping into a hasty identification of the sacred in Fanon and offering a Fanonian decolonial theology. Rather, I want to bring attention to a site in Fanon that often goes unnoticed. The few works that address Fanon and religion mostly draw on his critique of religion in which his engagement with religion is more evident. I am interested in going beyond his critique of religion and attend to the moments in which Fanon's generative vision insists on a certain figure of the sacred, however alternative or unnamed it may be. Might his work be viewed as a signpost that signals a new direction for rethinking the sacred—in/as Blackness? And if the answer is yes, what does this imply for the critical study of coloniality, modernity, and religion (secularism)? The remainder of this section explores these questions.

The concluding section of *Black Skin, White Masks* presents an interesting gesture as Fanon turns to a prayer: "O my body, make of me always a man who questions!"[47] The open-endedness of Fanon's prayer leaves us with many questions to consider in light of his struggle with his own masculinity. Many critics view Fanon's problematic understanding of gender as a hindrance to his contribution to decolonial thought. His problematic relationship with gender and sexuality is reflected not only in his observations of issues centered around women and their place in the anticolonial struggle, but also in many other constructive ideas that he has advanced. This evidences his unresolved struggle with his own problematic sense of masculinity and mastery. Fanon's anxiety over his own masculinity is inseparably linked to colonial racial anxiety. The Western norm of the human as the universalizing mode of being imprints not only a racialized ideal of humanity but also a gendered one. It continuously produces the binary that associates the white colonizer with masculinist traits and the colonized with effeminate images. Fanon's decolonial dialectic depicts the drama of the self who oscillates between two opposing poles of colonial anxiety and desire. In the process, the author moves from an intimate moment of confession and renunciation—which signals an undoing of colonial masculinity—to the affirmation of solutions that replicate and reinforce a certain ideal of mastery and masculinity.[48] Fanon's rejection of flesh in Césaire's poetics (which is also central to late Merleau-Ponty) can be also read from the same perspective. As Mayra Rivera observes, Fanon's rejection of Césaire's flesh reveals his anxiety and anger over the signs (colonial desire) of weakness projected onto his body. But Fanon's gesture also reveals his troubling association "between flesh and femininity, hypersexuality, and depravity."[49]

Addressing Fanon's issue with gender, or, better, hypermasculinity, Judith Butler also turns to Fanon's concluding prayer. What catches her attention is the displacement of subjectivity that takes place in the prayer. Fanon's prayer indicates a strong sense of alterity. His prayer is directed not to a god or spirits but to his own body, "one characterized precisely by what it does not yet know."[50] This gesture, a gesture that is not unusual for Fanon, who constantly expresses the desire for openness to and recognition by the other, indicates, for Butler, his recognition of the possibility of self-creation without violence. The question of violence (as well as gender) here begs more careful attention, and I will come back to it later. In particular, Butler's claim, that Fanon's prayer hints at the possibility of self-creation without violence, deserves more careful consideration. Here I want to focus for a moment on the religious dimension of the final prayer.

Joseph Winters's recent reading of Fanon's prayer suggests the possibility of reading it as Fanon's attempt to resignify the sacred. Discussing Charles Long's critical reading of Mircea Eliade's notion of the sacred, Winters points out that too often modern Western scholarship has construed and associated the sacred with a sense of establishing of foundation and order against disorder. It is far from difficult to see the connection between such conception of the sacred and the imperial ideology that has historically justified Europe's colonial enterprises. The ontological distinction that derives from this understanding of the sacred (and profane), Winters observes, carries deep racial signification in which sacredness stands for anti-Blackness.[51] Fanon's unusually religious gesture, Winters suggests, hints at a wholly different sense of the sacred that dislocates the sacred constructed by the modern/colonial imaginary.

Speaking about the crucial place of the embodied experience for feminist epistemology, M. Jacqui Alexander notes that the normative secularist framework displaces the sacred in personal (which is also social) embodied experience. She contends that spiritual work should be understood as a "body praxis," that is, in Nancy Scheper-Hughes's parlance, "habituating one's body."[52] If we follow Winters's lead in identifying the sacred in Fanon's prayer, we can say that the sacred Fanon envisions is oriented toward the body. The racist world displaces the self from its own body. Stripped of sanctity, the body becomes a suffocating hell for the Black self. Fanon's struggle to rethink the body radically anew and his appeal to religious language open the possibility of reading his reflection on the body as an endeavor to rethink and reclaim the sacred as a sacred oriented toward immanence over transcendence, openness over closure, and opacity over certainty. As Winters suggests, it might be "a sacred gone astray."[53]

As an advocate of secular humanism, Fanon was never concerned with theorizing religion. Yet he was keenly aware that political life in the colony was undetachable from the deep foundations of Western religion and its metaphysics. The colonial management of life (and death) is administered through theological commandments that underlie secular governance. Fanon's constructive response to the colonial theological nexus can be read as a decolonial reconception of the sacred: a sacred linked with the absolute existence of the self who fights for the present with one's whole being. Surely for Fanon this is an antisacred that disavows the very notion of the sacred itself. But it reveals the ambiguity that drives Fanon's often-conflicted desires that oscillate between attachment and denial. Fanon rejects Blackness in its symbolic and material signification, but he does not renounce it all together. Rather, he resignifies Blackness in ways that animate one's capacity to love and act, that is, to become a new human. Similarly, he refuses religion but this negation does not amount to renouncing the sacred that religion (as it is articulated and imposed by the West) cannot fully contain. Rather, he suggests a sacred to be reconstructed in one's faith in the body's capacity to refuse closure and to rebuild new reality, a sacred that animates the possibility of a new humanity amid wretchedness.

Decolonial Poetics and the Sacred

Fanon's struggle to repurpose the sacred leaves us with a host of critical questions. Reading through the optics of religion, his existential-phenomenological reflections gain a wider ground for interpretation. What happens when we read religion as a key fabric of social reality that constitutes both the colonial reality and the intellectual traditions that shaped his vision, regardless of how much Fanon was aware of it? What are the insights and perspectives me might gain when we view religion as a segue into decolonial resistance for Fanon? What happens when we pay more attention to the fact that his critical engagement with Merleau-Ponty's theology-infused corporeal schema concludes with a prayer to the unknown? The rather simplistic yet popular interpretation of Fanon's relationship to religion overlooks the numerous nuanced references to religion that he makes. He constantly appeals to religion even as he deliberately turns away from it. In a recent article on Fanon, Nelson Maldonado-Torres makes an important point on the reception of Fanon's writings by the contemporary academy. A frequent oversight when approaching Fanon's work, Maldonado-Torres observes, is to interpret it as a traditional academic text by taking his statements at face value, thus disregarding the complex layers of the clinical and revolutionary context within which he was writing. Religion, be it a conceptual apparatus or a constitutive element of the social fabric, occupies a substantial place in the formation of the anticolonial struggles and thoughts of which Fanon was a part. Both his critique of the pernicious presence of religion in social-political life and his gesture to repurpose religion (as a vessel to resignify

Blackness) remain underattended in Fanonian scholarship. His ambiguous view on religion is indicative of the larger secularist epistemic framework that informs his thinking. Reading Fanon and religion with these complexities in mind lends an interesting twist—and insight: Fanon's critique of religion (political theology) ends up being a critique of the secular (even when he is not naming it as such); his turn to the secularist language as an alternative to religion seems to suggest, in turn, an alternative notion of the sacred. The disavowal of colonial religion need not disclaim the diverse forms of religion-making that take place in and through various forms of decolonial movement and imagination. The sacred molds the spirit and movement of decolonial resistance in the colony. But unlike institutionalized forms (and categories) of religion, the diverse registers of the sacred usually take murky shapes. At times, they are presented as antithesis to the sacred, that is, as a disavowal of the dominant notion of the sacred (and of religion more broadly). Yet, even in negation, they are not renounced. In other words, his critique of religion winds up as a powerful critique of the secular. Contrarily, Fanon seeks refuge in the secular in order to resignify the human, but he ends up repurposing religion along the way. Perhaps, I submit, the poetics his writing invokes allows us to further reflect on the constructive possibilities that religion might offer to decolonial imagination. Poetics brings to light the enduring tie between the embodied experience of Blackness (and coloniality) and the reimagination of the sacred that many decolonial thinkers grapple with. As Paget Henry notes, in the Africana tradition, phenomenology often takes the form of poetics. Henry notes in the work of several Africana thinkers (including Fanon) a poetic reduction alongside the phenomenological reduction.[54]

Reflecting on the significance of poetics, Wynter articulates its worldmaking function. It is "in naming the world," she tells us, that we become human. The overrepresented Man relegates language to a utilitarian function. Man is the ultimate embodiment of the commodity culture that is premised on turning the other into a thing. The Wynterian analytic of Man raises numerous issues and questions lying behind the epoch of modernity/coloniality, but one thing she highlights in particular offers vital insights for thinking about religion and decoloniality: the function of language and poetics. Wynter's decolonial poetics is situated in continuity with the tradition of twentieth-century Caribbean poeticism. Whereas she never fully developed a systematic account of poetics, her articulation of Caribbean poetics helps us understand her project of reconfiguring the human as a project of political theology. Wynter views poetics as an insurrection against the order or Word of Man. Her reading of decolonial poetics troubles the religion/secular binary, a binary that reinstitutes the colonial order of knowing. Following the legacy of Aimé Césaire and Édouard Glissant, Wynter proposes decolonial poetics as a generative force that recasts the human against symbolic death.

The order of Man is enacted through both coercive power and knowledge (or language), that is, the Word of Man. Wynter pays close attention to the centrality of language in the constitution of this order. Language regulates human behaviors and it is through narratives, particularly founding narratives that human beings establish co-identification and kinship with each other.[55] The place of language and narrative in the order of Man reflects their place in the constitution of the human. Wynter insists that the storytelling function of the human is fundamentally important for resisting Man's reductionist definition of the human as bios—given, static, and predetermined. Challenging the order of Man requires the disruption of the dominant regime of knowledge that reinforces a normative mode of cognition, a particular regime of knowledge. This can only be done by rupturing the normative narrative of being.

How to imagine otherwise beyond the Word of Man? For Wynter, this is what the tradition of Caribbean poeticism testifies to. Poetics in the archipelago has always signaled the struggle to dismantle the narrative imposed by European universals. Caribbean poetics proposes a new mode of revolt against "the order of discourse and of its Word of Man."[56] Two figures occupy an important place in Wynter's understanding of Caribbean poetics: Aimé Césaire and Édouard Glissant. The works of Césaire and Glissant offer an inexhaustible source of inspiration for decolonial poetics in the Caribbean. Every form of decolonial resistance, Wynter remarks after Césaire and Glissant, alludes to poetics.

If decolonial poetics resists the secularizing project of Man, does it hint at the reconstruction of the human in religious terms? Does decolonial poetics resignify religion (the theological)? Or does religion reconstitute decolonial poetics? Does poetics recast the possibility of the "ceremony" that "must be found" for reconceptualizing the human?[57] Wynter identifies in Césaire's *Notebook of a Return to the Native Land* (*Cahier d'un retour au pays natal*) a "symbolic inversion of sacral metaphysics of blanchitude."[58] With this observation, she elucidates that whiteness for Césaire is a problem of religious metaphysics.[59] The invention of Man involves the invention of the modern category of race, a process that cannot be separated from the invention of the modern category of religion. And if whiteness is a theological problem, the problem of (anti)Blackness cannot be properly addressed without attending to the problem of theology.

Poetics seeks to break from the normative narrative by reconceptualizing symbols and meanings that constitute the world. Wynter observes that Glissant's thought hints at the anti-universal, "a claim to specificity."[60] Poetics, for Glissant, is a locally situated narrative of the particular that contends the universal, homogenizing narrative of the human. This local narrative is born in the painful terrain of history haunted by the Middle Passage and plantation life. It was Césaire, Glissant notes, who pioneered in elevating the local historical reality to the universal, seeking resonance with the stories and histories of suffering of people across the Americas, Africa, and the rest of the world.[61] Césaire's investment in decolonial poetics cannot be considered apart from his uncompromising Marxist analytic, which helped him to understand that coloniality is conditioned by material relations. Colonial relation is predicated not on "human contact, but relations of domination and submission," in which the sole objective is the exploitation of the Indigenous population that turns them "into an instrument of production."[62] Césaire's *Discourse on Colonialism* points to his poignant critique of the ritualistic construction of the modern European subject at the expense (sacrifice) of Blackness. Césaire's *Discourse,* J. Kameron Carter insists, should be read as a monumental critique of political theology. For Carter, Césaire understood the task of decolonization as a fundamentally politico-theological problem, one that "requires reckoning with how racial capitalism is lodged within... the sacrificial logic of the body (politic) as born out of the 'eucharistic matrix' of the Middle Ages."[63] Carter zooms in on the ambivalent function of language. Language is the medium that serves the double function of undoing symbolic (ontological) violence and resignifying the world. Language is also the very edifice of the Christian empire, an empire draped in blood (according to Gil Anidjar).[64] The Eucharistic liturgy that constitutes the empire operates through language, the words uttered from the altar over what is like a Eucharistic exchange of bread and wine transubstantiated as the body of Christ.[65] Carter takes his cue from a particular moment of French colonial history that Césaire describes. Discussing the colonial administrator Georges Bidault, who gave a public statement in the French Assembly about the anticolonial revolt in Madagascar, Césaire comments how Bidault was looking "like a communion wafer dipped in shit."[66] This colonial discourse, Carter comments, turns the body and the blood of the colonized into the sacrifice of the colonial Eucharistic ritual in which the colonized become the objects to be eaten and excreted. Seen this way, the colonial order for Césaire is born out of a secular iteration of the medieval Christian sacrament. The alchemy of the colonial discourse that organizes matter dissects the ceremoniality of colonialism.[67] This way, Carter amplifies the underexplored theological dimension that underpins Césaire's critique of coloniality in which Césaire expounds on how language (poetics) turns particular bodies into signifiers of certain values. If *Discourse* breaks down the ceremonial anatomy of coloniality, his *Notebook of a Return to the Native Land*, a text Wynter calls the "founding counterdiscourse of the Antilles," signals Césaire's attempt to reconstruct the ceremony for a new world and being.

Césaire's *Notebook* is an epic poem that is a ritualistic progression filled with religious imagery and metaphors. The first half of the poem is dedicated to portraying the reality of the colonized island in the state of absolute abjection: marked with the misery of poverty and the undying memories of violence, fear, ignorance, self-denial, and mournful crying. Toward the middle of the poem, Césaire starts to invoke the Christian language of confession, declaring his sin of being an apostate, a sinner who has deviated from the Western (Christian) ontological dogma: "I have assassinated God with my laziness with my words with my gestures / with my obscene songs / I have worn parrot plumes must cat skins / I have exhausted the missionaries' patience / insulted the benefactors of mankind / Deified Tyre / Deified Sidon / Worshipped the Zaembeze."[68] In this poem, the colonial abject signifies refusal. Césaire affirms that his negritude is an incorrigible dissenter of Western/Christian ontology. The ritual of penance is taken over by absolution. Redemption lies no longer in denying the racialized body or breaking out of the shameful flesh: the poet embraces his incurable body and flesh. The affirmation of a once-wretched being is overtaken by awe and wonder before the life-giving power of his own "perversity." Césaire's celebration and reassurance of negritude is proceeded by the sacramental chant "Voom rooh oh."[69] This interjection, which many critics call a *cri negre* (black cry/shout), marks the inauguration of a new language, a new reality called into being beyond the Word of Man. Decolonial poetics is driven by the desire to create a new being through new language. What vitalizes this poetics is cosmogony, that is, the creation of a new origin story (according to Wynter). Put differently, decolonial poetics is about beginnings. The last stanza of the cri negre is followed by a new stanza that opens up with the vexed question of beginning: "What can I do? / One must begin somewhere / Begin what? / The only thing in the world worth beginning: / The End of the world of course."⁷⁰ The perennial question of beginning (after trauma) haunts the imagination of many Caribbean thinkers. What draws attention is how Césaire pairs up beginning with the end of the world. Observing this link between beginning and apocalypse, John Drabinski comments that the apocalyptic word is a necessity that conditions "the move from abjection and torpor to ecstasy and possibility... [that] [a]t the end of the world, there is life."⁷¹ Decolonial poetics as beginning presupposes the abolition of the world as we know it.

Future—a future that signals the unknown, openness—occupies a central place in Caribbean decolonial imagination. Minkah Makalani comments that future orientation is a common characteristic of the Black Marxist radical tradition. He observes that many thinkers in the Black radical tradition have commonly rejected any notion of a knowable utopia or future. Rather, they share the Fanonian view that, "in refusing to decide the future, [it leaves] open the possibility of bringing into existence something entirely anew."⁷² Openness to an unknown future, I add, is also what characterizes the archipelagic imagination. It grounds the abyssal (groundless) decolonial poetics of the Caribbean archipelago. This openness finds an echo in the often-employed tropes of water in Caribbean literature and thought: the sea, the ocean, the abyss, the island, and the shoreline. Commenting on Césaire's poem *The Thoroughbred*, Drabinski observes that the sea, the witness of catastrophe and the holder of the abyssal silence, "transforms the metaphysics of landscape," producing the earth "without roots and empty." He adds, "The Sea changes everything. Césaire writes from and to the Sea."⁷³ The sea, the island, and the archipelago are the abiding objects of contemplation and boundless sources of poetics, a topic I will tap into further in chapter 5.

A key figure of the negritude movement and a pioneer of the Caribbean anticolonial tradition, Césaire holds unparalleled influence across the Black radical traditions of the twentieth-century global south. The philosophical and literary writings that emerged in the Caribbean from the mid-twentieth century and on are, in a way, in conversation with—and in many cases, a direct response to—Césaire's poetics. The profuse theological themes present in Césaire's work haunt the anticolonial poetics and imagination of the archipelago. For Wynter, poetics strives to reorient the human who is held captive by the secular Logos, that is, the Natural Logos of humanism that replaced the Christian Theologos of the Middle Ages. Her genealogical critique of modernity resonates with both Césaire's and Fanon's anticolonial critiques of the secular Logos. The Word of Man (as the sacral Word of the Sovereign) is predicated on the politico-theological ceremony of death.

Caribbean decolonial poetics, as glimpsed in Césaire and Fanon, bears testament to the collective struggle and imagination to reconstruct the dispossessed ceremony of life, the "ceremony [that] must be found" in order to create being anew.[74] Wynter and Césaire are not hinting at reverting back to the universals of Christian theological concepts as some Christian critics of secularism signal.[75] Rather, creating a rupture in the dominant order of discourse calls for a careful reconstruction of the counterritual, the counterceremony through which decolonial poetics weaves its new founding narratives, its new creolizing origin stories. Might poetics hint at the ceremony to resignify the human? Poetics suggests the possibility of reconceptualizing religion as it refuses to articulate the creation of the human (and of the world) apart from rethinking the sacred. Caribbean poetics as decolonial poetics points toward the relentless world-making struggle of communities that endure and survive the order of Man. The sacrament of Man transubstantiates its secular Logos into being. Decoloniality calls for disenchanting from this order and resignifying the world, a task that takes a careful examination of the deep and enduring theological root that undergirds the racist metaphysics of the West.

In his preface to Césaire's *Discourse*, Robin D.G. Kelly comments on the revolutionary nature of poetry: "It is poetry and therefore revolt. It is an act of insurrection."[76] Fanon's phenomenology of the political and of race is indebted, to a large extent, to Césairean poetics. Fanon's own work points to the powerful decolonial poetics that bears witness to the resilient world-making endeavors of those who are relegated to (no)thingness. Both Césaire and Fanon allude that burning down the old world and building it anew inevitably involves a theological process. The messianic call to an apocalyptic vision and to a new cosmogonic narrative that would ignite new beginnings is illustrated by various religious concepts and metaphors that overflow their writings. Read this way, in conversation with Césaire and Wynter, Fanon's reflection takes us to an incisive critique of the white, modern West as an institution that legitimizes itself through the ceremonial enactment of its universality over the racialized others, that is, the ritualistic consumption (sacrifice) of the other. Secularism's role in this process is crucial. It overshadows the theological transactions that undergird the colonial modern world, thus normalizing the everyday reality constituted by violence. Beyond the boundaries of religion and the secular, decolonial poetics rehabilitates the elemental ceremony that inaugurates new being, the sacred that organizes and animates life amid the colonial ruins.

Conclusion: Violence and Revolution

While it was not central to my analysis in this chapter, Fanon's prominence in global anticolonial/racist movements owes primarily to his theorization of revolutionary ideas and movements. In this sense, the Marxist revolutionary reception of Fanon's work precedes and outweighs the existential-phenomenological reception at the global scale. The provocative aspects of his thinking, particularly around violence and revolution, are often met with controversy in Western liberal academic discourses. By way of concluding, I want to reflect on the lingering question of violence and revolution in Fanon, which is the main topic of his reflection in "Concerning Violence." The problem of violence is also intricately connected to another lingering issue in Fanon that many critics have commonly pointed out: gender.

Western critics of various stripes have not been often favorable to Fanon's articulation of violence. Fanon is frequently accused of being an advocate of violence. Hannah Arendt strongly condemned Fanon's notion of violence by rejecting the association of violence with politics. For Arendt, violence as a means of politics jeopardizes politics as a whole, including the putative goal it purports to achieve. Arendt's position has been contested by many already. These critics point out Arendt's strictly instrumentalist understanding of violence.[77] Arendt's view also shows her oversight of the way violence constitutes politics, especially in the colony.

The dominant liberal notion of violence does not successfully capture the breadth of violence that constitutes the everyday ordinary reality of political life. Condemning certain forms of violence requires legitimation (and even sanction) of other acts of violence. As Ghassan Hage writes, the liberal notion of violence "involves a form of symbolic violence that forces us to normalize certain forms of violence and to pathologize others."[78] The justification of violence conjures up the sacred. Violence is sacralized—and sacralization often involves violence.

The decolonial violence Fanon advocates is absolute and intrinsic.[79] The decolonial violence that Fanon advances in "Concerning Violence," and *The Wretched of the Earth* more broadly, clearly indicates that he is not signaling a teleological goal of replacing one system with another. Decolonial violence exceeds teleological terms (particular acts of violence) that configure the conversations about violence. While he is not excluding the movement of revolutionary strikes in the Algerian Revolution, Fanon's notion of violence cannot be reduced to the particular. The Fanonian notion of violence indicates an absolute violence in the sense that "the substitution [of the particular system] is unconditional, absolute, total, and seamless."[80] As Samira Kawash comments, "Fanon makes it impossible to choose for violence or against. Fanon's violence of decolonization is always in excess and elsewhere to the instrumental violence of the colonized in struggle."[81] Decolonial violence is oriented toward the abolition of the current order that operates on the premise of violence. Seen this way, Fanon's "Concerning Violence" can be understood as a critique of violence. In it, he demystifies the violence that structures the politico-theological apparatus of the colonial sovereign.

Judith Butler recently weighed in on the problem of violence and gender in Fanon. She taps into the complexity of the problem of violence in revolutionary situation, a situation that was engulfing Fanon as he encountered Sartre's preface to *The Wretched of the Earth*. In his controversial preface, Sartre endorses the Third World's armed revolution against Europe by expressing an unambiguous support of Fanon's writings and the Algerian revolution. In doing so, however, Sartre renders decolonial revolution and violence a derivative of the colonizer's violence. He reads the violence of the colonizing Europe as the originary event while rendering anticolonial violence as a reaction to it. Fanon's resentful rejection of Sartre's reading aside, Butler pays close attention to the place of violence in the (re)formation of the self as the colonized appropriates or/and re-creates it, that is, the role of violence in the colonized's "route toward selfhood, agency, even life."[82] Is violence the only route? Butler asks, "Did Fanon think so?"[83] Sartre seems to believe that violence is crucial for the re-creation of the human. The dialectical confrontation with violence allows one to reconstitute the self. But for Fanon, Butler observes, the relationship with violence is much more complicated. While he may acknowledge the inevitable place of violence in decolonial struggle, "such conditions of oppression must be overcome in order for violence no longer to pervade social life."[84] Violence pervades and constitutes political life. It not only forms the everyday ordinary life in the colony, but also conditions the efforts to bring an end to it. Violence, however, cannot escape the burden of gender. Numerous critics have already pointed out the problematic link between gender (hypermasculinity) and violence in Fanon's work. These conversations tend to gravitate toward two opposing poles: either denouncing his sexist views—thus, discrediting his contribution as a whole or defending his position—or discrediting the charges coming from feminist critics.[85] Without fully reproducing this extensive debate here, I want to follow Butler's lead and make a few observations about hypermasculinity and violence in Fanon. Butler addresses these concerns without taking an either/or position. She takes the feminist critiques seriously but her sympathetic reading of Fanon invites readers to the inherent ambiguity in Fanon's own understanding of gender. She notices that Fanon's discussion of the hypermuscular fantasy of the colonized in "Concerning Violence" is not an endorsement but an observation, an acknowledgment of its inevitable and compensatory role that works as "a motivational component in the struggle" but "not a moral ideal toward which the decolonized should strive."[86] In his extensive commentary on Fanon and Fanonian scholarship, David Marriott addresses the "violent readings" that Fanon's account of violence has generated. Aside from Sartre and Arendt, Butler's reading of Fanon and violence also comes under scrutiny. Marriott gives Butler credit for a more sophisticated reading, compared to Sartre and Arendt, but he points out that her reading, too, is caught in instrumentalist framework: Butler associates Fanon's model of self-creation through anticolonial violence with hypermasculinity. Marriott is unambiguously clear in denouncing Butler's (and other feminist critics') readings. For Fanon, Marriott writes, "[violence] is neither positive nor negative, but marks the possibility of every relation in the colony (including ethics, politics, race, and gender), which is why violence is not opposed to the human but inextricable from its very possibility."[87] Marriott makes valid points when he points out that Butler is partially reproducing the common misreading of Fanon. These readings project the Fanonian notion of violence into particularity and an instrumentalist framework while at times downplaying the all-pervading character of violence. However, that Fanon's understanding of violence exceeds the narrow Western conception does not warrant an exemption from the lingering issue of gender that continuously haunts his worldview and writings. Regardless of one's position on Fanon and gender, whether one agrees with various critiques leveled against him or not, it is evidently clear that he struggled with the problem of gender: at times presented as a distorted sexist construction of women, or, at others, erasure (downplay) of their place in the revolution. Sometimes, it simply manifests in the form of an anxiety over his own masculinity. I do not find helpful some of the hasty accusations, often coming from Western liberal readers, leveled against Fanon that entirely dismiss the complexity of the context from which Fanon was writing. These hostile readings muffle the deep longing for openness, alterity, and love that Fanon's writings continuously signal. It is also equally as unhelpful to dismiss the analyses of the gender problem in Fanon simply as mischaracterization. In *Unthinking Mastery*, Julietta Singh proposes the notion of mastery as the axial pillar of the colonial logic of dominion: mastery over the other, the body, the nonhuman world. She reads the desire for mastery that looms in the writings of anticolonial thinkers who ironically denounce the logic of mastery and dominion of the colonizer. Fanon is one such example that embodies the conflicting and complex clash of desires for mastery and its undoing. In Fanon, Singh comments, the masculine colonial subject becomes the emerging countermaster: "He situates himself as a 'master' who has been 'crippled' by the force of the colonial relation."[88] Singh observes that mastery operates as the model of the human in these anticolonial narratives. Mastery is often gendered. Fanon's yearning for mastery is inseparable from his negation of body, desire, weakness, all of which are a menace to his own (secular-rational) masculinity. The contesting readings of Fanon around the issues of gender and violence beg a more careful approach to this complex question that refuses a simple, uniform answer. It is not my intention to discredit the rigorous readings done by critics over the past decades. Rather, I hope to underline the inherent ambiguity and complexity present in Fanon's work that cannot be reduced to the simple binary of either/or. Butler's reading also points toward this ambiguity.

Fanon's often-quoted concluding prayer in *Black Skin* beckons at alterity, an openness to the world. For Butler, this prayer—a prayer directed to his own body, instead of to gods—gestures not at a becoming (achieving of selfhood) driven by hypermasculinist anticolonial violence, but an openness to a future he does not yet know.[89] The charges of violence and hypermasculinity leveled against Fanon often eclipse the strong desire for love, care, and the other that his thought appeals to. Maldonado-Torres views love as one of the central axes that undergird Fanon's thoughts. Commenting on Fanon's cry in "The Lived Experience of the Black," Maldonado-Torres writes, "in Fanon's cry (shout) there is as much anger as love—indeed, one could argue that his anger stems out of love."[90] Fanon explains the painful sense of frustration he experiences when his desire for love and recognition is rejected: "What? While I was forgetting, forgiving, and wanting only to love, my message was flung back in my face like a slap. The white world, the only honorable one, barred me from all participation."[91] For Lewis Gordon, many of Fanon's writings indicate that one of the most fundamental and practical motivations driving Fanon's work and life was the craving for care and love demonstrated in his clinical encounter with his patients: the colonized who were living a life-in-death.[92]

The Fanonian account of the self resonates with Merleau-Ponty, for whom the self's formation and becoming is conditioned by (and given to) the world: "Why not the quite simple attempt to touch the other, to feel the other, to explain the other to myself? Was my freedom not given to me then in order to build the world of *you*?"[93] Meanwhile, the critiques directed at Fanon bring to light the tormenting absurdity of contradicting ideals and desires, the drama of frustration and anxiety, and, most important, the *failure* that marks his thoughts and writings. What is remarkable is that Fanon's ideas shine and excel precisely through the dialectical drama of contradicting affects that reveal his "passionate attachment" to his own weakness and failure, a failure that does not lead to resignation. The simultaneous denial and affirmation of these clashing affects indicate that he attends to them rather than running away from them; it indicates his openness to the impossible and to his own vulnerability, which might be better translated not so much as the completion of mastery but its undoing, the recognition that "the narrative of mastery is always fragile, threatened, and impossible."[94]

The sacred Fanon beckons at emerges through the constantly changing body, the intimacy and vulnerability of the flesh, which is the site where the re-creation of the self takes place. The racialized and gendered body is constituted not only by violence and negative affect, but also the unswerving desire and love that do not give up on life. Poetics is the ceremony that gives life to this generative power by calling it into being. The ceremony that Fanon strives to find (and found) evokes the messy and conflicting reality made of violence, denial, trauma, beauty, and vulnerability, all of which point at the most profound desire that drives his thinking and life: the desire for love and the other (recognition). This can only be achieved through the re-creation, that is, the total decolonization of the human. The sacred is the foundation and the expression of this undying desire—and also its failure and impossibility.

5

The fugitive ... far behind him he heard the dogs, but already the acacias had abducted him from the world of hunters....
The times were beginning again for him.

—ÉDOUARD GLISSANT, *Poetic Intention*

We who are born of the ocean can never seek solace in rivers.

—KAMAU BRATHWAITE, *Rights of Passage*

POETICS OF WORLD-MAKING
Creolizing the Sacred, Becoming Archipelago

I expounded in chapter 4 on the role and the place of poetics in Caribbean decolonial traditions. Read in dialogue with Aimé Césaire and Sylvia Wynter, we find in Fanon a decolonial poetics that denounces the secular-colonial ceremony of death that normalizes the everyday reality constituted by violence (the ritualistic sacrifice of the other). The genealogical trajectory of Caribbean decolonial poetics converges on the figure of Césaire whose poetics and significance I have already explored. Césaire is a key reference for the diverse orientations that Africana (Caribbean decolonial) critique takes across the twentieth century. Aside from his association with the negritude movement and the broader radical tradition that takes the Marxist revolutionary character (represented by figures such as C. L. R. James, Walter Rodney, and George Padmore), Césaire also occupies a pivotal place within the tradition of Caribbean poetics.[1]

The poeticist tradition is characterized by its use of imagination (imaginary), which is crucial for reinventing new conceptual and symbolic grammar to theorize the complex history and identity of Antilleanity. Put differently, many of these thinkers contributed to discerning and establishing what Aaron Kamugisha calls a Caribbean method.[2] If the modality of decolonial critique examined in chapter 4 via Fanon emerges primarily through the critical rearticulation of race (Blackness), the current of thought I examine in this chapter is generated through philosophical and poetic reflections on the transatlantic experience of displacement and violence that is the Middle Passage and plantation life. These contemplative and poetic reflections articulate the pain and the beauty of world-making amid the ruins: the stubborn force of life that unfolds upon the open horizon of history despite catastrophe. Aesthetics and ethics merge into one another. Aesthetic inquiry becomes an ethical duty in the aftermath of catastrophe, where what is left is deemed unworthy. Poetics offers the language to signify the unsignified, the unsignifiable. Poetics is an activating force that names new beings and animates new realities, rebuilding the world that violence has devastated, a world that violence has persistently foreclosed.

One of the most important and unique contributions to Caribbean decolonial poetics comes from the Martinican philosopher, essayist, and poet Édoaurd Glissant, who is the central focus of this chapter. Glissant's work demonstrates an original approach to engaging and theorizing the problem of coloniality in the Americas. His constructive use of imagination, along with the poetic vision of future imbued with deep philosophical texture, pushes language and being beyond the confines of the boundary conceived by the colonial vision. Like Fanon, Glissant does not often evoke religion explicitly. In Fanon, the murky shape of the sacred emerges as negation (of religion), whereas Glissant offers a more palpable—however opaque—contour. The various unsaid moments and figures Glissant's writings gesture at are often linked to a blurry image of the sacred that seems to ground the fragile possibility of survival, community, and future. Disarticulated from the baggage of colonial iteration, Glissant's sacred evokes a mystical disposition that conjures up the living and the dead, past and present, tragedy and awe, as well as the *entour* that is the whole environment that gives expression to poetics.

Glissant's attempt to reconfigure being in relation to poetics and the sacred suggests important insights and challenges for theorizing religion and (de)coloniality. Glissant challenges the registers of the Western/colonial ideal of being (Man) that abstract the complexity of particularity. The convoluted question of history, power, and violence (all of which are specific to place, that is, geography) that haunts the self is obscured in the abstract universal of being espoused by Western ontology. Glissant's visionary writings, filled with thought-provoking images and imaginaries, suggest ample constructive visions for reconfiguring the philosophical (and historical) registers that index being as a self-sufficient, isolated entity. Following the contemplative journey Glissant's reflections lead us to, we encounter a blurred figure of the unnamable slowly emerge along the journey. This opaque yet overwhelming figure, which refuses a simple (and single) linguistic designation, is often referred to as sacred in Glissant's corpus. This notion of the sacred exceeds a single name or meaning. It holds together and connects with many key ideas that are central to a Glissantian philosophy of creolization and Relation.

Glissant's work also pushes us to rethink the field's methodological orientation that operates on a reverse binary that tends to confine Afro-Caribbean religions to the domain of rituals and practices. As I discussed in chapter 1, the liberal corrective to past mistakes made by nineteenth-century scholarship of religion has normalized the asymmetrical dynamic that conditions the study of Afro-Indigenous religions. Whereas the traditional study of religion (the current that grew out of nineteenth-century European scholarship) took the large absence of texts in Afro-Indigenous religions as a sign of their inferiority, liberal theories of the late twentieth century rehabilitate this asymmetrical division by displacing West-centric categories of text and belief. I call this an asymmetrical division (or reverse binary) because it reinforces the binary association of Afro-Indigenous religions with ritual/practice and Western religion, with text. Disrupting the hierarchical categories in the study of religion does not guarantee the complete evacuation of hierarchical biases and categories inscribed in the dominant epistemic frameworks in which we operate. Displacing the hegemony of the text-centered approach is a much-needed and laudable endeavor. Yet texts are still ineluctably granted a more authoritative voice and agency compared to other elements and artifacts. Such inequity is more notable in the production of theory, as texts (authors' voices, be that canonical or vernacular) actively intervene in the realm of theory in ways that other artifacts do not. Practice, body, or ritual still primarily rely on theory (produced by text) in order to be thematized. Bodies without text, as is often the case with the study of Afro-Caribbean religions, rarely produce theory of their own in the current geography of knowledge in which the overwhelming hegemony of Euro-American theory (and the unequal structure of global knowledge production and distribution) is unchallenged. While there may not be canonical texts in Afro-Caribbean religions, there is an extensive body of literature that intervenes in issues that relate to religion, explicit and implicit. Glissant's work joins the ever-growing body of vernacular literature that is instrumental for theorizing Caribbean religions. And beyond Caribbean religions, I insist, Glissant offers important insights for rethinking the study of modern religion.

Against its initial intention to expand the narrow category of religion, the secularist orientation in the study of religion fomented by liberal theories often reifies boundaries that regulate the category of religion. These theories ensure that scholarship points toward the "right register" of religion by determining that the theoretical and methodological frameworks deployed in the study of religion are compatible with their liberal-secular criteria. However, the binary categories these theories enforce segregate religion in the works of many Caribbean thinkers, including Glissant's.

Glissant's work expands our register and term of religion in different directions. There are profuse ideas, imageries, and moments in Glissant's work that hint at a potential connection with religion. Many such moments go unnamed, which is indicative not of oversight but of potential. His poetic prose style is characterized with an abundance of unstated and unnamed moments. Glissant's writing invites the reader to name the unnamed, to realize the unrealized, to become the unimaginable. At times Glissant adopts the vague figure of the sacred to conjure up the various elements and images that appeal to a sense of religion. His notion of the sacred is nuanced and subtle. It is also different from the sacred proposed by Fanon. In Glissant's world, the sacred, whether named or not, offers a center of gravity in the place where foundation (both metaphysical and historical) is evacuated. An in-depth look at the intrinsic link between the generative ideas Glissant offers and the sacred allows us to resituate religion in decolonial thinking and imagination beyond the boundaries set by the secular-liberal theories and epistemic frameworks.

In what follows, I reflect on Glissant's work with a particular emphasis on the significance his poetics offers. In conversation with his Caribbean interlocutors such as Aimé Césaire, Derek Walcott, and Sylvia Wynter, I seek to highlight the broad theoretical and philosophical significance his thought bears for a critical reading of European (and Eurocentric) modernity from the standpoint of the colonial archipelago. My intention in this chapter, and elsewhere, is not to make ontological claims about the sacred. Rather, my goal is to locate and thematize the scattered articulation of the sacred in

Glissant's work that goes unnoticed and unexplored. I do not limit my reading of religion in Glissant to the figure of the sacred since religion cannot be reduced to the sacred alone. Likewise, religion in Glissant's oeuvre cannot be fully contained in the figure of the sacred. Nevertheless, the sacred serves as an important reference for guiding our journey into the world of poetic imaginaire Glissant opens for us, a world of endless becoming (creolizing) that bears witness to life that persists after (and despite) loss. This persisting force of life, which is both an *elsewhere* and *right here,* and the future it opens, signals the reconstruction of a renewed sense of the sacred. Putting down roots and creating home is deemed sacred in various streams of the Caribbean intellectual tradition. The sacred indicates both the resilient spirit of world-making and a renewed understanding of wholeness. Glissant's sacred points at the multiple registers of possibilities that weave the fabric of this new history, the cosmogony of beginning again after catastrophe.

The Abyss: Poetics of Place

Glissant's reflections begin with the problem of history. Modern Caribbean history is marked or fractured by a narrative born out of violence. The problem for Glissant (and for many Antillean thinkers of his generation) lies in the collective consciousness's inability and unwillingness to come to terms with history, which he diagnoses as the problem of "nonhistory."[3] Nonhistory refers not only to an oblivious attitude toward history, but also to the collective lethargy before a history that fails to generate any meaning other than tragedy. A traumatic history marked with horrendous violence and shock perhaps does not offer any meaning worthy to the present. However, for Glissant, the painful task of making sense of history is unavoidable in order to think about the present and future of Caribbean identity. In *Caribbean Discourse* he writes, "The past, to which we were subjected, which has not yet emerged as history for us, is, however, obsessively present. The duty of the writer is to explore this obsession, to show its relevance in a continuous fashion to the immediate present."[4] The task of exploring this obsession that is engaging with the traumatic collective history consists of staring straight into the very heart of the abyss of loss. The specific historical site that he turns to in *Poetics of Relation* is the Middle Passage, the site of both death (trauma) and life (future). The opening essay, "The Open Boat," carefully and contemplatively expands on the traumatic dimension of the violent displacement and voyage. The essay illustrates the image of the slave ship in the

Middle Passage with overloaded, crammed bodies in miserable conditions and bodies that are thrown overboard, dead or alive. The horrendous scene is paradoxically juxtaposed with the ship being steered into the open ocean, sailing toward the infinitely open (and beautiful) horizon. The unfathomable dimension of this violence and terror is one that haunts Glissant's writings through his career.

The encounter with the new land marks a beginning, however tragic the journey is. The abyss of the depth of the ocean, however traumatic, is also generative. Those who survived the Middle Passage "rose up on this unexpected, dumbfounded land."[5] The ship and the Middle Passage as the site of death is also the womb that gives birth to new life and community. It is a "site of initial destruction, which is, paradoxically, also a site of initial creation," as Stanka Radovich comments.[6] This is not, however, the all-too-familiar account that glorifies resilience and normalizes suffering. The Glissantian account of beginning is one that is perpetually haunted by "drowned bodies that sowed in its depths explosive seeds of absence."[7] Glissant's philosophical writings are, in this sense, a memory project.[8] In wrestling with the undying memory of colonial specters, he beckons at both the past and the future at the same time. Theorizing the persisting force of life, thinking about beginning requires, for Glissant, continuously reflecting on the traumatic memory that haunts the collective consciousness without surrendering to the nostalgic fixation on tragedy. The ocean is the site of paradox: an open grave that is also the fecund site of world-making.

Imagination is central to Glissant's thought, and the ocean is the key concept and metaphor that drives his generative vision. As I will explore more later, Glissant's thought presents original philosophical challenges to traditional epistemological and ontological grammar of Western philosophy that often alienates the thinking subject from *place*. The Western ideal of Man as transcendent of place is indicative of Europe's privilege, which make it blind to its own root in place. For people whose history begins with forced dislocation, place becomes crucial for one's identity and belonging (thus, it shapes thinking). Finding and founding place is one of the primary orientations of people born out of placelessness, out of rootlessness. Spatial metaphors and concepts are thus key: the sea, the ocean, the ship, the island, the mangrove, and the archipelago. Glissant's philosophical work recounts the narrative of the being whose journey of becoming is inseparably rooted in the landscape of the archipelago. Spatial concepts are not mere metaphors but imaginaries (*imaginaire*) that aim at producing a new modality of thinking and, eventually, of being. The French word *imaginaire* needs to be distinguished from imagination as it does not have a direct equivalent in English other than the neologism "imaginary." The former denotes an active relation and possibility for change between knowing and being, between the self and its relation to the world.[9] *Imaginary* rejects the binary between thinking and being, between aesthetics and politics.

The overwhelming historical memory that exceeds speech parallels the beauty and the intensity of the archipelago's landscape, which also fails to find expression in language. The archipelagic landscape bears the sole witness to the history of violence and survival, the account that goes unrecorded in history books. Poetics gives expression to that testimony—the archipelagic landscape that has witnessed history; the history of catastrophe and the life that persists despite violence. Discussing the histories of maroon resistance, slaughter, and deaths that taint the entire landscape of the island, Glissant writes, "So history is spread out beneath this surface, from the mountains to the sea, from north to south, from the forest to the beaches. Maroon resistance and denial, entrenchment and endurance, the world beyond and dream. (Our landscape is its own monument: its meaning can only be traced on the underside. It is all history)."[10] Caribbean decolonial poetics is always already a poetics of place, of the archipelagic landscape.

Glissant's emphasis on place draws a contrast with the ways the Western imaginary is constructed as a universal worldview. The construction and projection of universalism often presupposes a depoliticized geography. As I discussed in previous chapters, numerous critics of the global south have pointed out that the modern West is a product of the imperial geography of reason. The Eurocentric configuration of the current world order cannot be properly articulated apart from its history of colonialism. Attention to place and geography unveils the dynamics of power that conditions social relations across modern/colonial space. Elizabeth DeLoughrey writes about the "cartographic hierarchy" that reflects the (post)colonial power relations across the globe. The very distinction between continent and island is, to a certain extent, arbitrary, and it reflects geography's ingrained cultural and political assumptions in which "islands [are] usually associated with small islands, former colonies, close to the equator, exotic, remote."[11] This is why critique in the Americas is always a critique of place, a critique of colonial cartography and its construction of place.

Space is neither neutrally given nor devoid of meanings. Critical geographers and theorists of the late twentieth century shifted their attention from the abstracted concept of space to the "production" of space as *place*. For the Marxist French philosopher Henri Lefebvre, space is the result of social production. Space as a means of production conceals the productive forces that produce it: "Things lie, and when having become commodities, they lie in order to conceal their origin, namely social labor, they tend to set themselves up as absolutes. They become more real than reality itself—the productive activity itself, which thus they take over."[12] That space is socially constructed does not mean it can be reduced to the cultural or social alone. Many important thinkers and theorists of space have argued that place is an essential element to being human.[13] And, as I reviewed in chapter 4, phenomenology regards place as central to our perception and creation of the world. However, our construction of the world (space/place) goes beyond our inner conceptual perception of it, since neither our body nor our mind is free from the sociopolitical forces that produce the matrix in which we are situated. Thus, the Brazilian geographer Milton Santos writes, "Each geographic place corresponds, in each moment, to a set of technologies and instruments that result from a specific combination that is historically determined."[14] He adds, "In any given moment the world selects particular places and rejects others, and in doing so it modifies the set of places, and space as a whole. To become space, the world becomes on the virtualities of place."[15] For both Lefebvre and Santos, the production of modern space is part of the secular process of rationalization. Santos calls this process the "disenchantment of geographic space," a process oriented to globalizing (homogenizing) actions.[16] Lefebvre highlights the religious dimension of space even further as he writes, "The act of creation is a process. For it to occur it is necessary for a society's practical capabilities and sovereign powers to have at their disposal special places: religious and political sites. A further necessity: space should come into being inhabited by a higher reality."[17]

The close correlation between space and religion had already caught the attention of key twentieth-century scholars of religion. In his influential work, *The Sacred and the Profane*, Mircea Eliade draws on the metaphor of space to articulate what he deems to be the "essence" of religious experience, that is, the sacred. For Eliade, the sacred plays the key function of meaning-making in an otherwise meaningless world. In a (profane) world of homogeneous spaces where no meaning or direction is derivative, the sacred manifests by drawing boundaries, thus creating the nonhomogeneous space, a space that is different and separate: a new reality. Such experience is "a primordial religious experience" for Eliade and it "precedes all reflection on the world."[18] In the existential-phenomenological language, the former, that is, the profane experience of sameness and chaos, indicates nothingness while the latter (the sacred) represents being.[19] Because the sacred creates new reality (and space), it can be equated with cosmogony that is the founding of the world. In creating the world, the human situates itself at the center of the world. Eliade writes, "*If the world is to be lived, it must be founded*—and no world can come to birth in the chaos of the homogeneity and relativity of the profane space. The discovery or projection of a fixed point—center—is equivalent to the founding of the world."[20]

There are numerous questionable complications that Eliade's theory of religion bears not only for the study of religion but also for the study of coloniality and race. These various ramifications aside, the close link Eliade draws between religion and space deserves our attention. Religion is, first of all, conceived as a spatial act and phenomenon. Eliade views religion as the human being's attachment, the primordial need to *belong* in place. It is, however, not an act of finding one's place in space. Rather, one creates or founds place: by claiming its place in the chaotic array of sameness and becoming its own center.

Despite the important and useful link between religion and space/place, Eliade's theory of religion carries significant problems for theorizing religion in the twenty-first century. As I discussed already, Eliade's notion of the sacred relies on essentializing categories and concepts (Christian-centric) that grant religion a transcendental character detached from history and power. While Eliade situates the human being in place, he does so by applying a generic and universalizing category, thus failing to historicize the human and its place. It is also not difficult to draw a possible association between Eliade's theory with histories of settler colonialism, considering that settling and inhabiting the territory occupies a central role in his theory of the sacred. Eliade's work of world-creating involves the bloody destruction of the enemy, the monster:

> For what is involved is *undertaking the work of creation of the world that one has chosen to inhabit*. Hence it is necessary to imitate the work of gods, the cosmogony. But this is not always easy, for there are also tragic, blood-drenched cosmogonies; as imitator of divine gestures, man must reiterate them. Since the gods had to slay and dismember a marine monster or a primordial being in order to create the world from it, man in his turn must imitate them when he builds his own world, his city or his house.[21]

Religion, for Eliade, bespeaks the existential necessity *essential* to all humans, a necessity that projects the innermost desire to find and found order in an otherwise orderless (meaningless) world. In manifesting itself, the sacred inspires human beings to imitate the cosmogonic work of gods, driving them to found worlds by inhabiting space, conquering chaos (otherness), and establishing order. Aside from reducing religion to a matter of inner reflection, Eliade associates religion with the spatial imaginary of congruity and stability. In his critical commentary on the history of the study of religion, Jonathan Z. Smith observes the field's tendency to identify religion primarily with congruency and conformity. Spatial metaphor is central to Smith's commentary as the primary target of his critical reflection is Eliade's theory of religion. He calls this model a "locative map of the world,"[22] a cartographic imaginary that reflects the imperial ideology. It projects a world-view of order and congruity devoid of tension.[23] Religion, construed by this imperial model, produces space as a locatable and controlled ground of stability that guarantees meaning. Spaces of the unknown, the unpredictable, haunt Eliade. A deep fear for the chaos of otherness: the abyss terrifies him. This way, religion for Eliade amounts to cosmogony, the founding of a world of order and meaning. In many ways, Caribbean poeticism also turns to the trope of cosmogony in order to reenvision Antilleanity. This is why "beginning" as an act of second creation occupies an important place for many Caribbean writers.

Tomoko Masuzawa has elaborated extensively on how equating religion with origin stories reflects the Western-centric view of religion. For Masuzawa, Eliade reduces all activities of the "archaic man" to the beginning of time. His archaic man is eternally held captive to cosmogonic nostalgia. Masuzawa observes the conservative nature of Eliade's schema, the archaic man perpetually dwelling on the timeless mystical horizon of repetition: "Terrorized by the continual threat of the new and the meaningless, he resorts to compulsory and compulsive repetition. He repeats, and he refers, time and time again, to the Self-identical beginning."[24] Cosmogony takes a different meaning in Caribbean decolonial thinking. It disavows the origin-oriented theories of religion. Caribbean thinkers' use of origin defies the myth of origin, yet it retains the sense of world-making in that it testifies to the creativity that negotiates meaning for one's (not only individual but also collective) existence.[25]

Glissant's attachment to place, particularly his insistence on the specificity of the Antillean archipelago, points to a sharp contrast between what he calls *la pensée continentale* (continental thinking) and *la pensée archipélique* (archipelagic thinking). Continental thinking is characterized by clear boundaries and limits that demarcate continental geography. The archipelagic mode of thinking (and being) calls for a radical reconfiguration of one's relationship to place, to the world. It emerges from "poetics and imaginary of the world . . . a non-systematic, inductive thought, [that] explor[es] the unforeseen of the whole-world . . ."[26] As Michael Dash writes, Glissant's central concern lies in "how we might inhabit the world poetically or how we might renounce territorial claims in earthly dwelling."[27] Dash implies here that poetics reconfigures the subject's sovereign agency in relation to the world, that is, entour. Renouncing territoriality does not indicate giving up geographic specificity, including its materiality, that is, the land.

Rather, it indicates revolting against the imperial cartographic imagination that conditions our relation to place (the world). It signals liberating the place (land) from the colonial category of territoriality that is used for its dispossession, enclosure, and privatization. In this sense, Glissant's project as a poetics of place seeks to reclaim space, that is, the universality of the particular place disavowed by the West. Continental imagination (la pensée continentale) presupposes its clearly demarcated boundaries across the connected landmass as the precondition of wholeness (universality). From the viewpoint of continental thinking, the archipelago signifies insularity and fragmentation. For Glissant, the archipelagic imagination views "each island [as] embod[ying] openness. The dialectic between inside and outside is reflected in the relationship of land and sea."[28] He abolishes the very notion of the universal and the particular, or center and periphery.[29] Renouncing of territoriality means, in this sense, reclaiming the universality of Antilleanity. "Loss of territoriality," Dash comments, "opens Glissant's marroner to poetic dwelling or archipelagic thought."[30] The insular and fragmented archipelago and its islands represent a limitless openness, a *tout-monde*: the Caribbean as a Whole World.

In many ways, the Caribbean is the inseparable other of European modernity. If the Americas was crucial for the emergence of European modernity, the Caribbean can be regarded as the womb, the womb inseminated with the blood of Africa that delivered the Atlantic.[31] Because of its inception in the modern Western imaginary, the Caribbean has been the site of the West's economic experimentation and appropriation. While it provided the material resources that drove mercantile capitalism at the global level, the Caribbean also created an unprecedented form of local social edifice that was entirely structured and run by the plantation. It was a society whose single raison d'être was the extraction of profit in which the entire people was deemed a mere object of exploitation. As George Lamming comments, it was a society in which "people were brought for one purpose and one purpose only... [which was] to be transformed from persons into instruments of production."[32] The plantation is the name of the socioeconomic system and worldview that facilitated the material production and the circulation of the modern world order and imagination.

The problem of plantation modernity has been recently rearticulated in environmental humanities, particularly in conversations about the anthropocene. The anthropocene was recently introduced and popularized as a term that captures the new geological epoch in which the human relation to the earth is fundamentally altered, resulting in changes to the earth's ecosystem and climate. Building on this conversation, newly coined terms such as *capitalocene* and *plantationocene* seek to extend the anthropocene discourse beyond the perimeter of traditional environmentalism. They attempt to broaden the link of current ecological crisis to human-initiated activities that bear a devastating cost to the earth, with capitalism (capitalocene) and the plantation (plantationocene) as models of exploitative and extractive systems of exchange.[33] Plantationocene, in particular, draws the historical continuity between the plantation as a constitutive element of colonial modernity and the current globalized capitalist system of production, which reduces the land, environment, human labor, and nonhuman lives into commodified tools of exploitation and mass production.

The impact and the implication that the current ecological crisis bears on the global scale cannot be articulated aside from its continuity with the history of colonial modernity and the mode of production and extraction it has built through mass violence inflected on Black and Indigenous peoples. Reversely, colonial history is always a history of experimentation and exploitation, not only of humans but also nonhumans, the land, and control of local peoples' mode of relating with the surrounding world. Slave gardens and imperial botanical gardens are often drawn as contrasting examples of this bio/environmental dimension of colonialism. As Donna Haraway explains, slave gardens open spaces that are "nurtured even in the harshest circumstances," an "underexplored world" that provides critical resources for both humans and biodiversity.[34] Ros Gray and Shela Sheikh observe that, despite the utopian association gardens have in Western imagination, they are riven with "questions concerning who is displaced in order to demarcate their boundaries, and whose labour is exploited to maintain them as sites of nourishment and enjoyment."[35] DeLoughrey adds the religious layer to the issue when she points out that Caribbean islands are often associated with the Christian allegory of paradise despite its history of violence.[36] The notion of plantation modernity as well as the emerging conversations about the plantationocene seek to fill the missing link of race, (racial) capitalism, and colonialism in the discourse of the anthropocene.[37] They offer an important perspective for the study of the connection between the current climate crisis, predatory (racial) capitalism, and colonialism. For instance, Ray and Sheikh observe, after Londa Schiebinger, that botanists were "agents of empire" whose scientific systems of classification and taxonomy served the colonial agenda.[38] Ray and Sheikh add, "Imperial science... excluded other, 'minor' histories and systems of knowledge (ecologies of knowledge), as well as modes of being-in-the-world that are not premised upon the value, profitability and usefulness of plants that underpins the vampire logic of capitalism towards nature."[39] The term *anthropocene*, some critics point out, depoliticizes the broader problem of global coloniality by reducing its cause to the environment. For Jairus Grove, this broader global order (which he names the *Eurocene*) needs to be approached from the event of 1492, as a colonial configuration of the world order driven by geopolitical (motivated by economic profit) goals in which war (extraction and destruction of life) becomes an essential mode of life: "The Eurocene conceptually demarcates forms of martial life that emerged at the expense of other forms of life and other ecological order often by means of annihilation..."[40] The continuing cycle of destruction that led to the current ecological crisis cannot be attributed to speciesism alone but geohistoric and geopolitical causes that reconfigured the global order as we know it.[41] A discourse of ecological crisis that fails to attend to the root cause of colonial-capitalist-modernity might reproduce what Renato Rosaldo calls "imperialist nostalgia," which is when "agents of colonialism... often display nostalgia for... the very forms of life they intentionally altered or destroyed."[42] The problem, as Rosaldo diagnoses, is that this nostalgia presents "a pose of 'innocent' yearning both to capture people's imaginations and to conceal its complicity with often brutal domination."[43] Along the same vein, Grove emphasizes that what it takes to build a political system to confront environmental justice is "the kind of struggle taken up by W. E. B. Du Bois and Frantz Fanon in the name of self-determination and anticolonialism," rather than extracting Indigenous knowledge and practice.[44]

Glissant articulates the problem of colonial modernity in relation to place, the landscape, the nonhuman world in ways that create generative resonance across the diverse voices that point to the link between the current ecological crisis and colonial (plantation) modernity. Glissant's concern for place, for the non- or other-than-human world is born out of the long Caribbean tradition of anticolonialism, a tradition deeply linked to the struggle against the extractivist violence of racial capitalism and the plantation economy. The poetics of place we witness in Glissant begs a distinction from Western liberal environmentalist projects that often attempt to misappropriate and domesticate his thought.[45]

Reclaiming the Caribbean as tout-monde (Whole World) against the universalizing imperial cartography of the West solicits a commitment to renew one's sense of territoriality by renouncing it. Renouncing one's territorial claim does not mean renouncing place (land) but reclaiming and re-creating it. The creation of imperial geography involved deracination of an entire people. Revolting against this order means for Glissant reinventing rootlessness (placelessness) as wholeness. Affirming rootlessness need not lead to renouncing the root. Rather, what Glissant suggests is to reconfigure the conceptualization of place based in continental thinking. Thinking from the archipelago, it is place-creating from exile. Poetics is the work of world-making. The plantation as "*place* was closed, but the world derived from it remained open."[46] Glissant's project as a poetics of place is one that grapples with this world that remains open, one that seeks to give it a meaning. Archipelagic thinking offers a wholly different mode of thinking and being in the world, a vision of inhabiting the world that refuses the confining cartographic boundaries drawn by imperial reason. The Cartesian self-assured subject loses itself in archipelagic thinking. The creolized self engenders the larger web of Relation that constitutes the world, the archipelago and its landscape.

Glissant's poetic vision of the world is based in his philosophy of creolization. As the authors of *Éloge de la créolité* write, creolization is less a theoretical concept crafted by intellectual discourses than a living testimony to survival.[47] Creole as a linguistic and cultural tool has been the means of communication, resistance, and solidarity among slave communities across the Caribbean. Creole indicates survival rather than an active and organized form of resistance when the overwhelming presence of violence leaves the community with scarce means for resistance. In this sense, creolizing is a testament to the creative force and persistence of life that goes on despite devastating violence. Likewise, the poetic witness we find in Glissant's writings is the figure of the lone, dumbfounded survivor, "the opaque wanderer who refuses speech."[48] His silence points at the silence of the landscape, the silence of the world.[49] The figure of the silent survivor, however, does not signal renunciation or despair, but beginning. For despite his emphasis on the past, Glissant's writings are future oriented. The pressing question lies in thinking about beginning again from the ruins of catastrophe. Antillean poetics is a testament to the collective history of creolization that is resilience and survival: beginning again on the stranded island. Derek Walcott writes:

> Deprived of their original language, the captured and indentured tribes create their own, accreting and secreting fragments of an old, an epic vocabulary, from Asia and from Africa, but to an ancestral, an ecstatic rhythm in the blood that cannot be subdued by slavery or indenture, while nouns are renamed and the given names of places accepted like Felicity village or Choiseul. The original language dissolves from the exhaustion of distance like fog trying to cross an ocean, but this process of renaming, of finding new metaphors, is the same process that the poet faces every morning of his working day, making his own tools like Crusoe, assembling nouns from necessity, from Felicity, even renaming himself.[50]

This is where poetics meets politics of creolization. Beginning again is an act of renaming the new reality in the place of the lost, original name. Creolizing is the persistent process of renaming and rebuilding the world, wholly anew. Walcott adds:

> The stripped and naked man, however abused, however disabused of old beliefs, instinctually, even desperately begins again as craftsman. In the indication of the slightest necessary gesture of ordering the world around him, of losing his old name and rechristening himself, in the arduous enunciation of a dimmed alphabet, in the shaping of tools, pen or spade, is the whole, profound sigh of human optimism, of what we in the archipelago still believe in: work and hope. It is out of this that the New World, or the Third World, should begin.[51]

The work of the poet consists of re-creating the world from the shipwreck, from the shard of the lost vocabulary, the fragments of drowned memories. The myth of purity and wholeness yields to creolized ontology. The self, the landscape, and the future are always already creolized.

Creolization carries a spiritual connotation. No aspect of the Caribbean worldview and culture can be sharply separated from the sacred. Despite Christianity being the predominant religion in the region, the strict distinction of secular and the sacred has never found its place in the Caribbean. Discussing the crucial place of religion in Caribbean intellectual history, Kamugisha observes that the secularist orientation of contemporary scholarship puts restrictive barriers on our understanding of Caribbean intellectual history. He writes, "Religion and spirituality as a site of embodied cultural memory, a galvanizing force for marronage, a practice of freedom with a theory of diaspora, and a commitment to transnationalism emerges here as the absent presence in a tradition of scholarship on intellectual history that has remained resolutely secular, a limitation in need of address."[52] Religion in the Caribbean has been the animating force of culture and history. It has provided the fertile soil on which decolonial creativity and imagination are nurtured and cultivated. Decolonial poetics gives expression to the process in which the sacred is preserved and re-created through continuous processes of creolization. The figure of the sacred, like the trope of the root, is one that cannot be lived without. It needs to be continuously reinvented to ensure the collective survival. The sacred in Caribbean poetics signals immanent movements of encounter and exchange, the journey and trajectories of becoming, all that creolization symbolizes. If the sacred is understood to take place in and through movements, its theologizing (however secular it may be) happens through poetics. Poetics holds the space in which untamed notions of the sacred are born.

In *Water Graves*, Valérie Loichot traces the figure of the sacred in Caribbean artistic and philosophical works. She reads the production of these works as a counterritual to the "unritual" that marks the historical experience of the Middle Passage. Unritual, Loichot writes, "is the privation of ritual." It indicates "the obstruction of the sacred in the first place."[53] Reading the transatlantic works of literary, artistic, and philosophical production as a ritual against the unritual imposed by colonial modernity provides numerous important benefits for grasping the complex constitution and manifestation of power in the Americas.

One of the primary and recurring observations that *The Coloniality of the Secular* makes is religion's indispensable place in the constitution of power (relations) in the Americas. The dominant concepts and methods currently employed in the study of religion do not adequately consider the way religion constitutes power or, to be more specific, coloniality in Latin America and the

Caribbean. As I have elaborated already, the study of Caribbean religions is usually reserved for social scientific methods that often deem the Caribbean as the site of the production of data but not theory. While Loichot does not develop her reading into a full-blown theory of religion, she signals a new methodological possibility that would help us incorporate Caribbean intellectual production as a critical resource for theorizing religion.

In her reading of Glissant, Loichot observes the link between the sacred and the production of poetry. She writes, "The sacred in the face of the unritual can only function with the ecological help of the *entour*." Here entour means "the whole environment comprising the poem, human and nonhuman animals, vegetation, rocks, lavas, and 'nature' and 'culture.'"[54] In other words, the sacred is linked to the production of not only poetry but also place. Poetics creates place, and the sacred is often linked to the process through which poetics creates place.

Writing about place, Edward Casey links cosmogony to the creation of place. He writes, "Cosmogenesis is topogenesis."[55] The initial creation, for Casey, is the negation of void, the notion of no-place. "To create 'in the first place,'" he writes, "is to create a *first place*."[56] Casey's insight is useful for making the connection between Caribbean decolonial poetics, the creation of place, and the sacred more concrete. I will come back to the sacred in Caribbean poetics and in Glissant toward the end of this chapter.

The Shoreline: Creolization

Creolization as a method and tool goes far beyond the notion of survival. The vision that creolization suggests distinguishes clearly from the bleak Fanonian diagnosis of colonial existence: "living simply means not to die. To exist means staying alive."[57] It also differs significantly from the pessimists' vision that denies the possibility of Black social life in a world constituted by anti-Blackness. Creolization is indeed a tactic of survival, but its goal extends far beyond mere survival. It refers to the rich process of world-making, of a new reality in which new beings flourish in wholeness and freedom.

Jean Bernabé, Patrick Chamoiseau, and Raphaël Confiant, the authors of *Éloge*, attribute the notion of creoleness to Césaire and Césairean negritude: "Cesairian Negritude is a baptism, the primal act of our restored dignity. We are forever Cesaire's sons."[58] Negritude was the first intellectual attempt to uplift Africana identity, born out of the transatlantic cultural encounter. But its vision was rooted in a rather essentializing understanding of Blackness, tying Blackness back to Africa. Bernabé, Chamoiseau, and Confiant explain that Glissant succeeds Césairean negritude by recasting it into Antilleanity, thus overcoming the confining identitarian vision of negritude.[59] Glissant revealed that Caribbeanness (Antilleanity) lies in self-knowledge. And self-knowledge can be accessed through an interior vision. Accepting one's creoleness is imperative in order to reach to the depth of this interior vision: "We cannot reach Caribbeanness without interior vision. And interior vision is nothing without the unconditional acceptance of our Creoleness. We declare ourselves Creoles."[60]

Despite *Éloge*'s important contribution to the theory of creoleness, Glissant distanced himself from the concept of creoleness by distinguishing creolization (*créolisation*) from creoleness (*créolité*). In fact, his first use of the term occurs in the context in which he distinguishes Antilleanity from creoleness, a term that is based in linguistic kinship. Glissant's vision of Caribbeanness goes far beyond the linguistic distinction toward cultural formations that unites the various experiences of the repeating islands across the archipelago.[61] Despite *Éloge*'s claim that creoleness signifies "to live the world, the whole world" (*a vivre le monde, ou le tout-monde*), Glissant finds creoleness essentializing and confining.[62] Creoleness "only works in the Caribbean. Creolization, on the other hand, is not an essence but a universal process."[63] Creolization bases the notion of Relation that Glissant later develops. Creolization and Relation offer important philosophical registers that stretch to broader ramifications for thinking about the self, ethics, and politics.

In "The Muse of History," Derek Walcott illustrates the dilemma with Caribbean history and identity, the backdrop from which creolization as a method and tactic emerges. He contrasts the way history is approached by the New World poets who are subject to what he calls the "muse of history." They have constantly created "a literature of recrimination and despair, a literature of revenge by the descendants of slaves or a literature of remorse written by the descendants of masters."[64] Those who seek to break from the past are also held hostage to coloniality with their overinvestment in the new world as an exceptional moment of history. Coloniality outlasts the revolutionary break from history. The desire of wanting to break from the past itself might end up reinstating a new myth, a mythological past. Walcott writes:

> This self-torture arises when the poet also sees history as language, when he limits his memory to the suffering of the victim. Their admirable wish to honour the degraded ancestor limits their language to phonetic pain,

the groan of suffering, the curse of revenge. The tone of the past becomes an unbearable burden, for they must abuse the master or hero in his own language, and this implies self-deceit. Their view of Caliban is of the enraged pupil. They cannot separate the rage of Caliban from the beauty of his speech when the speeches of Caliban are equal in their elemental power to those of his tutor.[65]

Walcott finds a different approach in the great poets of the Americas whose "vision of man in the New World is Adamic."[66] By Adamic, Walcott refers to the capacity to wonder, the capacity to recognize the beauty of Caliban's speech, to see it as victory, not servitude.[67] The task of the poet that Walcott suggests is not to contemplate the shipwreck in "an oceanic nostalgia for the older culture and a melancholy at the new," but to name and build the new place out of the shipwreck.[68] Here Walcott captures graciously what creolization attends to. Creolization is future oriented. It bears both the weight of the past and the pressure of the present in the singular and absolute act of beginning. Creolization reclaims the dispossessed present, the fragmented and bastardized cosmogony of the dislocated community by reinventing it through a new language and parameter of wholeness. Referring to the shipwreck in his poem "Crusoe's Journal," Walcott writes that "... out of such timbers / came our first book, our profane Genesis / whose Adam speaks that prose / which, blessing some sea-rock, startles itself / with poetry's surprise / in a green world, one without metaphors." Decolonial thought and politics in the Caribbean inevitably entails rethinking aesthetics. Decolonial aesthetics, as suggested by Glissant and Walcott, attends to the work of love and perseverance of the second Adam, whose second beginning is as whole as the first beginning. Walcott reclaims the sense of beauty in the political and aesthetic praxis that harnesses brokenness into wholeness, as he writes in this famous passage: "Break a vase, and the love that reassembles the fragments is stronger than that love which took its symmetry for granted when it was whole."[69] For Walcott, the aesthetics of creolization points at the work of love and care that gathers the broken, ill-fitting pieces together; it is the work of persistence as a testimony to the life that goes on after catastrophe. Similarly, creolization as envisioned by Glissant suggests the figure of the lone survivor and witness in the new land. The dumbfounded witness Glissant portrays is one who wanders along the haunted shoreline in silence and solitude yet who is capable of *wonder*. This second beginning is also the becoming-of-place that is the creolization of place.

The often-evoked trope of the abyss in Glissant's work is indicative of the question of home(lessness) and root(lessness) in his thought. The abyss is often used to refer to the indeterminate state of the voyage in the Middle Passage, the bottomless depth of the ocean in which the traumatic pain and cries of memory are drowned along with the bodies that were thrown overboard. It also indicates the land, the community, and the future that have yet to emerge. Glissant's use of the trope of the abyss deserves attention here. It is not an accident that he uses *abyss* instead of *void* since the two beg distinction from one another. The two terms are often conflated but the distinction is clear. As I have elaborated in *The Decolonial Abyss*, void refers to vacancy, the state of emptiness. The abyss, contrastingly, indicates indeterminacy in which the boundary between finitude and infinity is blurred.[70] In other words, the abyss is a space of not only negativity but also infinite possibility. For Glissant, the ocean as abyss represents the site in which being is creolized. The endless state of exile, of placelessness (rootlessness), that haunts the Caribbean imagination and identity is also creolized in the oceanic abyss of becoming. Being and its intimate tie to place and home is radically reconceived. Glissant writes, "We create our landscape.... Whoever finds the earth thus suspended in space, and who will come near, will nonetheless not experience the ecstasy of the One. For other stars will join themselves as pendants to this unique ball, which will obsess the traveler. We must exhaust our landscapes, in other words, realize them. But we must not fear discovering them endlessly: new, tempting, possibly prohibited."[71]

Glissant's tactic for reclaiming the dispossessed land consists of reconstructing the sense of place. Place (geography) is constructed by colonial imagination and exploration. Cartography is not a reflection of the existing reality but a construct. Writing (and thinking) in the Caribbean is an act of exploring the landscape and the geography that was distorted by imperial cartography. In this sense, it must be reminded that when Glissant says "we must not fear discovering them endlessly," he is not referring to the Western imperialist mode of exploring "uncharted territories." Rather, creolization's method can be described as the "anti-explorer's method" as Brian Russell Roberts and Michelle Stephens call it after Walcott.[72] In offering an answer to the question "what is the nature of an island?" Walcott writes that he does not know how to answer the question "except by ... the opposite method to the explorer's."[73] Movements across the earth's terrain mark significant disparities that reflect the colonial difference between the explorer and the creolized people. Glissant notes that, in the ancient West, voyages and exiles were viewed as a necessary experience to achieve "being's complete fulfillment."[74] The ancient saga of heroic adventures continues as a powerful narrative that drives the Western imaginary. DeLoughrey observes that "the self made male who accidentally colonizes a desert isle has been a powerful and repeated trope of empire building and of British literature of the eighteenth and nineteenth centuries."[75] In contrast, the anti-explorer's mode of wandering and exploring the world seeks to reclaim exile and affirm displacement as the condition of being and multiplicity. Glissant writes, "Having no place, the seer founds exile... for exile did not arise yesterday: it began with the departure of the first caravel. It is not a state, but a passion..."[76] Reclaiming place is a crucial operation for displacing the universal, its logic of One and the center/periphery binary. He follows Deleuze and Guattari's notion of rhizomatic multiplicity and suggests "submarine roots" to resist the traditional Western metaphysics that renders multiple a replication of sameness.[77] Submarine roots suggest a different mode of being, "not fixed in one position in some primordial spot but extending in all directions in our world through its network of branches."[78] Reclaiming place and root eventually suggests a new mode of being in the world, a creolized ontology. The notion of being as essence gives way to relation or, better, Relation. Likewise, the Caribbean landscape refuses to be determined by the Euclidean set of lines. Glissant writes, "The land has ceased to be essence, it becomes relation."[79]

Relation displaces ontology. The notion of Relation points to the heart of the philosophical vision that Glissant has signaled consistently through his intellectual trajectory. In *Caribbean Discourse*, originally published in 1981 as *Le discours Antillais*, he discusses diversion as a tool of decolonial resistance. Diversion is incomplete without reversion, which does not indicate a return to an origin or "to some immutable state of Being, but a return to the point of entanglement, from which we were forcefully turned away."[80] As we can see, he is putting forward the notion of relational entanglement that defies the traditional metaphysical notion of being as essence. Creolization rejects the ontological definition of being as an individuated and immutable essence. Reflecting on the philosophical register and significance of Glissant's work, John Drabinski comments, "The Middle Passage changes everything."[81] Being is buried in the abyssal depth of the ocean. Paradoxically, this is the site in which a new possibility emerges. In *Poetics of Relation*, Glissant develops this concept into the notion of Relation. He calls the slave ship and the depth of the ocean—central objects of reflection in the opening chapter—the "womb abyss." It is the site in which being in its most material sense, as *body*, dissolves. Yet this womb gives birth to people, however painful and traumatic. Relation attests to these sedimented layers of shared experience and knowledge that constitute creolizing solidarity across different singularities of the repeating islands: "Relation is not made up of things that are foreign but of shared knowledge."[82] Glissant further explains that this knowledge, while particular, is part of the universal, one that folds back into the whole, that is, Relation: "Not just a specific knowledge, appetite, suffering, and delight of one particular people, not only that, but knowledge of the Whole, great from having been at the abyss and freeing knowledge of Relation within the Whole."[83] He carefully captures the work of the abyss that "dissolves" and "expels" (gives birth to) being. Terror and freedom.

Neither Relation nor creolization seeks to romanticize (and water down) the arduous work and struggle involved in the process. Michael Monahan's articulation of creolization is helpful here as he defines creolization as a practice of relation and liberation, "the maintenance of a *relation* that affirms and builds upon human agency, understood as constitutively social."[84] This mode of being, as a praxis of relation and liberation, ultimately signals freedom. As Glissant explains, creolization is an ontology of multiplicity that "allow[s] each person to be there and elsewhere, rooted and open, lost in the mountains and free beneath the sea, in harmony and in errantry."[85] Such a notion of freedom begs a distinction from the Western notion of freedom informed by liberal values of individual rights, which include property ownership, movement, and exchange. The creolizing ontology of multiplicity and errantry Glissant's Relation advocates is conceived in the abyss of the Middle Passage, in the bottomless depth of the shared collective memory that exceeds language. The possibility of a new beginning is seeded in the fragile name of the community that is yet to emerge. Survival is not predicated on the individual's heroic determination. Rather, it is conditioned by the other who solicits future. Glissant writes, "To live the relation may very well be to measure its convincing fragility."[86] However fragile, the other beckons at the unknown future. A future that *insists* in the present despite loss: "Time constitutes itself there, but it does not begin, nor is it fixed: *it continues for us*...."[87] This is why, Glissant writes, exile (or, I would say, creolization), is not a state but passion. Freedom lived in Relation, for people who emerge out of the abyss, signals the capacity to sail into the unknown future, an unknown that no longer terrifies.[88] Language fails to name this sense of freedom. Only time, the landscape, and poetics give witness to it.

The Ocean: Poetics

The genealogy of Caribbean poetics signals both testimony (of survival) and ceremony (of world-making). Poetics bridges past and future, the dead and the yet to come. Reflecting on the dilemma of Caribbean history, the authors of *Éloge* write, "[The events] happened with no witnesses, or rather with no testimonies..."[89] In this context, history as archived by the colonial chronicle fails to access Caribbean history. Rather, they add, only poetic knowledge and artistic expression will do. Similarly, discussing the crucial function of poetics for articulating the history of social violence in the Caribbean, Antonio Benítez-Rojo writes, "The culture of the Peoples of the Sea expresses the desire to sublimate social violence through referring itself to a space that can only be intuited through the poetic..."[90] Thinking about poetics as a form of decolonial resistance presupposes rethinking any fixed notion of resistance that reduces poetics, artistic expressions, and rituals to a narrow conception of aesthetics. Decolonial aesthetics suggested by the Caribbean intellectual traditions is driven by the political responsibility to reconfigure normative definitions of beauty: wholeness, purity, origin/tradition, and lineage.

Decolonial aesthetics hints at the epistemic revolt that overthrows the normative modality of thinking and suggests a different modality, an archipelagic imaginary. Achille Mbembe articulates the deeper meaning of slave revolt as he writes, "A slave uprising signals not only liberation but also radical transformation... of the mechanism of its redistribution so of the foundations for the reproduction of life itself."[91] Slave resistance cannot be reduced to armed revolt alone. Mbembe clarifies the significance of slave resistance found in unlikely sites, such as the community, rituals, artistic expressions, and language. It is through these exchanges that "slaves always remained human..." and, thus, "they continued to create a world."[92] Poetics seeks to locate unknowable forms of world-making in unexpected sites and exchanges. Similarly, religion also nurtures the cultural soil out of which various forms of world-making were seeded and cultivated.

In his commentary on West Indian anti-imperial historiography, Wilson Harris diagnoses West Indian historians' erasure of religion and ritual that resulted in "consolida[ting] an intellectual censorship of significant vestiges of the subconscious imagination which they needed to explore if they were to begin to apprehend a figurative meaning beyond the real or apparently real world."[93] These historians, even in their rightful denouncement of imperialist historiography, "reinforced old colonial prejudices by relegating Caribbean religious expression to irrational superstitions."[94] Referring to the specific examples of limbo and Vodou, Harris calls these rituals an "art of creative coexistence... [which] is of utmost importance and native to the Caribbean, perhaps to the Americas as a whole."[95] The diagnosis I offer in the introduction and throughout the book about the reduction of religion in the study of power relations in the (post)colonial Americas finds an important resonance in Wilson Harris, who observes that many historians have drawn a "uniform pattern of imperialism" in the Americas, overlooking the subtle and broader reach of power, thus reinstating colonial epistemic categories.[96] These modern secularist methods keep us from properly locating and identifying creative forces of imagination that inhabit unlikely sites and temporalities. With this comment, Harris implies that the boundary between the sacred and mundane, religion and the secular, the "real world" and myth, is itself questionable. The figurative meaning that lies beyond the boundaries of "the real world" might be liberative; it might point at something that the real world, that is, "the prison of history" fails to capture.[97] In this sense, Harris adds, Caribbean religions may point at the possibilities of "a language of variables in art which would have a profound revolutionary cultural and philosophical significance for Caribbean man."[98]

Confining language and poetics to the narrow function of communication draws a parallel with the way the rich matrix of religions in the Americas is reduced to a narrow concept. Religion as a critical resource and force of world-making has always existed since before—and beyond—the arrival and adoption of colonial religions. Likewise, poetics as a revolt against colonial modernity has never ceased to mobilize communities in the Americas beyond the imposed Word of Man. This is why, Walcott writes, "The revolution is here. It was always here."[99] For the metropolitan elites, revolution must be carried out with a certain aura of conscientization, a banner of self-proclamation, an ideological infusion, theorization and tactics in intellectual terms. But for the peasants, "the inevitably rooted man," Walcott claims, revolution has always been there.[100] Power continuously shifts form. It inhabits and conditions unlikely sites, unpredictable temporalities, and unnamable modalities. Reflecting on the nature of power, Mbembe explains that power exceeds a given single form because, "in its very nature, it participates in the surplus."[101] For Mbembe, the essence of power lies in its capacity to change form. He adds, "To have power is therefore to know how to give and receive forms. But it is also to know how to escape existing forms...."[102] Power, as a force of death, is capable of "entering into new relationships with destruction, loss and death"; also, power, as a force of life, is capable of transforming "the source of death into a seeding strength, or [converting] the resources of death into the capacity for healing."[103] What makes resistance revolutionary is the capacity to reject the dominant discourses that institute and reinforce normative *forms* of power, both in their oppressive capacity and resisting force. Poetics (and poetic musings on the sacred we find in Caribbean thought and literature) animates our capacity and sensibility to read the many forms of power that constantly shift its form as well as our reality.

In *Caribbean Discourse*, Glissant discusses in detail the place of poetics as a method of decolonial resistance. Poetics as a method of survival in the colonial ruins emerges as a "forced option" that is born when "a need for expression confronts an inability to achieve expression."[104] For this reason, Glissant calls it forced poetics or counterpoetics. The creole folktale as a prototype of forced poetics shows the example of a poetics that, instead of a naive glamorizing poetry, serves as a signpost of survival: "[It] leaves no room for quiet rest. No time to gaze at things ... there are no soothing shadows or moments of sweet langour. You must run without stopping, from a past order that is rejected to an absurd present. The land that has been suffered is not yet the land that is offered, made accessible."[105] A pressing sense of political urgency drives the creole folktale as a form of forced poetics. Both the community and the land(scape) are yet to emerge. Colonial cartography and imagination have radically dislodged the archipelagic landscape. The task of poetics (and politics) is to explore and realize the landscape that is yet to emerge from the abyss, the community that is yet to materialize: "This is what each hopes to see: *the earth emerging from the abyss and thickening before oneself.*"[106] There is a stern sense of materiality driving Glissant's poetics, a materiality that seeks to free the landscape from the tyranny of colonial geography, to retrieve the land and the ocean that were ravaged with violence and oblivion. Glissant writes, "I build my language out of rocks."[107]

Philosophy and poetics of creolization are a testimony to the ceremony of beginning after catastrophe. This second beginning is marked with both the overwhelming haunting trauma of history and the elemental awe of life: "For every poet it is always morning in the world. History a forgotten, insomniac night; History and elemental awe are always our early beginning, because the fate of poetry is to fall in love with the world, in spite of History."[108] Poetics refers to the act of naming the world. In calling the world into being, the poet re-creates himself/herself. Commenting on Glissant's poetics, Wynter articulates the world-making function of poetics through which one becomes human: "For to name the world is to conceptualize the world; and to conceptualize the world is an expression of active relation."[109] Poetics is the agent of resistance to the colonial order of commodification that calls people into thingness, rather than being, death rather than life—an order in which relations between beings are mediated only through commodification, subjugation, and exploitation. By referencing what Aimé Césaire calls "dysbeing," Wynter observes that ontological lack (lacking the quality of Man) signifies a symbolic death.[110] In contrast, world-making and re-creating the self is generative. Poetics as poiesis is life-giving—against the colonial denial of life, the (fore)closure of the world.

Wynter locates in Fanon's concept of sociogeny the generative function of social poetics. Our perception of the self that emerges through social relations redirects and repurposes our biological constitution. The generative potential of poetics rests in its function of identifying and activating relations that have been muted and foreclosed. By reconceptualizing the world otherwise, poetics gives life to relations that were deemed unrecognizable, unreadable, and absent. These social relations reconstitute the self in return. Refusing the ontogenic reduction of the human to bios (biological determinism), Wynter resignifies the human as both *mythos* and *bios*. Poetics of Antilleanity restores the mythos of the human against the ontogenic reduction: in resonance with "Cesaire's revalorization of the *nègre*, Fanon's genial replacement of ontogeny with sociogeny, and Glissant's projection of *l'etant* in place of *l'Etre*..."[111] Wynter's commentary implies that Glissant rearticulates being as a dynamic event, a process of becoming over the static meaning of being as being-there (*es gibt/l'etant*). Caribbean poetics displaces Man and reconstitutes the human "beyond the Word of Man."

Naming the world does not indicate an idyllic art in Caribbean poetics. Caribbean poetics as decolonial praxis explores the limits that confine one's being and place to static ontological boundaries. The work of poetics we glimpse in Glissant can be projected into the figure who is exiled on the island. This unnamed figure, faced with the limits of the land, takes to the sea in search of landscape, in search of new horizon, a new center of gravity, however groundless that may be: "The exigency for exile does not abdicate being; it must always take to the sea. The poet, in the margins of his world recreates a world: from the steps of exile, he manages a solitude more populated than any empire's land."[112] The world evoked and redesigned by

Caribbean poetics calls for the reconfiguration of ontological categories that segregate the self from the other, the landscape, and the world. Poetics as a life-giving praxis explores the self's relation to the other as well as its own situatedness in the ever-changing materiality that constitutes him/her: the body, the river, the land, the sea.

The Word of Man encloses the illimitable cartography of the archipelago; the excess of animacy and life that comprises the repeating islands becomes yet another passive landscape to be named/explored. Poetics names the obstinate persistence that is the landscape: the enduring landscape that reveals *essence*.[113] It is not that the poet as the subject of speech gives name to the lifeless nonhuman world. Rather, poetics is more akin to a testimony that attends to the patience of the landscape that encloses the self, the survival and witness of the self and of the earth/world. Caribbean poetics evokes a mode of being human that is oriented toward the world, who is given to the world; the human is evoked by the poetic enunciation of the other, whose thoughts and words are molded by the ever-changing materiality of the archipelagic landscape. The essence (in its old sense) of this land has died. And now it is reborn with people who give it a new meaning: "It is an island, and it is no longer one. Its sea is fordable; the horizon does not enclose. The land has ceased to be essence. It becomes relation. Essence was ravaged by the action of the transporters, but relation is interred in the suffering of the transported."[114]

Poetics often speaks in the language of negation. Meaning is inseparable from opacity: "No, it doesn't reveal; it unveils with gravity."[115] The other inscribed at the heart of the self indicates an ephemeral, ceaselessly fleeting alterity. Poetics is oriented toward the impossible and the unspeakable. For speech is already dictated by the Word and the grammar of Man. The colonized takes refuge not in word but opacity. Opacity, Celia Britton explains, does not simply consist of hiding. There is simply no hinterland in the Caribbean where slaves can hide, just as there is no historical hinterland to which they can withdraw. Opacity is a tactic of survival and resistance, like Creole, which has offered itself historically as a site of protection and resistance for the colonized.[116] Through time, various Africana thinkers have resorted to music, rhythm, and the oral tradition to resist the tyranny of the Word. Brathwaite is especially dedicated to the use of nonword expressions in his poetry. The Senegalese philosopher and one of the founding figures of negritude, Leopold Senghor, also refers to rhythm as the being of the being.[117] While Glissant did not develop nonwritten forms of expressions, he acknowledges their potential when he associates the written with non-movement and oral expression with movement.[118]

There is an intrinsic connection between the sacred in Glissant and the production of poetry as Loichot has recently pointed out. But Glissant's notion of poetry, Loichot reminds us, "only functions with the ecological help of the *entour*."[119] This means that Glissant does not confine the meaning of poetry to the narrow sense of the poem. If the production of poetry depends on the entour, it means that the production of poetry is also the production of place—and the creation of the self *in* place. In other words, Glissant refers to the broader meaning of poetics when he often talks about poetry. Occasionally, the sacred takes a double meaning in Glissant's works. He sometimes draws on the figure of the sacred to designate colonial modes of knowing and relating. For instance, in his critique of filiation as a Western (imperial) mode of relating, he calls it the "sacred legitimacy of filiation."[120] In discussing the hegemony of the root metaphor in contrast to the rhizomatic model, he also associates the root with the sacred.[121] However, the poet quickly reinvents the negative figure of the sacred into what amounts to the "founding books of community"[122] But unlike their "epic claims of collective consciousness, triumph, and dogmatic certainty," the renewed figure of the sacred houses "the rhizome of multiple relationship with the Other" and it is the base of "every community's reason for existence . . . which would be, all in all, a Poetics of Relation."[123] Glissant is claiming that the sacred occupies a foundational place in the poetics of Relation.

In *Philosophie de la Relation*, he elaborates extensively on the sacred by drawing on the figure of the original poem, the sacred word (*parole sacree*) that precedes the creation of the world. Glissant opens *Philosophie* with an intriguing chapter that starts with an enigmatic passage about the sacred: "Il y eut, qui s'élève, une parole sacree. Or le poeme, alors le poeme, de soi engendre, commenca d'etre reconnu" (There was a sacred word that was emerging. Or the poem, then the poem, self-generated began to be recognized).[124] The opening chapter of *Philosophie* is reminiscent of the biblical account of Creation in which Glissant reflects on the originary sacred that emerges from the primordial collapse (*effondrement*) of the world, that is, the original hollow/abyss.[125] The original poem as the sacred word grounds the counterorigin narrative Glissant writes through *Philosophie*. Unlike the primordial Word of the biblical narrative that begets essence, this word, the language of the ever-emerging chaos and entour of the earth, the bastardized language of Caliban, engenders Relation in place of essence: "Il n'approche aucune essence, précisément, il établit un autre sacre, dans la relation, non pas de ceci á cela mais de tout a tout" (It does not come to any essence, precisely, it establishes another sacred, in relation, not from this to that but from everything to everything).[126] The sacred word Glissant directs us toward is a poetics to be inhabited by all. The sacred is another name for the fragile possibility or name of the we, the community: "The sacred is of us, of this network, of our wandering, our errantry."[127] The sacred in this sense makes survival possible. A poetics of duration, Glissant adds, is "one of the first principles of the sacred."[128] Walcott resonates with Glissant when he writes, "Survival is the work of stubbornness, and spiritual stubbornness, a sublime stupidity is what makes the occupation of poetry endure, when there are so many things that should make it futile."[129]

The sacred, I submit, plays two different functions in Glissant. On the one hand, it indicates the undying resilience and creativity that animate world-making. On the other hand, the sacred works as a parameter or, better, placeholder of a renewed sense of wholeness. Poetics of creolization disavows the traditional Western categories of purity and origin by reinventing its cosmogony as an orphan narrative (Loichot). The flight from the dualistic categories of purity, completeness, and stasis finds refuge, a new center of gravity, in the sacred. The sacred serves as the groundless ground that hosts and nurtures a new sense of wholeness based on multiplicity, porosity, and becoming. This sacred diverts from the sacred that is mutually co-constitutive of metaphysics, the sacred that hosts and reinforces traditional metaphysical categories.

In many ways, decolonial poetics is a testimony to the overwhelming excess of creolized existence and of the tragedy and the beauty of the patient yet tenacious landscape and its people who have witnessed devastating history but never ceased to creolize and make worlds, each time anew. Decolonial poetics is a testimony to this excess and enigma; it is a testimony to the mystery and awe of (the force of) *life*. Alessandro Corio adopts Roberto Esposito's expression to read Glissant's work from the perspective of biopolitics. With his "openness toward an affirmative and plural biopolitics," Corio writes, Glissant offers "a politics that is no longer over life but *of* life."[130] Naming and constructing the world is not so much about the self's heroic act of determination and creation (ex nihilo) but an act of witnessing and testifying to the power of life that unfolds against the force and politics of death. As Corio comments, poetry, for Glissant, is not an "approriat[ion of] the expression of the living" but it "constantly searches for a grasp on the living, not to capture it or isolate it ... but rather to touch and expose its inherent ungraspable nature..."[131] Glissant's poetics seeks to give an expression to this uncontainable excess. His resignification of the world refuses mastery. Rather, he offers a testimony to the living—to its patience, dizziness, shock, pain, beauty, persistence: vertigo. In his article on Glissant, the French philosopher François Noudelmann writes, "Glissant insisted on opacity and the trembling of thought. He appealed not so much for disciples as for witnesses." In Noudelmann's reading, the key to uplifting the particularity of Antillean experience to universal significance without appealing to the universal is in witnessing: "As bearers of a code, we become also the bearers of this witness without knowing exactly to what he is witness. But in any case, this witness is handed on to us and we bear witness not 'for' this witness but to the existence of a witness without a message whose value is as a touchstone. He transmits an experience, and through it, perceptions, emotions, concepts, and *imaginaires*."[132]

This is how the particular becomes the bearer of the universal. The emphasis is not so much on the event to which one is witness but on the event of witnessing. In order to highlight the enigmatic aspect of witnessing, Noudelmann insists that "what passes is, in itself, meaningless: it is the movement of passing, the transition itself, that gives meaning to what passes."[133] This should not be read as an attempt to erase or reduce the singularity of the particular. As I have already discussed extensively, the particular is central to Glissant's thought. The historical experience and the specific geographic site of the Caribbean is the very womb from which his reflection is born. The particular historical experience Glissant transmits is itself absolute and singular. But what grants Glissant's reflection its universal meaning to those who might not be directly implicated in this shared experience is the singularity of his witnessing, his testimony to the living. It is this enigma that solicits becoming-Caribbean, becoming-archipelago, calling each of us to the journey of re-creating (decolonizing) being and the world. Language and metaphysics fail to give expression to the force of the living, the persistence of the present, and the future that *insists* despite catastrophe. Only poetics gives witness to it.

Glissant's writing as a poetics of place itself performs this ritual of witnessing. Witnessing is filled with opacity and ambiguity. Its language seldom points at clarity. There are important registers of the sacred in witnessing that is filled with the unknown and the unsaid. Glissant invites us to rethink religion by reflecting on the unspoken registers inscribed in these testimonies.

The Island: The Sacred

In "The Muse of History," Walcott discusses the place of religion in colonial Antilles. The imposed religion (with its anthropomorphic monodeity) and secular humanism's replacement with religion seemed to indicate surrender but it was in fact a redemption. Religion is creolized so that "what seemed the loss of tradition was its renewal."[134] While most thinkers I engage in this chapter discuss religion only sporadically, it is not their deliberate reference to religion that captures my attention. When they discuss religion, the most creative insights these thinkers offer are often domesticated by the conceptual tools that inform their understanding of religion. After all, critically theorizing and decolonizing religion was not the primary concern of most of these thinkers. My observation is that the most important and insightful reflections about religion emerge in their discussion of "secular topics." In the writings about memory, community, becoming, history, and future, I find some of the most profound and thought-provoking articulations about religion. Regardless of their differences and interests—or lack thereof—in exploring religion, many of these thinkers view religion as an indispensable (and inexhaustible) source of decolonial thinking. Contrastingly, they often diagnose the secular as a platform or project of colonial modernity. I want to pay particular attention to the alternative models of the sacred these thinkers offer. The creatively reinvented sacred in their work serves as the countermetaphysical root or ground for the poetics and politics of creolization. They hint at important insights that might help us undo the study of modern religion that is profoundly informed by coloniality.

With religion in mind, it is far from difficult to read, following Wynter's suggestion, the work of Glissant and his fellow decolonial visionaries as a rewriting of cosmogonic narratives. One can say that Glissant's poetics is in a constant search for the ceremony that it takes to re-create the human, to found the world. For Wynter, this ceremony (which is yet to emerge, yet to be found) must address the problem of religion (that is, the secular) as it must "entail the un/writing of our present normative defining of the secular mode of the Subject."[135] If, as Wynter tells us, modernity was instigated by the desire to release the human from Christian Theologos, decoloniality as a project seeks to disenchant us with the spell of the colonial secular Theologos.

The new cosmogony that Caribbean poeticism crafts is not a genesis that retreats back to the myth of lineage and origin. Rather, for Glissant, this cosmogony materializes in multiple new beginnings, singular and absolute each time. Creolization is the conceptualization (and praxis) of new beginnings. It is the weapon of the displaced and dispossessed. Dispossessed of their world, the colonized re-create, that is, creolize, the world. The tenacity of beginning again indicates the spiritual dimension of creolization. As the authors of *Éloge* write, creolization is the sacred moment of deepening the inner vision to reconstruct the collective self.[136] The slave ship in Glissant's *Poetics of Relation* projects a cosmogonic image.[137] In it, Glissant reconceives the oceanic grave as the site of genesis.

Speaking about the religion of the oppressed, Charles Long observed the primordial desire that oppressed communities have for an original, "first creation" of their image against the image that was created and imposed by the oppressors. The religion of the oppressed seeks an authentic, original creation of the self beyond the dichotomic structure set by the oppressor: "... in seeking a new beginning in the future, it must perforce imagine an originary beginning."[138] This new beginning, the new creation for the oppressed communities must be, for Long, an originary act, a first beginning/creation that goes beyond the "original" beginning. Long's articulation of an authentic (or originary) beginning finds profound resonance in Glissant and Walcott who also view the second beginning as absolute and singular.

The second creation or beginning again is as originary as the first creation and beginning. Every beginning, for Glissant, is sacred. Reflecting on the enigma of beginning in Walcott and Glissant, Drabinski observes the synchronicity of arrival and (as) beginning. He writes, "The Middle Passage carries the sacred event of beginning again. How to write this sacred is one of Glissant's great tasks as a poet..."[139] Glissant re-creates displacement and rootlessness as wholeness by reading (re)beginning as a second creation. The sacred plays a pivotal role in this process of reinvention as it serves as the placeholder of wholeness. Glissant evokes the figure of the sacred when discussing the renewed sense of wholeness as well as the problem of beginning and root(edness). He writes, "The founding books have taught us that the sacred dimension consists always of going deeper into the mystery of the root, shaded with variations of errantry. In reality, errant thinking is the postulation of an unyielding and unfading sacred."[140] Errantry is not uprootedness. It is rhizomatic in that the trajectory of its movements embodies multiplicity. It is rooted, yet it refuses the notion of the arboreal, single root.[141] Glissant's errantry suggests a model of rootedness and movement that materializes multiplicity. The sacred that Glissant's poetics signals is derivative of the renewed sense of root, ground, and being.[142]

The linkage between the sacred and the problem of groundlessness expressed in Glissantian notions such as home(lessness), root(lessness), and exile also finds resonance in the work of the Barbadian writer George Lamming. Discussing his novel *Of Age and Innocence*, Lamming links the character's national spirit to the feeling of "possessing and being possessed by the whole landscape of the place where you were born..."[143] He clarifies that this is "not a material possession but a spiritual possession of the landscape in which you live."[144] In essence, Lamming is referring to the sense of being rooted in one's home as a spiritual experience that defines nationalism in the context of decolonial struggle. The marriage between the root metaphor and the figure of the sacred is worth noting as he further describes this experience by evoking "the silent and the sacred communion between you and the roots you have made on this island. It is the bond between each man and that corner of the earth which his birth and his work have baptised with the name, home."[145] The struggle to put down one's roots and to create home is conceived as sacred in Caribbean decolonial poetics. To repeat the point I made already, the sacred plays two different functions in Glissant. On the one hand, it indicates the undying resilience and creativity that animate world-making. On the other hand, it works as a parameter of a renewed sense of wholeness. The sacred that emerges in Caribbean poetics reconfigures our understanding of religion; it is an always and already creolized (and creolizing) sacred that attends to the generative spirits and struggles of world-making against the secularist narrative of coloniality. The unritual of coloniality deprives the sacred. Decolonial poetics, as a counterritual in-the-making, suggests a figure of the sacred that takes shape in and through the archipelagic landscape and imaginaire, one that is rooted in the oceanic abyss, in the relational communion and solidarity with the other and the entour.

Abyssal Islands

In *Desert Islands*, Gilles Deleuze reflects on the figure of the island as a conceptual framework for thinking about the reconstruction of the world as an act of new beginning, an act of absolute singularity. The island represents the creative tension marking the singularity of beginning, for beginning is always a new act, of starting from scratch, alone and separate, like the island that drifts away from a continent. However, Deleuze adds, "the island is also that toward which one drifts."[146] Though separate and perhaps alone, it is the site of a new creation and new beginning. It represents the singularity of each event or act of becoming.

Islands evoke Deleuze's ontology of becoming in which being signals a new beginning: a beginning that starts from separation (from other continents), "being lost and alone." But insularity implies that the island is "also the origin, radical and absolute."[147] Every beginning signifies an absolute singularity. When thinking from the perspective of the humans encountering and populating the island, the new beginning on the island can be viewed as a rebeginning, a second origin. This second origin surpasses the meaning of original beginning. Referencing the biblical story of the Flood, he writes, "The ark sets down on the one place of the earth that remains uncovered by water, a circular and sacred place, from which the world begins anew."[148] Second origin takes place in the middle of the ocean: *a sacred island*. The island turns us to that which precedes beginning: the absolute solitude of the island surrounded by the abyssal sea; the solitude of the being who must take on the work of creating the world without gods. Beginning is abyssal.

Deleuze's imaginary of islands as second origin finds an interesting resonance in the works of Glissant and Walcott.[149] The landscape of the archipelago, particularly the figure of the island in its relation to the sea, symbolizes the abyss that overwhelms the self, revealing both the colonial difference conditioning the present—like the insular island surrounded by the sea—and the possibilities such difference signals (like the sea that connects the island to limitless shorelines).

Islands, Deleuze writes, "drift away from continent."[150] The drifting island is separated from the continent by the abyssal ocean. The repeating islands in the archipelago are separated from each other by the sea. The unfathomable depth of history and memory marking the blurred shorelines of the repeating islands is neglected by continental tourists who, Walcott writes, "love" the islands as the destination for a short vacation, "meaning that someday they plan to return for a visit but could never live there."[151] From the continental perspective, the repeating islands become a mere repetition of sameness. Out of necessity, Walcott continues, islanders sell themselves the "high-pitched representation of the same images of service that cannot distinguish one island from the other."[152] In the continental imaginary, the archipelago signifies a homogeneous tropical paradise that offers an idyllic break to nomadic explorers. But the thresholds that draw the thin contours of the islands trouble boundaries: the boundary between beginning and end, between limits and possibilities. Thresholds open room for abyssal thinking, the radical indeterminacy lurking in the space of the "in-between." The abyss nests both finitude and possibilities. Antilleanity and its geography cannot be contained by the cartographic boundaries of the imperial imaginary. Walcott writes, "There is a territory wider than this—wider than the limits made by the map of an island—which is the illimitable sea and what it remembers."[153]

In Glissant's oeuvre, the figure of the abyss merges with the historical reality of colonial experience, particularly the historical memory of the Middle Passage: "Experience of the abyss lies inside and outside the abyss. The torment of those who never escaped it; straight from the belly of the slave ship into the violent belly of the ocean depths they went ... the panic of the new land, the haunting of the former land, finally the alliance with the imposed land, suffered and redeemed. The unconscious memory of the abyss served as the alluvium for these metamorphoses."[154] The impasse of the Caribbean writer rests on the burden of coming to terms with a past marked by trauma and making sense of the equally fragmented present.

The specters of terrifying memory refuse to die. Yet future does not wait to be born at the very shoreline in which the end of the ocean marks the beginning of land. In this sense, the island marks a beginning, a rebeginning from the ruins. This is not a glamorous beginning, but "lowly, paradoxical, and unspectacular."[155] Beginning on the island does not signal the ecstatic modality of transgressive becoming envisioned by continental nomadism.

For both Glissant and Walcott, loss (singular and irreparable, therefore absolute) need not be conducive to resignation. Beginning on the island hints at the ritual of creolization. It consists of working with the elemental force, with the "shipwreck of fragments, these echoes, these shards of a huge tribal vocabulary, these partially remembered customs."[156] Such is the future for creolized people and creolized islands. Abyssal islands promise no shorelines. Both the insularity and the infinite openness solicit an exilic consciousness. Glissant glimpses the possibilities of a new being at the site of loss. As Celia Britton writes, the unbearable pain of "transportation destroys the idealist conception of being as permanent essence. However, this perdition opens up the possibility of relation instead of essence."[157] Creolization is the political reinvention of displacement as the means for reassembling the fragmented self and to affirm the life that goes on after catastrophe. Creolization is about living exile passionately: a passionate search and exploration of unmaterialized possibilities.

Glissant's vision of creolization presupposes the place of the other at the heart of the self. The notion of the coherent self yields its place to the other, for there is an ineluctable otherness, an indelible trace of alterity prior to and inherent in the texture of the self, an alterity that materializes only in the name of the community. The other on the colonial island points at the ties of relation from which the self emerges, and through whom it survives the horror of colonial violence. The freeing power of creolized ontology lurks in the shared experience and knowledge that survives history: "knowledge of the Whole, greater for having been at the abyss and freeing knowledge of Relation within the Whole."[158] This experience and knowledge is the fertile soil from which the persistence and creativity of being elsewhere and everywhere is born. Reflecting on the ocean and the sacred, M. Jacqui Alexander writes, "Being elsewhere was the only way to evade capture and to ensure the permanence of change—one of the Truths of the Ocean."[159] In Glissant's parlance, it is a mode of being "there and elsewhere, rooted and open, lost in the mountains and free beneath the sea, in harmony and in errantry."[160]

Thinking about the future from the abyssal islands suggests the abyss as a method and figurative framework for reconsidering the self and its world. The figure of the abyss recurring in the Neoplatonic and medieval mystical tradition points at indeterminacy. The abyss does not indicate a static temporality. Rather, it is associated with movement: passion, rather than resignation. The abyss refers to the work and prayer, the reordering and re-creating of the world, a (re)beginning: not from nothing or pure potentiality, but out of the shipwreck, fragments of haunting memory, shards of broken vocabulary, and the other who marks both the limit and the possibility of the self's abyssal becoming. Having lost its original name, the self, creolized, renames itself, renames gods, finding new metaphors and assembling new vocabulary, which resembles "[the] process that the poet faces every morning of his working day, making his own tools like Crusoe, assembling nouns from necessity..."[161] For both Walcott and Glissant, the re-creation of the world, the creolization of the self and the future, is sacred.

Can writing redeem the past? Does poetics reconstitute the self? What is loss to the future? Writing starts with absence and silence, in absolute solitude, as an absolute singularity. Words fail, as do names. It is not history that we are talking about but devastation, not memory but mourning: a self, dumbfounded in the stupor and absurdity of the unjust and the unspeakable. The silent wanderer walking along the shoreline of the abyssal island, who nevertheless signals not despair but beginning. Beginning again is an act of solitude and singularity. Contesting Heidegger's notion of world, Derrida writes:

The worlds in which we live in are different to the point of the monstrosity of the unrecognizable... the absolutely unshareable... the abyssal unshareable—I mean separated, like one island from another by an abyss beyond which no shore is even promised which would allow anything, however little, to happen, anything worthy of the word "happen"—the abyssal un-shareable, then, of the abyss between the islands of the archipelago and the vertiginous untranslatable, to the point that the very solitude we are saying so much about is not even the solitude of several people in the same world,... but the solitude of worlds, the undeniable fact that there is no world, not even one and the same world, no world that is one.[162]

What kind of world and what kind of self does poetics of creolization gather between the abysses that do not promise shores? Perhaps there is no world that is shareable, but a world to be created, each time anew: the solitude of creating the world without gods, the solitude of creating gods without the world. The fate of poetry, Walcott writes, is "to fall in love with the world, in spite of History."[163] Beginning on the abyssal island is a work of love, "stronger than that love which took its symmetry for granted when it was whole."[164] Like the poet who begins from scratch without reference or metaphor, creolized (and creolizing) future survives on the thin hope borne out of the shared vulnerability that constitutes the fragile name of the community.

A new creation narrative is born here on the island, on its burning beach. An orphan narrative, a bastardized lineage: the work of love that gathers the broken pieces of the lost wor(l)d, more whole than the first creation. A blurred figure of the unnamable emerges alongside the lone wanderer who walks on the burning beach. The burning beach is the name Glissant gives the volcanic beach in Le Diamant, a landscape of ever-cycling movements ceaselessly shaped by waves and volcanic sediments, the chaosmodic repetition of creation. The burning beach indicates the subterranean life of the living island, its submarine roots that inhabit both the land and the ocean. Might the sacred, often employed along the metaphor of roots in Glissant, signify the subterranean root, ground, and life of the living island and its people? A center of gravity that provides refuge and a new foundation to the place that was deprived of its ground? Before the unritual of coloniality that deprives the sacred, decolonial poetics as a ritual in-the-making suggests the notion of the sacred that takes shape in and through the archipelagic landscape and imaginaire. The murky figure of the creolized sacred that Glissant's writings evoke invites the reader to dwell right here and become elsewhere, to become the archipelago, to become the unrealized.

The open horizon of the unknown future beckons upon the repeating islands, revealing the scars holding the ill-fitting fragments together. The possibility of envisioning the future is murmured in the solitude of the self drifting on the abyssal ocean between openness and insularity; in an abyss that does not guarantee shorelines but promises new beginnings; in the generosity of Relation that does not exhaust; and in which future is another name for the sigh of optimism, of the fragile hope that remains in the aftermath of survival.

CONCLUSION

Contemporary academic study of religion is overshadowed by the long history of the academic discipline that has evolved alongside the emergence and formation of colonial modernity. Teaching the history of this academic discipline can be a challenging task for any instructor in twenty-first-century classrooms. One could say that the history of any modern academic discipline is tainted with its own dark side. The problem with the study of religion is that its history is not just tainted by overtly racist and imperialist views. Rather, the very historical foundation of the discipline is constituted by such views—hence the troubling questions of how to teach it or even whether it should be taught. In *In Search of a Dreamtime*, Tomoko Masuzawa examines the once-dominant paradigm in the study of religion, which was geared toward seeking "the origin of religion." The trouble is, as Masuzawa articulates eloquently, that, as the foregone founders of the discipline are buried alongside the old paradigm, contemporary students of religion are given the disciplinary duty of "the guardian of these tombs, obliged to stand at once venerating and condemning the dead."[1] Despite her focus on the quest for the origin, I believe Masuzawa's critical reflections on the disciplinary tendency and practices bear broader ramifications that speak to various issues implicated in the study of modern religion, especially considering that the primary objects and artifacts of academic research have usually been non-Western, tribal religions.[2] I want to reiterate Masuzawa's sense of trouble and ambivalence about contemporary scholars of religion's ambiguous relationship with the dead (the dead "founding fathers"). Her sense of uneasiness resonates with the sense of confusion and frustration often coming from students when I teach these materials, a sense of trouble that inevitably draws us to the larger question about the legitimacy and the very essence of an academic discipline whose founders' crucial contributions to the field parallel Europe's imperialist enterprises in colonial frontiers. What does this troubling history tell us about the epistemic foundation, theoretical orientation, and the analytic frameworks that constitute the discipline and the history of its scholarship? How does one reckon with the ambiguous place these foregone founders (and their theories) have in the study of modern religion? What exactly is it with our ambivalent relationship with these foregone theories as we position ourselves constantly between renunciation and veneration? More important, what does such history tells us about the field today? One of the great liberal fantasies I come across often today is liberalism's self-assurance of its own corrective capacity. A common reaction from students I have witnessed when teaching these materials is how their frustration and rage are often followed by relief. A sense of relief based on the assumption of a redeemed present. The strong sense of resentment for these past views reflects, in a way, the presumption that these mistakes belong to a foregone past and that the highly enhanced liberal sensibilities of the present make us immune to past mistakes.

Like any other academic discipline, the study of religion has made continuous advancements over time. The diversification of methods and the interdisciplinary expansion of theory for the study of religion have enriched the academic conversations enormously. Important interventions have continuously renewed and helped us recalibrate our approach to the study of religion. Our sense of what (the study of) religion is and how to study it has been constantly challenged and reconceived. Largely unchanged despite renewed efforts is, however, the fundamental epistemic framework that structures the broader scholarly inquiry, which brings us back to the problem of knowledge production. Addressing the asymmetrical structure of knowledge production cannot be reduced to the simple issue of equity and representation (which is not to say that equity or representation is a simple problem).

Contemporary scholars' complicated relationship with the founders of the field is translated into the anxiety or illusion of an "irreversible severance from the past."[3] The desire or fantasy for "such an exit," Masuzawa observes, is linked to the hope that this exit will "locate us on the clean slate of the present."[4] The illusion of a redeemed present is inseparable from the liberal fantasy of its own corrective capacity. Man is now capable of recognizing his own mistakes. He is ready and willing to acknowledge his own blind spots and show the way out of this impasse—as if the present warrants a vantage point that puts us in a categorically different relationship with the past.

Critical study of the field's classics, Masuzawa suggests, is not about "gaining a new vantage point unencumbered by past prejudices"; rather, its goal is to "venture a little further into the present epistemic mire, into our own time."[5] I reiterate, following Masuzawa, that turning to decolonial thinkers of the global south does not warrant yet another vantage point that will eventually let us articulate novel forms of knowledge without ever reproducing violence. What we get from these traditions is a different genealogy and trajectory of thinking, an epistemic and conceptual framework with a different point of origin and orientation, a form of thinking that operates on a different conceptual register than the one that the West has been reproducing. The impasse of theory today parallels the predicament of the endless loop of the West's self-referentiality in which "the narrative returns the West to itself despite its various transformation."[6] The West's self-referentiality is reproduced even in its very critique of the West and colonial modernity.

Many recent studies of secularism suggest that the formation of secularism in the modern West was mediated by colonial encounters. Europe's understanding of what religion is (and is not) was significantly shaped by its experiences and encounters in the colonial frontier. Similarly, we must think about the secular in conjunction with the colonial imaginary. The secular as a conceptual framework foundational to the Western modern imaginary requires the colonial imaginary. The Western politico-theological imagination of secular modernity is constituted by the colonial other. The unmarked secularity and coloniality of the conceptual and theoretical tools produced in the West present an inherent inadequacy for untangling the complex knot of power that binds race and religion in the historical matrix of colonial modernity.

The tradition of decolonial thinking and struggle has long denounced the secular manifested in various shapes of social norms and political institutions. Numerous thinkers of the global south view the secularity of theory as one of the many facets of theory's coloniality. The trajectory of decolonial movements and imaginations has continuously and constantly intersected with various forms and expressions of religion in the Americas. Because of their presumably secular orientation, these diverse registers of religion have rarely been considered as a source for the study of religion. I am not arguing for a need to prescriptively redefine these theories, imaginations, and movements as religion. Rather, my intention is to challenge and revisit the rather problematic conceptual and analytic framework through which we process the various registers of religion manifesting across broader spheres of the social-cultural matrix.

The persisting struggle and quest for a decolonial otherwise invite us to reconsider the place of religion in mobilizing movements and imaginations beyond the narrow categories that determine the boundaries of knowing and being. The genealogy of alternative modernities in the Americas denounces the presumable secularity of the Western liberal order as equally as theological—in that it is ridden with ideologically loaded values, sectarian worldviews, and exclusionary norms, and it is as dogmatically positioned as any theology. When we uncritically accept the problematic binary of religion and the secular, it makes us blindly embrace the normative ideal of the secular that runs on the premise of its colonial/white/heteropatriarchal/capitalist theology while losing sight of the myriad struggles and imaginations that religion has continuously inspired. The various thinkers I have engaged in this book sought creative ways to articulate different modes of imagining and building new worlds. In doing that, they attend to the deeper dimension of life and the many affects, symbolic and material capacities, or imagination to relentlessly seek an alternative way of relating with the self and each other. The imagination and the praxis of mobilizing a different way of being, a different mode of social relations, they tell us, is an active philosophical work and an active religious intervention.

Notes

Introduction

Earlier versions of the introduction and chapter 1 appeared as "A Decolonial Theory of Religion: Race, Coloniality, and Secularity in the Americas," *Journal of the American Academy of Religion* 88, no. 4 (2020): 947–80.

1. Walcott, *What the Twilight Says*, 52.
2. Walcott, *What the Twilight Says*, 52.
3. The colonial sublation turns the colonized into a Eucharistic offering, a cannibalistic transubstantiation that feeds the modern colonial West. As I will unpack further in chapters 3 and 4, I follow J. Kameron Carter's recent reading of Césaire's passages in *Discourse on Colonialism* in which Césaire employs the metaphor of the Christian Eucharist to analyze the dialectical relationship between the cannibalistic killing of colonial insurrectionists and the modern Christian bourgeoise Europe. See Césaire, *Discourse on Colonialism*, 48.
4. Césaire, *Notebook*, 19.
5. Maldonado-Torres, "Religion, Modernity, and Coloniality," 547.
6. Asad, Brown, Butler, and Mahmood, *Is Critique Secular?*, vii, xix.
7. Wynter, "Beyond the Word of Man," 641.
8. Wynter, "Beyond the Word of Man," 641.

9   Wynter, "Beyond the Word of Man," 641.

10 Mbembe, *Out of the Dark Night*, 14.

11 Mbembe, *Out of the Dark Night*, 14.

12 Chakrabarty, *Provincializing Europe*, 29.

13 If, as many contemporary social scientists have contended, secularism regulates religion in social-political domains, then similarly, "the secular" as a conceptual category, rhetoric, and imaginary effectively regulates religion in discursive domains, including conceptual and epistemic frameworks. See Mahmood, "Secularism, Hermeneutics, and Empire"; Agrama, "Secularism, Sovereignty, Indeterminacy"; Brown, "Civilizational Delusions"; and Van der Veer, *The Modern Spirit of Asia*.

14 Mignolo, *Local Histories/Global Designs*; Mastnak, *Crusading Peace*; Anidjar, *The Jew, the Arab*; Maldonado-Torres, "Race, Religion, and Ethics"; Heng, *The Invention of Race*; Keel, *Divine Variations*.

15 Mignolo, *Local Histories/Global Designs*, 27–29; Maldonado-Torres, "AAR Centennial Roundtable," 637.

16 Long, *Significations*; J. Smith, "Religion, Religions, Religious"; Chidester, *Empire of Religion*; Nongbri, *Before Religion*; Maldonado-Torres, "AAR Centennial Roundtable"; Topolski, "The Race-Religion Constellation."

17 Jennings, *The Christian Imagination*; Maldonado-Torres, "Race, Religion, and Ethics"; Maldonado-Torres, "AAR Centennial Roundtable."

18 Some of the key figures who laid down the foundation of contemporary decolonial theory are Aníbal Quijano, Enrique Dussel, Walter Mignolo, Maria Lugones, Nelson Maldonado-Torres, Catherine Walsh, Ramon Grosfoguel, and Santiago Castro Gomez. Some recent literature that addresses decoloniality and the study of religion are Rivera, *The Touch of Transcendence*; Jennings, *The Christian Imagination*; Isasi-Diaz and Mendieta, *Decolonizing Epistemologies*; Maldonado-Torres, "Race, Religion, and Ethics"; Slabodsky, *Decolonial Judaism*; Tayob, "Decolonizing the Study of Religions."; An and Craig, *Beyond Man*.

19 See Moraña, Dussel, and Jáuregui, "Colonialism and Its Replicants," 6; and An, *The Decolonial Abyss*, chap. 1.

20 Johnson, *African American Religions, 1500–2000*, chap. 3; Mendoza, "Decolonial Theories in Comparison."

21 Asad, *Genealogies of Religion*; Chidester, *Savage Systems*; King, *Religion and Orientalism*; Van der Veer, *Imperial Encounters*; Fitzgerald, *Religion and the Secular*.

22 The institutional religion's presence in the process of colonialization was all-pervading, including in military, judicial, cultural, and political spheres. More important, as Willie Jennings notes, the religion-based

encomienda system forced a radical reconfiguration of Andean peoples' relationship to land and space—a central element to their worldview. See Jennings, *The Christian Imagination*, 75–81.

23 While Wilfred Cantwell Smith has already problematized the notion of religion over half a century ago it was not until decades later that the category of religion was probed through the lens of colonialism. See W. Smith, *The Meaning and End of Religion*; Long, *Significations*; and Asad, *Genealogies of Religion*. More recently, Nelson Maldonado-Torres has produced important works that explore the connection between the category of religion, race, and colonialism. See Maldonado-Torres, "Race, Religion, and Ethics"; and Maldonado-Torres, "Religion, Modernity, and Coloniality."

24 Long, *Significations*.

25 Asad, *Genealogies of Religion*.

26 Fitzgerald, *The Ideology of Religious Studies*; Fitzgerald, *Religion and the Secular*.

27 Chidester, *Savage Systems*; Chidester, *Empire of Religion*.

28 Casanova, *Public Religions in the Modern World*; Connolly, *Why I Am Not a Secularist*; Asad, *Formations of the Secular*; Habermas, "Religion in the Public Sphere"; Taylor, *A Secular Age*; Jakobson and Pellegrini, *Secularisms*; Calhoun, Juergensmeyer, and Van Antwerpen, *Rethinking Secularism*; Calhoun, Van Antwerpen, and Warner, *Varieties of Secularism in a Secular Age*; Bilgrami, *Secularism, Identity, and Enchantment*; Josephson Storm, *The Myth of Disenchantment*; Balibar, *Secularism and Cosmopolitanism*.

29 Connolly, "Europe," 75.

30 Dressler and Mandair, *Secularism and Religion-Making*; De Roover, *Europe, India, and the Limits of Secularism*; Mahmood, *Religious Difference in a Secular Age*; Gole, *Islam and Secularity*.

31 King, *Religion and Orientalism*; Van der Veer, *Imperial Encounters*; Van der Veer, *The Modern Spirit of Asia*; Asad, *Formations of the Secular*; Masuzawa, *The Invention of World Religions*.

32 The broad significance of political theology's contribution—particularly as it was advanced by Schmitt and his interlocutors—for analyzing the complex organizing mechanism of the political is far-reaching. See De Vries and Sullivan, *Political Theologies*; Žižek, Santner, and Reinhard, *The Neighbor*; Kahn, *Political Theology*; Robbins, *Radical Democracy and Political Theology*; Crockett, *Radical Political Theology*.

33 Dressler and Mandair, *Secularism and Religion-Making*, 4–5.

34 Dressler and Mandair, *Secularism and Religion-Making*, 10–11.

35 Long, *Significations*; Chidester, *Savage Systems*; Van der Veer, *Imperial Encounters*; King, *Religion and Orientalism*; Asad, *Formations of the Secular*;

Masuzawa, *The Invention of World Religions*; Nongbri, *Before Religion*; Mahmood, *Religious Difference in a Secular Age*.

36 Anidjar, "Secularism," 56.

37 Anidjar, "Secularism," 54.

38 Mignolo, "I Am Where I Think."

39 Alexander, *Pedagogies of Crossing*, 295.

40 Farred, *What's My Name?*, 11–12; Drabinski, *Glissant and the Middle Passage*, 205–12.

41 I want to thank Beatrice Marovich for inspiring this phrase.

42 Loichot, *Water Graves*.

Chapter 1: Modernity/Coloniality/Secularity

Earlier versions of the introduction and chapter 1 appeared as "A Decolonial Theory of Religion: Race, Coloniality, and Secularity in the Americas," *Journal of the American Academy of Religion* 88, no. 4 (2020): 947–80.

1 Kahn and Lloyd, *Race and Secularism in America*, 5.

2 Kahn and Lloyd, *Race and Secularism in America*, 5.

3 Kamugisha, "The Promise of Caribbean Intellectual History," 52.

4 Kahn and Lloyd, *Race and Secularism in America*, 15.

5 Quijano, "Colonialidad y modernidad/racionalidad"; Quijano, "Colonialidad, poder, cultura y conocimiento en American Latina."

6 Quijano, "Coloniality of Power," 534–40.

7 Mignolo and Walsh, *On Decoloniality*, 144.

8 Dussel, "Europe, Modernity, and Eurocentrism."

9 Wallerstein, *The Modern World-System*, vol. 1; Wallerstein, *The Modern World-System*, vol. 2.

10 Dussel, "World-System and 'Trans'-Modernity," 224.

11 Mignolo and Walsh, *On Decoloniality*, 24. It is also important to note the Jewish aspect of Levinas's notion of exteriority that Dussel wrestled with. As Santiago Slabodsky observes, it was precisely the Jewishness of Levinas's thought that inspired Dussel's refinement of his geopolitics of knowledge. Slabodsky traces the exchange between Levinas and Dussel and argues that this encounter shaped not only Dussel's thought, as it is well known, but also Levinas's thought. For more, see Slabodsky, *Decolonial Judaism*, chap. 6.

12 Dussel, "Europe, Modernity, and Eurocentrism," 223–24; Mignolo, *Local Histories/Global Designs*, 30.

13 Wallerestein, "The Insurmountable Contradictions of Liberalism," 1163; Mignolo, *Local Histories/Global Designs*, 56–57.

14 Mignolo and Walsh, *On Decoloniality*, 141.

15 Mignolo, *Local Histories/Global Designs*, 61–62.

16 Mignolo, *Local Histories/Global Designs*, 27–29.

17 Mignolo, *The Darker Side of Western Modernity*, 8.

18 Anidjar, *The Jew, the Arab*, xvii.

19 Anidjar, *The Jew, the Arab*, xii.

20 Numerous scholars have contributed to this important line of inquiry. Just to name a few, see Mastnak, *Crusading Peace*; Anidjar, *The Jew, the Arab*; Sayyid and Vakil, *Thinking through Islamophobia*; Slabodsky, *Decolonial Judaism*; Renton and Gidley, *Antisemitism and Islamophobia in Europe*; and Abbasi, "Islam, Muslims, and the Coloniality of Being."

21 Save a few occasional appearances as a foil, that is, religion as the driving force of missionary activities and colonial oppression.

22 Maldonado-Torres, "Race, Religion, and Ethics," 691–92.

23 Wynter, "Beyond the Word of Man"; Wynter, "Unsettling the Coloniality of Being/Power/Truth/Freedom."

24 Jennings, *The Christian Imagination*, 75–76.

25 Hanke, *Aristotle and the American Indians*, 124.

26 Aristotle, *The Politics*, 1254 a8.

27 Hanke, *Aristotle and the American Indians*, 47.

28 Koskenniemi, "Empire and International Law," 13.

29 Koskenniemi, "Empire and International Law," 16. The first system of modern international law is conceived upon this juridico-theological concern that regards Europe's colonial interests. By calling the exercise of *dominium* on oversea property "natural rights of rational humanity," Vitoria makes the exchange between people a crucial sign of humanity—a sign that indicates Indians' ability for self-governance. With Vitoria, the Greek notion of hospitality is turned into a right under *Ius gentium* (law of nations), "the right of natural partnership communication" (*naturalis societas et communicationis*): "It is considered inhuman to treat travelers badly without some special cause, humane and dutiful to behave hospitably to strangers." See Pagden, *The Fall of Natural Man*; Denying Europeans' access to their land signaled a failure to abide by the universal principle of hospitality, "a violation of the law of nature," a contradiction to the key faculty that testifies to their humanity. See, Pagden, "Human Rights, Natural Rights, and Europe's Imperial Legacy."

30 Wynter, "Unsettling the Coloniality of Being/Power/Truth/Freedom," 265–85.

31 Wynter, "Unsettling the Coloniality of Being/Power/Truth/Freedom," 265.

32 Wynter, "Unsettling the Coloniality of Being/Power/Truth/Freedom," 275–82.
33 Wynter, "Unsettling the Coloniality of Being/Power/Truth/Freedom."
34 Anzaldúa, *Borderlands/La Frontera*, 102.
35 Anzaldúa, *Borderlands/La Frontera*, 25.
36 Anzaldúa, *Borderlands/La Frontera*, 51.
37 Anzaldúa, *Borderlands/La Frontera*, 50-51.
38 Anzaldúa, *Borderlands/La Frontera*, 82.
39 Ortega, *In-Between*, 35.
40 See Saldaña-Portillo, "Who's the Indian in Aztlan?"; and Ortega, *In-Between*, 33.
41 Lugones, "The Coloniality of Gender," 2.
42 Lugones, "The Coloniality of Gender," 5.
43 Lugones, "Toward a Decolonial Feminism," 743.
44 These critics argue that Lugones misses gender's central role in precolonial Indigenous societies. Paredes, *Hilando fino desde el feminismo comunitario*; Segato, "Género y colonialidad"; Mendoza, "Coloniality of Gender and Power."
45 Marcos, *Taken from the Lips*, 115.
46 Marcos, "Beyond Binary Categories," 118–21.
47 Marcos, "Mesoamerican Women's Indigenous Spirituality," 39–42.
48 Cruz, "La revolución india de Fausto Reinaga," 4–5.
49 Cruz, "Del socialismo indio al Reino de la Verdad y la Vida," 64.
50 Reinaga *América india y el occidente*, 158.
51 Reinaga, *La razón y el indio* 195, 204.
52 Morris, "Vine Deloria, Jr.," 125.
53 Morris, "Vine Deloria, Jr.," 101.
54 Deloria, *God Is Red*, 88–89.
55 Cusicanqui, *Chi'ixinakax utxiwa*, 56–60.
56 See Grosfoguel, "Epistemic Extractivism."
57 Gilroy, *The Black Atlantic*.
58 Robinson, *Black Marxism*, 26
59 Beliso-De Jesús, "Confounded Identities."
60 De Sousa Santos, *The End of the Cognitive Empire*, 6.
61 Connell, "Meeting at the Edge of Fear," 20.
62 Fanon, *The Wretched of the Earth*, 6.

63 Taking a cue from Lewis Gordon, who first coined the term *Manichean theodicy*, I have elsewhere elaborated on the notion of Manichean theodicy in Fanon. See An, "On Violence and Redemption." See also Gordon, "Fanon and Development."

64 Alexander Weheliye makes a compelling critique of Agamben's analysis of the bare life. See Weheliye, *Habeas Viscus*.

65 An, "On Violence and Redemption."

66 Wynter, "Beyond the Word of Man," 642.

67 McKittrick, *Sylvia Wynter*, 31.

68 Wynter, "Beyond the Word of Man," 639.

69 Glissant, *Poetics of Relation*, 22.

70 Walcott, *What the Twilight Says*, 70.

71 Walcott, *What the Twilight Says*, 69.

72 Walcott, *What the Twilight Says*, 75.

73 Diawara, "One World in Relation," 6.

74 Johnson, *African American Religions, 1500–2000*, 109.

75 An, *The Decolonial Abyss*, chaps. 4–5.

76 Jantzen, *Power, Gender, and Christian Mysticism*, 12; King, *Religion and Orientalism*, 8–10; Hollywood, "Introduction," 7.

77 See Wiebe, "The Failure of Nerve"; Strenski, *Religion in Relation*; Segal, "In Defense of Reductionism"; Fitzgerald, *The Ideology of Religious Studies*; and McCutcheon, *Manufacturing Religion*.

78 The diversification of method/approach in the study of religion pushed the study of religions beyond text and belief, often centered around single figures. However, such a push has never displaced the still predominant figure/text-based approach in the study of Western religions. Contrastingly, the study of non-Western religions, particularly Africana and Indigenous religions, has not always orbited around text/figure, but practice. While the pre-twentieth-century scholarship of Asian religions was dominated by the text-centered approach, the focus on text was limited to "religious canons." In this sense, even in some non-Western religions in which the study of text was heavily emphasized, the meaning of the text did not include the various vernacular (philosophical, literary, and political) writings that formed a key function in the intellectual production. This tendency is even more conspicuous in Africana and Indigenous religions in which the notion of religious text is much more ambiguous. Thus, the prevailing tendency in the field reinforces the division in which the study of the former keeps producing theories based in text, figure, and thought, while the latter is usually limited to ritual and practice.

79 Mahmood, *Religious Difference*, 21.

80 Mahmood, *Religious Difference*, 21.
81 Johnson, *African American Religions, 1500–2000*, 88.
82 Sexton. *Amalgamation Schemes*; Wilderson, *Red, White, and Black*.
83 Wilderson, *Red, White, and Black*, 58.
84 Moten, "Blackness and Nothingness," 739.
85 Moten, "Blackness and Nothingness," 774.
86 Calvin Warren rightly points out that Moten turns to Black mysticism in search of a refuge as he flees from ontology. Warren, "Black Mysticism," 222.
87 Moten, "Blackness and Nothingness," 750.
88 Moten, "Blackness and Nothingness," 751.
89 Mbembe, "Necropolitics," 16, 27.
90 Thomas, "Afro-Blue Notes"; Gordon, *Freedom, Justice, and Decolonization*, chap. 5.
91 Warren, *Ontological Terror*, 5–6.
92 Sharpe, *In the Wake*, 11.
93 Glissant, "The Indies," 91.

Chapter 2: Crisis and Revolutionary Praxis

An earlier version of chapter 2 appeared as "Secularism Meets Coloniality: Mariátegui's Andean Political Theology," *Political Theology* 18, no. 8 (2017): 677–92.

1 Miguez Bonino, *Doing Theology in a Revolutionary Situation*.
2 Gutiérrez, *Teología de la liberación*, 34–40.
3 This categorization is made by Horacio Cerruti Guldberg. See Cerruti Guldberg, *Filosofía de la liberación latinoamericana*; and Cerruti Guldberg, "Situación y perspectivas de la filosofía de la liberación latinoamericana."
4 Scannone, "La filosofía de la liberación," 61.
5 Scannone, "La filosofía de la liberación," 61 (translation mine).
6 Salazar Bondy, *Existe una filosofía de nuestra america?*, 72–73.
7 Salazar Bondy, "Historia de las ideas en el peru contemporaneo," 458–59, cited in Schutte, *Cultural Identity*, 100.
8 Salazar Bondy, *Existe una filosofía de nuestra america?*, 41.
9 As Ofelia Schutte observes, eventually, Salazar Bondy challenges the universality of Western philosophy to a certain extent. In a Hegelian-dialectic fashion, Salazar Bondy argues that Western philosophy was unable to achieve liberation due to its position as the oppressor. It was in the Third World that the possibility of liberation opened up for the first time in history. This way, Third World philosophy aims at liberating its people as well

as the oppressor. See Salazar Bondy, *América Latina: Filosofía y liberación*, 50–51, cited in Schutte, *Cultural Identity*, 103.

10   Zea, *América como conciencia*, 22–24.
11   Zea, "En torno a una filosofía latinoamericana," 65–66.
12   Dussel, *Filosofía de la liberación*, 158–60.
13   Dussel, "World-System and 'Trans'-Modernity."
14   Dussel, *The Invention of the Americas*, 11.
15   Dussel, *Philosophy of Liberation*, 1–2.
16   Dussel, *Philosophy of Liberation*, 3
17   Dussel, *Philosophy of Liberation*, 5.
18   Dussel, *Philosophy of Liberation*, 17.
19   Dussel, *Towards an Unknown Marx*, xvii.
20   Dussel, *Towards an Unknown Marx*, 7.
21   Dussel, *Towards an Unknown Marx*, 7.
22   Dussel, *Towards an Unknown Marx*, 10–11.
23   Dussel, *Beyond Philosophy*, 9.
24   Dussel, *Philosophy of Liberation*, 8.
25   Dussel, *Philosophy of Liberation*, 96.
26   Dussel, *Philosophy of Liberation*, 96.
27   Dussel, *Twenty Theses on Politics*, 30–31.
28   Dussel, *Philosophy of Liberation*, 97.
29   Dussel, *Philosophy of Liberation*, 97.
30   Dussel, *Philosophy of Liberation*, 97.
31   Dussel, *Philosophy of Liberation*, 98.
32   Schutte, *Cultural Identity*, 188.
33   Maldonado-Torres, *Against War*, 181–85.
34   Schutte, *Cultural Identity*, 179; Castro-Gómez, *Crítica de la razón latinoamericana*.
35   Dussel, *Philosophy of Liberation*, 157.
36   I have elsewhere elaborated extensively on negativity in Hegel's dialectics that refuses a simplistic, totalitarian reading. The complexity of the negative is more pronounced in his early work, *Phenomenology of Spirit*. See An, *The Decolonial Abyss*, chap. 3.
37   Dussel, *Filosofía de la liberación*, 188.
38   Indeed, Dussel's reading of Hegelian dialectics as the champion of totalitarian ontology can be viewed, to a certain extent, as a misplaced accusation.

Hegel too insists that consciousness "must acknowledge its opposite as its own actuality"(*Phenomenology of Spirit*, 284)—a point Dussel argues for with the notion of immanent transcendence. Many readers of Hegel argue, against the common accusation that dialectics is totalitarian, that dialectics is structured around the principle of recognition (of otherness). In this sense, Hegel's racist view of history betrays the very principle that structures his own philosophical system. For more, see An, "Breaking from Within."

39 Miller, *Reinventing Modernity in Latin America*, 47.
40 Mariátegui, *Siete ensayos*, 140–42.
41 Mariátegui, *José Carlos Mariátegui*, 85, 147.
42 Quijano, *Coloniality of Power*, 564–74.
43 Mariátegui, *Siete ensayos*, 136–51.
44 Mariátegui, *Siete ensayos*, 135.
45 Mariátegui, *Siete ensayos*, 151.
46 Mariátegui, *José Carlos Mariátegui*, 383.
47 Mariátegui, *José Carlos Mariátegui*, 387.
48 Rouanet, "Irrationalism and Myth," 65.
49 Sorel, *Reflections on Violence*, 27–29.
50 Rouanet, "Irrationalism and Myth," 51.
51 Rouanet, "Irrationalism and Myth," 67.
52 Tager, "Myths and Politics," 629.
53 Vernon, *Commitment and Change*, 61–71; Vincent, "Interpreting Georges Sorel," 243.
54 Schutte, *Cultural Identity*, 39.
55 Mariátegui, *José Carlos Mariátegui*, 208.
56 Mariátegui, *José Carlos Mariátegui*, 209.
57 Mariátegui, *José Carlos Mariátegui*, 210.
58 Quijano, "Prologo: Jose Carlos Mariategui: Reencuentro y debate," in Mariátegui, *Siete ensayos*, lxxvi.
59 Mariátegui, *José Carlos Mariátegui*, 383.
60 Mariátegui, *José Carlos Mariátegui*, 383.
61 Mariátegui, *Siete ensayos*, 160 (translation mine).
62 Paris, *El Marxismo latinoamericano de Mariátegui*, 14; Dessau, "Literatura y sociedad"; Messeguer, *Jose Carlos Mariátegui*, 136–41.
63 Feretti, "Del misticismo decadentista a la religiosidad revolucionaria," 86.
64 Schutte, *Cultural Identity*, 43–44.
65 Mariátegui, *José Carlos Mariátegui*, 387.

66 Mariátegui, *José Carlos Mariátegui*, 387.
67 Rivera-Pagán, *A Violent Evangelism*; Althaus-Reid, *Indecent Theology*; Bedford, "To Speak of God from More Than One Place"; Maldonado-Torres, "Liberation Theology"; Rivera, *The Touch of Transcendence*; Rieger, *Christ and Empire*; Tamayo, *La teología de la liberación*; Miguez, Rieger, and Sung, *Beyond the Spirit of Empire*; Pimentel-Chacon, *Teologías latinoamericanas de la liberación*; Drexler-Dreis, *Decolonial Love*; Panotto, "A Critique of the Coloniality of Theological Knowledge"; Maia, *Trading Futures*.
68 For example, Mayra Rivera finds in the work of Ignacio Ellacuría a theological model of God that challenges models of transcendence that have served as the metaphysical foundation of colonial ideology/theology. See Rivera, *The Touch of Transcendence*, chap. 3.
69 Gutiérrez, *Teología de la liberación*, 67.
70 Schutte, *Cultural Identity*, 47–48.
71 Gutiérrez, *Teología de la liberación*, 56.
72 Irvine, "Liberation Theology"; Valiente Nunez, "Liberation Theology and Latin America's Testimonio"; Drexler-Dreis, *Decolonial Love*.
73 Mignolo, "Decolonizing Western Epistemology," 23–25.
74 Gutiérrez, *The Power of the Poor in History*, 212.
75 Gutiérrez, *The Power of the Poor in History*, 212.
76 Segundo, "Capitalism-Socialism," 110–11.
77 Dussel, *Teología de la liberación*, 105.
78 Dussel, *Teología de la liberación*, 105.
79 Dussel, *Beyond Philosophy*, 33–34.
80 Dussel, *Ethics and Theology*, 150, 162.
81 Dussel, *Ethics and Theology*, 152, 162.
82 Dussel, *Desintegración de la cristiandad colonial y liberación*, 29.
83 Dussel, *Beyond Philosophy*, 30, 34.
84 Dussel, *Teología de la liberación*, 111.
85 For instance, it gave birth to pedagogy of liberation and psychology of liberation. See Freire, *Pedagogia do oprimido*; Girardi, *Por una pedagogia revolucionaria*; and Baro, *Psicología de la liberación para American Latina*.
86 Hinkelammert, *Las armas ideológicas de la muerte*, 9–64.
87 Hinkelammert, "La visibilidad de lo invisible," 50.
88 Hinkelammert, "La visibilidad de lo invisible," 56.
89 Hinkelammert, "La crítica de la religión neoliberal," 154.
90 Hinkelammert, "La crítica de la religión neoliberal," 154 (translation mine).

91 Nichols, *Theft Is Property!*, 65.
92 Gebara, *Longing for Running Water*; Tamez, *Las mujeres en el movimiento de Jesús, el Cristo*; Bingemer, *O segredo do mistério*.
93 Da Silva, *Existe um pensar teologico negro?*; Lopez Hernandez, *Teología India*; Wagua, *Principios de la teofanía guna*.
94 Marcella Althaus-Reid does not use the term *coloniality* as the term was still in its early nascent period of development when she was writing her first books, but the way she articulates power in post/decolonial terms gets to the heart of the term *coloniality*.
95 Althaus-Reid, *Indecent Theology*, 12, 15.
96 Althaus-Reid, *Indecent Theology*, 20.
97 Althaus-Reid, *Indecent Theology*, 166.
98 Althaus-Reid, *Indecent Theology*, 166.
99 Althaus-Reid, *Indecent Theology*, 4.
100 Althaus-Reid, *Indecent Theology*, 4.
101 Althaus-Reid, *Indecent Theology*, 25.
102 Althaus-Reid, *Indecent Theology*, 25.
103 Althaus-Reid, *Indecent Theology*, 31.
104 Althaus-Reid, "Gustavo Gutierrez Goes to Disneyland."

Chapter 3: Phenomenology of the Political

1 Casanova, *Public Religions in the Modern World*; Taylor, *A Secular Age*; Habermas, "Secularism's Crisis of Faith."
2 Schmitt, *Political Theology*, 36.
3 Benítez-Rojo, *The Repeating Island*, 5.
4 Mbembe, *Necropolitics*, 27.
5 Kahn, "Political Theology and Liberalism."
6 Settler, "Religion in the Work of Frantz Fanon," 5.
7 Settler, "Religion in the Work of Frantz Fanon," 24.
8 Fanon, *The Wretched of the Earth*, 18–20.
9 Fanon, *The Wretched of the Earth*, 19.
10 Slisli, "Islam," 99.
11 Slisli, "Islam," 97.
12 Slisli, "Islam," 104.
13 Fanon, *A Dying Colonialism*, 143.

14. Fanon, "Social Therapy in a Ward of Muslim Men," in Fanon, *Alienation and Freedom*.
15. Fanon, "Social Therapy in a Ward of Muslim Men," 365.
16. Fanon, "Daily Life in the Douars," in Fanon, *Alienation and Freedom*, 384.
17. Fanon, "Daily Life in the Douars," 379–81.
18. Fanon, "Daily Life in the Douars," 381–83.
19. Lackey, "Frantz Fanon on the Theology of Colonization," 3.
20. Césaire, *Discourse on Colonialism*, 48.
21. Carter, "The Excremental Sacred." See also Lloyd, "Introduction," 1.
22. Fanon, *The Wretched of the Earth*, 6.
23. Fanon, *The Wretched of the Earth*, 3.
24. Fanon, *The Wretched of the Earth*, 5.
25. Fanon, *The Wretched of the Earth*, 18.
26. Fanon, *The Wretched of the Earth*, 7.
27. Kahn, *Sacred Violence*, 115.
28. Kahn, *Political Theology*, 23.
29. Kahn, *Political Theology*, 31.
30. Schulman, "Pluralizing Political Theology."
31. Carter, "The Politics of Atonement."
32. Mbembe, "Necropolitics," 11.
33. Mbembe, "Necropolitics," 24.
34. Mbembe notes that "war has become the Sacrament of our time." See Mbembe, "Necropolitics," 2. Nelson Maldonado-Torres also uses the term *war paradigm* to describe colonial ontology. See Maldonado-Torres, *Against War*.
35. Agamben, *Homo Sacer*, 6.
36. Alexander Weheliye argues that barelife and biopolitics fall short of the analysis of racialization. See Weheliye, *Habeas Viscus*, introduction.
37. Fanon, *The Wretched of the Earth*, 4. For "war paradigm," see Maldonado-Torres, *Against War*.
38. Mbembe, "Necropolitics," 139.
39. McKittrick, *Sylvia Wynter*, 31.
40. Wynter, "Beyond the Word of Man," 639.
41. Wynter, "On Disenchanting Discourse," 237.
42. Wynter, "Beyond the Word of Man," 641.

43 Rubenstein, *Strange Wonder*.
44 Asad, *Formations of the Secular*; Van der Veer, *The Modern Spirit of Asia*.
45 Mbembe, *On the Postcolony*, 111.

Chapter 4: Phenomenology of Race

1   Ahmed, *Queer Phenomenology*, 27.
2   Lewis Gordon's work is a great example that shows this dimension of Fanon's work. See Gordon, *Existentia Africana*; and Gordon, "Through the Zone of Nonbeing."
3   Wynter, "Beyond the Word of Man," 639.
4   Fanon, *Black Skin, White Masks*, 109.
5   Fanon, *Black Skin, White Masks*, 116.
6   Donald Landes, "Translator's Introduction," in Merleau-Ponty, *Phenomenology of Perception*, xl.
7   Merleau-Ponty, *Phenomenology of Perception*, lxxx.
8   Merleau-Ponty, *Phenomenology of Perception*, 5.
9   Merleau-Ponty, *Phenomenology of Perception*, 141. As the translator Donald Landes notes, the original phrase in French, "je sui a l'espace et au temps," implies the rich and complex character of the French preposition, as the phrase could translate as both "I am toward space and time" or "I am at space and time." See Merleau-Ponty, *Phenomenology of Perception*, 525.
10 Merleau-Ponty, *Phenomenology of Perception*, lxxiv.
11 Fanon, *Black Skin, White Masks*, 109.
12 Guenther, "Critical Phenomenology," 12. The quotation is from Merleau-Ponty, *The Visible and the Invisible*, 100.
13 Merleau-Ponty, *The Visible and the Invisible*, 72.
14 Fanon, *Black Skin, White Masks*, 110.
15 Ahmed, *Queer Phenomenology*, 138.
16 Ahmed, *Queer Phenomenology*, 139.
17 Fanon, *Black Skin, White Masks*, 109.
18 Fanon, *Black Skin, White Masks*, 113.
19 Merleau-Ponty, *Phenomenology of Perception*, 101.
20 Merleau-Ponty, *Phenomenology of Perception*, 102.
21 Fanon, *Black Skin, White Masks*, 110.
22 Fanon, *Black Skin, White Masks*, 112.
23 Wynter, "Beyond the Word of Man," 640.

24 Merleau-Ponty, *The Visible and the Invisible*, 30.

25 Merleau-Ponty, *The Visible and the Invisible*, 179.

26 Merleau-Ponty, *The Visible and the Invisible*, 3.

27 Merleau-Ponty, *The Visible and the Invisible*, 103.

28 Orion, *Things Seen and Unseen*, 21.

29 Merleau-Ponty's philosophical vision's close connection with Christian theology has been explored by many already. See Ward, *Christ and Culture*; Kearney, *Anatheism*; Nordlander, "Figuring Flesh in Creation"; and Orion, *Things Seen and Unseen*.

30 Eugene Fink, "Die Phenomenologische Philosophie Edmund Husserls in der gegenwartigen Kritik," 350, cited in Merleau-Ponty, *Phenomenology of Perception*, 309.

31 Merleau-Ponty, *Phenomenology of Perception*, lxxvii.

32 Merleau-Ponty, *The Visible and the Invisible*, 151.

33 "Shock reveals the inessentiality of things; awe reveals the thingliness of inessentiality. Shock brings us out of 'subject-object' relations; awe brings us into being-toward. Shock demolishes autonomy; awe frees us for freedom. Shock unworks; awe makes sense. Shock punctuates; awe enchains. In shock, thinking loses everything, and in awe, everything returns, at once more or less than thinking had thought it to be" (Rubenstein, *Strange Wonder*, 128).

34 Merleau-Ponty, *Phenomenology of Perception*, lxxxv.

35 Rivera, *Poetics of the Flesh*, 62.

36 Fanon, *Black Skin, White Masks*, 112.

37 Fanon, *Black Skin, White Masks*, 116.

38 Fanon, *Black Skin, White Masks*, 140.

39 Brinkema, *Forms of the Affects*, 16–17.

40 Brinkema, *Forms of the Affects*, 17.

41 Moten, "The Case of Blackness," 181.

42 Moten, "The Case of Blackness," 181–82.

43 Barad, "What Flashes Up," 60.

44 Barad, "What Flashes Up," 53, 56.

45 Hong, *Death beyond Disavowal*, 16. She adds: "Insofar as our ability to live protected lives depends upon their inability do to so, a politics that registers vulnerability to death simply as something to be eradicated and sees these deathly subjects simply as those we have yet to bring into protection of life merely advances the validation of life that legislates their deaths. In so doing, we replicate the conditions that create these deathworlds by making life the only site of meaning or political possibility" (16).

46 Hong, *Death beyond Disavowal*, 16.
47 Fanon, *Black Skin, White Masks*, 232.
48 Singh, *Unthinking Mastery*.
49 Rivera, *Poetics of the Flesh*, 119.
50 Butler, *Senses of the Subject*, 193.
51 Winters, "The Sacred Gone Astray," 247–49.
52 Alexander, *Pedagogies of Crossing*, 295–97.
53 Winters, "The Sacred Gone Astray."
54 Henry, "Africana Phenomenology," 12.
55 Wynter, "Columbus and the Poetics of Propter Nos," 261.
56 Wynter, "Beyond the Word of Man," 639.
57 Wynter, "The Ceremony Must Be Found."
58 Wynter, "Beyond the Word of Man," 641.
59 Negritude was initially criticized for its essentializing view of Blackness and Africanness. Its reception was met with the suspicion that negritude is unradical and unrevolutionary. We must distinguish, however, Césaire's negritude from Leopold Senghor's. Many key Caribbean intellectuals, including Fanon, acknowledge their intellectual debt to Césaire. See Garraway, "What Is Mine"; and Hiddleston, "Aimé Cesairé and Postcolonial Humanism."
60 Wynter, "Beyond the Word of Man," 641.
61 Glissant, "Aimé Cesairé," 120.
62 Césaire, *Discourse on Colonialism*, 42.
63 Carter, "The Excremental Sacred," 156.
64 Carter, "The Excremental Sacred," 165.
65 Carter, "The Excremental Sacred," 172.
66 Césaire, *Discourse on Colonialism*, 48.
67 Carter, "The Excremental Sacred," 159.
68 Césaire, *Notebook*, 19.
69 Césaire, *Notebook*, 20–21.
70 Césaire, *Notebook*, 22.
71 Drabinski, "Cesaire's Apocalyptic Word," 568.
72 Makalani, "The Politically Unimaginable," 33.
73 Drabinski, "Cesaire's Apocalyptic Word," 579.
74 Wynter, "The Ceremony Must Be Found."
75 Here I am thinking about radical orthodoxy.
76 Robin D.G. Kelly, "Preface," in Césaire, *Discourse on Colonialism*, 28.

77 Frazer and Hutchins, "On Politics and Violence," 103.

78 Hage, "Comes a Time We Are All Enthusiasm," 72.

79 I discuss violence in Fanon and develop an analysis of violence through the lens of theodicy in "On Violence and Redemption." There I also distinguish between the dominant conception of violence and Fanon's notion of decolonial violence.

80 Fanon, *The Wretched of the Earth*, 3.

81 Kawash, "Terrorists and Vampires," 237.

82 Butler, *Senses of the Subject*, 185.

83 Butler, *Senses of the Subject*, 185.

84 Butler, *Senses of the Subject*, 189.

85 Bergner, "Who Is That Masked Woman?"; McClintock, *Imperial Leather*; Fuss, *Identification Papers*; Chow, "The Politics of Admittance"; Sharpley-Whiting, *Frantz Fanon*; Dubey, "The 'True Lie' of the Nation"; Seshadri-Crooks, "I Am a Master"; Marriott, *Whither Fanon?*

86 Butler, *Senses of the Subject*, 189.

87 Marriott, *Wither Fanon?*, 371.

88 Singh, *Unthinking Mastery*, 70–71.

89 Butler, *Senses of the Subject*, 193.

90 Maldonado-Torres, *Against War*, 137.

91 Fanon, *Black Skin, White Masks*, 114–15.

92 Lewis Gordon, *What Fanon Said*, 75–78.

93 Fanon, *Black Skin, White Masks*, 231.

94 Singh, *Unthinking Mastery*, 18.

Chapter 5: Poetics of World-Making

1 To apply a loose typology, the poeticist tradition (represented by Wilson Harris, Édouard Glissant, Sylvia Wynter, Derek Walcott, Kamau Brathwaite, and Maryse Condeé, to name a few) maintains an overall Pan-African orientation—like the radical revolutionary tradition—while emphasizing the particularity of Caribbeanness. The loose taxonomy I employ here is not meant to reify said categories, as the lines that draw the boundaries between traditions are often less than clear. Many of these writers often cross and overlap multiple boundaries. While acknowledging its risks and limits, here I employ a loose typology in order to situate this chapter's central figures within the twentieth-century Caribbean intellectual genealogy.

2 Kamugisha, "The Promise of Caribbean Intellectual History," 53.

3 Glissant, *Caribbean Discourse*, 62.

4   Glissant, *Caribbean Discourse*, 63.
5   Glissant, *Poetics of Relation*, 6.
6   Radovich, "The Birthplace of Relation," 476.
7   Glissant, *Poetics of Relation*, 9.
8   Drabinski, "Shorelines," 6.
9   Wiedorn, *Think Like an Archipelago*, xiv.
10 Glissant, *Poetics of Relation*, 10–11.
11 DeLoughrey, *Routes and Roots*, 2.
12 Lefebvre, *The Production of Space*, 81.
13 Sack, *Conceptions of Space in Social Thought*; Casey, *The Fate of Place*; Malpas, *Place and Experience*.
14 Santos, *The Nature of Space*, 31.
15 Santos, *The Nature of Space*, 235.
16 Santos, *The Nature of Space*, 206, 229, 235.
17 Lefebvre, *The Production of Space*, 34.
18 Eliade, *The Sacred and the Profane*, 21.
19 Eliade, *The Sacred and the Profane*, 64.
20 Eliade, *The Sacred and the Profane*, 22.
21 Eliade, *The Sacred and the Profane*, 51.
22 J. Smith, *Map Is Not Territory*, 178.
23 J. Smith, *Map Is Not Territory*.
24 Masuzawa, *In Search of Dreamtime*.
25 J. Smith, *Map Is Not Territory*, 178.
26 Glissant, *Introduction a une poetique du divers*, 44 (translation mine).
27 Dash, "The Stranger by the Shore," 356.
28 Glissant, *Caribbean Discourse*, 139.
29 Parham, "Breadfruit, Time and Again," 132.
30 Dash, "The Stranger by the Shore," 368.
31 Benítez-Rojo, *The Repeating Island*, 5.
32 Lamming, "The Imperial Encirclement," 85.
33 The term *capitalocene* was first adopted by Jason Moore to situate contemporary conversations about the anthropocene in the modern framework of capitalism. See Moore, "The Capitalocene, Part I." *Plantationocene* was first coined in a conversation among several scholars of critical theory, which was published as Haraway et al., "Anthropologists Are Talking—about the Anthropocene."

34   Haraway, "Anthropocene, Capitalocene, Plantationocene, Chthulucene," 159–65.
35   Ray and Sheikh, "Introduction," 165.
36   DeLoughrey, *Allegories of the Anthropocene*, 35–36.
37   An important tension within this nascent discourse is well delineated by Janae Davis and others, who argue that the multispecies framework of anthropocene obscures the centrality of the problem of race. See Davis et al., "Anthropocene, Capitalocene, . . . Plantationocene?"
38   Ray and Sheikh, "Introduction," 165; Schiebinger, *Plants and Empire*, 5, 11.
39   Ray and Sheikh, "Introduction," 165.
40   Grove, *Savage Ecology*, 110.
41   Grove, *Savage Ecology*, 195.
42   Rosaldo, "Imperialist Nostalgia," 107–8.
43   Rosaldo, "Imperialist Nostalgia," 108.
44   Grove, *Savage Ecology*, 196.
45   I have elsewhere written on Rosi Braidotti's misappropriation of Glissant. See An, "Beginning in the Middle."
46   Glissant, *Poetics of Relation*, 75.
47   "Proclaiming creoleness . . . do[es] not stem from theory or learned principles. They are akin to testimony" (Bernabé, Chamoiseau, and Confiant, *Éloge de la créolité*, 75).
48   Dash, "The Stranger by the Shore," 359.
49   Édouard Glissant, *L'intention poetique*, 47, cited in Oakley, "In Citations to the Chance," 34.
50   Walcott, *What the Twilight Says*, 70.
51   Walcott, "The Caribbean," 13.
52   Kamugisha, "The Promise of Caribbean Intellectual History," 56.
53   Loichot, *Water Graves*, 7.
54   Loichot, *Water Graves*, 28.
55   Casey, *The Fate of Place*, 5.
56   This powerful insight is eclipsed by his use of Eliade's famous quote, "settling in a territory is equivalent to founding a world." As Joseph Winters examines, Eliade's proposition comes with the package of colonial expansion and conquest in which taking of a new land is translated into the colonial logic of transforming profane land into a sacred world (Casey, *The Fate of Place*, 5). See also Winters, "The Sacred Gone Astray."
57   Fanon, *A Dying Colonialism*, 232.
58   Bernabé, Chamoiseau, Confiant, *Éloge de la créolité*, 80.

59 Bernabé, Chamoiseau, Confiant, *Éloge de la créolité*, 83–84.
60 Bernabé, Chamoiseau, Confiant, *Éloge de la créolité*, 87.
61 Chancé, "Creolization," 263.
62 Bernabé et al., *Éloge de la créolité*, 100.
63 Gilles Anquetil, quoted in Chance, "Creolization," 264.
64 Walcott, *What the Twilight Says*, 37.
65 Walcott, *What the Twilight Says*, 38–39.
66 Walcott, *What the Twilight Says*, 37.
67 Walcott, *What the Twilight Says*, 39.
68 Walcott, *What the Twilight Says*, 42.
69 Walcott, *What the Twilight Says*, 69.
70 An, *The Decolonial Abyss*, 8–9.
71 Glissant, *Poetic Intention*, 11.
72 Roberts and Stephens, "Archipelagic American Studies," 20.
73 Walcott, "Isla Incognita," 52.
74 Glissant, *Poetics of Relation*, 13.
75 DeLoughrey, *Routes and Roots*, 13.
76 Glissant, *Poetic Intention*, 106.
77 Deleuze and Guattari, *A Thousand Plateaus*, 21.
78 Glissant, *Caribbean Discourse*, 67.
79 Glissant, *Poetic Intention*, 182.
80 Glissant, *Caribbean Discourse*, 26.
81 Drabinski, *Glissant and the Middle Passage*, 62.
82 Glissant, *Poetics of Relation*, 8.
83 Glissant, *Poetics of Relation*, 8.
84 Monahan, *The Creolizing Subject*, 202.
85 Glissant, *Poetics of Relation*, 34.
86 Glissant, *Poetic Intention*, 19.
87 Glissant, *Poetic Intention*, 219.
88 "We know ourselves as part and as crowd, in an unknown that does not terrify" (Glissant, *Poetics of Relation*, 9).
89 Bernabé, Chamoiseau, Confiant, *Éloge de la créolité*, 99.
90 Benítez-Rojo, *The Repeating Island*, 17.
91 Mbembe, *Critique of Black Reason*, 37.
92 Mbembe, *Critique of Black Reason*, 48.

93   Harris, "History, Fable and Myth in the Caribbean and Guianas," 156.
94   Harris, "History, Fable and Myth in the Caribbean and Guianas," 156.
95   Harris, "History, Fable and Myth in the Caribbean and Guianas," 158.
96   Harris, "History, Fable and Myth in the Caribbean and Guianas," 158.
97   Harris, "History, Fable and Myth in the Caribbean and Guianas," 156.
98   Harris, "History, Fable and Myth in the Caribbean and Guianas," 164.
99   Walcott, *What the Twilight Says*, 57.
100 Walcott, *What the Twilight Says*, 57.
101 Mbembe, *Critique of Black Reason*, 131.
102 Mbembe, *Critique of Black Reason*, 132.
103 Mbembe, *Critique of Black Reason*, 132.
104 Glissant, *Caribbean Discourse*, 120.
105 Glissant, *Caribbean Discourse*, 131.
106 Glissant, *Poetic Intention*, 11.
107 Glissant, *Poetic Intention*, 43.
108 Walcott, *What the Twilight Says*, 79.
109 Wynter, "Ethno or Sociopoetics," 87.
110 Wynter, "Beyond the Word of Man," 641–42.
111 Wynter, "Beyond the Word of Man," 645.
112 Glissant, *Poetic Intention*, 108.
113 Glissant, *Poetic Intention*, 64.
114 Glissant, *Poetic Intention*, 182.
115 Glissant, *Poetic Intention*, 42.
116 Britton, *Édouard Glissant and Postcolonial Theory*, 25.
117 McKittrick, O'Shaughnessy, and Wiltaszek, "Rhythm or on Wynter's Science of the Word," 870.
118 Glissant, *Caribbean Discourse*, 122.
119 Loichot, *Water Graves*, 28.
120 Glissant, *Poetics of Relation*, 52.
121 Glissant, *Poetics of Relation*, 147.
122 Glissant, *Poetics of Relation*, 33.
123 Glissant, *Poetics of Relation*, 15–16.
124 Glissant, *Philosophie de la relation*, 11 (translation mine). Valérie Loichot offers an informative and insightful reading of this passage. See Loichot, *Water Graves*, 55.
125 Glissant, *Philosophie de la relation*, 15.

126 Glissant, *Philosophie de la relation*, 148 (translation mine).
127 Glissant, *Poetics of Relation*, 56.
128 Glissant, *Poetics of Relation*, 33.
129 Walcott, *What the Twilight Says*, 75.
130 Corio, "The Living and the Poetic Intention," 919; Esposito, *Bios*, 11.
131 Corio, "The Living and the Poetic Intention," 922, 928.
132 Noudelmann, "Édouard Glissant's Legacy," 873.
133 Noudelmann, "Édouard Glissant's Legacy," 874.
134 Walcott, *What the Twilight Says*, 43.
135 Wynter, "The Ceremony Must Be Found," 22.
136 Bernabé, Chamoiseau, Confiant, *Éloge de la créolité*, 85–86.
137 Radovich, "The Birthplace of Relation," 477.
138 Long, *Significations*, 184.
139 Drabinski, *Glissant and the Middle Passage*, 48.
140 Glissant, *Poetics of Relation*, 21.
141 Deleuze and Guattari, *A Thousand Plateaus*, 39.
142 "If there is a sacred in Glissant, it is one anchored in the lives of human communities, often suffering, dispossessed" (Cailler, "Reves sur les funerailles religieuses d'Edouard Glissant," 246).
143 Lamming, "Nationalism and Nation," 112.
144 Lamming, "Nationalism and Nation," 112.
145 Lamming, "Nationalism and Nation," 112.
146 Deleuze, *Desert Islands*, 10.
147 Deleuze, *Desert Islands*, 10.
148 Deleuze, *Desert Islands*, 13.
149 The connection between Deleuze and Glissant has been explored by many theorists. See Britton *Édouard Glissant and Postcolonial Theory*; Nesbitt, "Deleuze, Glissant, and the Production of Postcolonial Concepts"; Hallward, *Absolutely Postcolonial*; Braidotti, *Transpositions*; Noudelmann, "Édouard Glissant's Legacy"; Hantel, "Rhizome and the Space of Translation"; An, "Beginning in the Middle"; Wiedorn, *Think Like an Archipelago*; Drabinski, *Glissant and the Middle Passage*.
150 Deleuze, *Desert Islands*, 10.
151 Walcott, *What the Twilight Says*, 77.
152 Walcott, *What the Twilight Says*, 81.
153 Walcott, *What the Twilight Says*, 82.
154 Glissant, *Poetics of Relation*, 7.

155 Michael Dash, "Preface," in Glissant, *Caribbean Discourse*, xii.
156 Walcott, *What the Twilight Says*, 70.
157 Britton, *Édouard Glissant and Postcolonial Theory*, 15.
158 Glissant, *Poetics of Relation*, 7.
159 Alexander, *Pedagogies of Crossing*, 289.
160 Glissant, *Poetics of Relation*, 34.
161 Walcott, *What the Twilight Says*, 70.
162 Derrida, *The Beast and the Sovereign*, 108.
163 Walcott, *What the Twilight Says*, 79.
164 Walcott, *What the Twilight Says*, 69.

Conclusion

1 Masuzawa, *In Search of Dreamtime*, 1.
2 Various issues are entangled in the quest for the origin of religion, one of them being the issue of comparative religion or the treatment of non-Western religions. While her primary focus in *In Search of Dreamtime* is on "the quest for the origin," the problem of the study of non-Western religions (and the unmarked universality of Western/Christian framework) becomes a more central part of her research later in *The Invention of World Religions*.
3 Masuzawa, *In Search of Dreamtime*, 31.
4 Masuzawa, *In Search of Dreamtime*, 32.
5 Masuzawa, *In Search of Dreamtime*, 33.
6 Mandair, *Religion and the Specter of the West*, 4.

Bibliography

Abbasi, Iskander. "Islam, Muslims, and the Coloniality of Being: Reframing the Debate on Race and Religion in Modernity." *Journal for the Study of Religion* 33, no. 2 (2020): 1–31.

Agamben, Giorgio. *Homo Sacer: Sovereign Power and Bare Life*. Redwood City, CA: Stanford University Press, 1998.

Agrama, Hussein Ali. "Secularism, Sovereignty, Indeterminacy: Is Egypt a Secular or a Religious State?" *Comparative Studies in Society and History* 52, no. 3 (2010): 495–523.

Ahmed, Sara. *Queer Phenomenology: Orientations, Objects, Others*. Durham, NC: Duke University Press, 2006.

Alexander, M. Jacqui. *Pedagogies of Crossing: Meditations on Feminism, Sexual Politics, Memory, and the Sacred*. Durham, NC: Duke University Press, 2006.

Althaus-Reid, Marcella. "Gustavo Gutierrez Goes to Disneyland: Theme Park Theologies and the Diaspora of the Discourse of the Popular Theologian in Liberation Theology." In *Interpreting Beyond Borders*, edited by Fernando Segovia, 36–58. Sheffield: Sheffield Academic Press, 2000.

Althaus-Reid, Marcella. *Indecent Theology: Theological Perversions in Sex, Gender, and Politics*. London: Routledge, 2000.

Althaus-Reid, Marcella. *The Queer God*. London: Routledge, 2003.

An, Yountae. "Beginning in the Middle: Deleuze, Glissant, and Colonial Difference." *Culture, Theory and Critique* 55, no. 3 (2014): 286–301.

An, Yountae. "Breaking from Within: The Dialectic of Labor and the Death of God." In *Common Goods: Economy, Ecology, and Political Theology*, edited by

Catherine Keller, Elias Ortega-Aponte, and Melanie Johnson-DeBeaufre, 248–66. New York: Fordham University Press, 2015.

An, Yountae. *The Decolonial Abyss: Mysticism and Cosmopolitics from the Ruins.* New York: Fordham University Press, 2016.

An, Yountae. "On Violence and Redemption: Fanon and Colonial Theodicy." In *Beyond Man: Race, Coloniality, and Philosophy of Religion*, edited by An Yountae and Eleanor Craig, 204–25. Durham, NC: Duke University Press, 2021.

Anidjar, Gil. *The Jew, the Arab: A History of the Enemy.* Redwood City, CA: Stanford University Press, 2002.

Anidjar, Gil. "Secularism." *Critical Inquiry* 33, no. 1 (2006): 52–77.

Anzaldúa, Gloria. *Borderlands/La Frontera: The New Mestiza.* San Francisco: Aunt Lute Books, 1987.

Aristotle. *The Politics.* Manchester, UK: Penguin, 1981.

Asad, Talal. *Formations of the Secular.* Redwood City, CA: Stanford University Press, 2003.

Asad, Talal. *Genealogies of Religion: Discipline and Reasons of Power in Christianity and Islam.* Baltimore: Johns Hopkins University Press, 1993.

Asad, Talal, Wendy Brown, Judith Butler, and Saba Mahmood. *Is Critique Secular? Blasphemy, Injury, and Free Speech.* New York: Fordham University Press, 2013.

Balibar, Étienne. *Secularism and Cosmopolitanism: Critical Hypotheses on Religion and Politics.* New York: Columbia University Press, 2018.

Barad, Karen. "What Flashes Up: Theological-Political-Scientific Fragments." In *Entangled Worlds: Religion, Science, and New Materialisms*, edited by Catherine Keller and Mary-Jane Rubenstein, 21–88. New York: Fordham University Press, 2017.

Baro, Ignacio Martin. *Psicología de la liberación para American Latina.* Guadalajara: ITESO, 1990.

Bedford, Nancy. "To Speak of God from More Than One Place: Theological Reflections from the Experience of Migration." In *Latin American Liberation Theology: The Next Generation*, edited by Ivan Petrella, 132–67. Maryknoll, NY: Orbis Books, 2005.

Beliso-De Jesús, Aisha. "Confounded Identities: A Meditation on Race, Feminism, and Religious Studies in Times of White Supremacy." *Journal of the American Academy of Religion* 86, no. 2 (2018): 307–40.

Benítez-Rojo, Antonio. *The Repeating Island.* Durham, NC: Duke University Press, 1996.

Bergner, Gwen. "Who Is That Masked Woman? Or, The Role of Gender in Fanon's *Black Skin, White Masks*." *PMLA* 110, no. 1 (1995): 75–88.

Bernabé, Jean, Patrick Chamoiseau, and Raphaël Confiant. *Éloge de la créolité / In Praise of Creoleness.* Paris: Gallimard, 1993.

Bilgrami, Akeel. *Secularism, Identity, and Enchantment.* Cambridge, MA: Harvard University Press, 2014.

Bingemer, Maria Clara. *O segredo do mistério: Ensaios de teología na ótica da mulher.* Petropolis: Vozes, 1991.

Braidotti, Rosi. *Transpositions: On Nomadic Ethics*. New York: Polity, 2006.
Brathwaite, Edward Kamau. *Rights of Passage*. Oxford: Oxford University Press, 1968.
Brinkema, Eugenie. *Forms of the Affects*. Durham, NC: Duke University Press, 2014.
Britton, Celia. *Édouard Glissant and Postcolonial Theory: Strategies of Language and Resistance*. Charlottesville: University Press of Virginia, 1999.
Brown, Wendy. "Civilizational Delusions: Secularism, Tolerance, Equality." *Theory and Event* 15, no. 2 (2012), https://muse-jhu-edu.libproxy.csun.edu/pub/1/article/478356. 10/8/2020.
Butler, Judith. *Senses of the Subject*. New York: Fordham University Press, 2015.
Cailler, Bernadette. "Reves sur les funerailles religieuses d'Edouard Glissant." *Revue des sciences humaines*, no. 309 (2013): 239–50.
Calhoun, Craig, Mark Juergensmeyer, and Jonathan Van Antwerpen, eds. *Rethinking Secularism*. Oxford: Oxford University Press, 2011.
Calhoun, Craig, Jonathan Van Antwerpen, and Michael Warner, eds. *Varieties of Secularism in a Secular Age*. Cambridge, MA: Harvard University Press, 2013.
Carter, J. Kameron. "The Excremental Sacred: A Paraliturgy." In *Beyond Man: Race, Coloniality, and Philosophy of Religion*, edited by An Yountae and Eleanor Craig, 151–203. Durham, NC: Duke University Press, 2021.
Carter, J. Kameron. "The Politics of Atonement." *Immanent Frame*, July 18, 2011. https://tif.ssrc.org/2011/07/18/the-politics-of-the-atonement/.
Carter, J. Kameron. *Race: A Theological Account*. Oxford: Oxford University Press, 2008.
Carvalhaes, Claudio. *Liturgies from Below: Prayers from People at the End of the World*. Nashville, KY: Abingdon, 2020.
Casanova, José. *Public Religions in the Modern World*. Chicago: University of Chicago Press, 1994.
Casey, Edward. *The Fate of Place*. Berkeley: University of California Press, 1997.
Castro-Gómez, Santiago. *Crítica de la razón latinoamericana*. Barcelona: Puvill Libros, 1996.
Cerruti Guldberg, Horacio. *Filosofía de la liberación latinoamericana*. Mexico City: FCE, 1983.
Cerruti Guldberg, Horacio. "Situación y perspectivas de la filosofía de la liberación latinoamericana." *Concordia* 1, no. 15 (1989): 65–83.
Césaire, Aimé. *Discourse on Colonialism*. New York: Monthly Review Press, 2000.
Césaire, Aimé. *Notebook of a Return to the Native Land*. Middletown, CT: Wesleyan University Press, 2001.
Chakrabarty, Dipesh. *Provincializing Europe: Postcolonial Thought and Historical Difference*. Princeton, NJ: Princeton University Press, 2000.
Chancé, Dominique. "Creolization: Definition and Critique," In *The Creolization of Theory*, edited by Françoise Lionnet and Shu-mei Shih, 262–68. Durham, NC: Duke University Press, 2011.
Chidester, David. *Empire of Religion: Imperialism and Comparative Religion*. Chicago: University of Chicago Press, 2014.

Chidester, David. *Savage Systems: Colonialism and Comparative Religion in Southern Africa*. Charlottesville: University Press of Virginia, 1996.

Chow, Rey. "The Politics of Admittance: Female Sexual Agency, Miscegenation, and the Formation of Community in Frantz Fanon." In *Frantz Fanon: Critical Perspectives*, edited by Anthony Alessandrini, 34–56. London: Routledge, 1999.

Connell, Raewyn. "Meeting at the Edge of Fear: Theory on a World Scale." In *Constructing the Pluriverse: The Geopolitics of Knowledge*, edited by Bernd Reiter, 19–38. Durham, NC: Duke University Press, 2018.

Connell, Raewyn. "Rethinking Gender from the South." *Feminist Studies* 40, no. 3 (2014): 518–39.

Connolly, William. "Europe: A Minor Tradition." In *Powers of the Secular Modern*, edited by David Scott and Charles Hirschkind, 75–92. Redwood City, CA: Stanford University Press, 2006.

Connolly, William. *Why I Am Not a Secularist*. Minneapolis: University of Minnesota Press, 1999.

Corio, Alessandro. "The Living and the Poetic Intention: Glissant's Biopolitics of Literature." *Callaloo* 36, no. 4 (2013): 913–30.

Crockett, Clayton. *Radical Political Theology: Religion and Politics after Liberalism*. New York: Columbia University Press, 2013.

Cruz, Gustavo. "Del socialismo indio al Reino de la Verdad y la Vida: Utopías de Fausto Reinaga." *Utopías y praxis latinoamericana año* 21, no. 75 (2016): 59–71.

Cruz, Gustavo. "La revolución india de Fausto Reinaga: Ideología y filosofía política descolonizadora." *Interticios de la política y la cultura* 1, no. 2 (2012): 1–11.

Cusicanqui, Silvia. *Chi'ixinakax utxiwa: Una reflexión sobre prácticas y discursos descoloniales*. Buenos Aires: Tinta Limon Ediciones, 2010.

Dash, Michael. "The Stranger by the Shore: The Archipelization of Caliban in Antillean Theatre." In *Archipelagic American Studies*, edited by Brian Russell Roberts and Michelle Ann Stephens, 356–72. Durham, NC: Duke University Press, 2017.

Da Silva, Antônio Aparecido. *Existe um pensar teologico negro?* São Paulo: Paulinas, 1998.

Davis, Janae, Alex Moulton, Levi Van Sant, and Brian Williams. "Anthropocene, Capitalocene, ... Plantationocene? A Manifesto for Ecological Justice in an Age of Global Crisis." *Geography Compass* 13, no. 5 (2019): 1–15.

Deleuze, Gilles. *Desert Islands and Other Texts, 1953–1974*. Translated by Mike Taormina. Los Angeles: Semiotext(e), 2004.

Deleuze, Gilles, and Félix Guattari. *A Thousand Plateaus*. Translated by Brian Massumi. Minneapolis: University of Minnesota Press, 1987.

Deloria, Vine. *God Is Red: A Native View of Religion*. Golden, CO: Fulcrum Publishing, 2003.

DeLoughrey, Elizabeth. *Allegories of the Anthropocene*. Durham, NC: Duke University Press, 2019.

DeLoughrey, Elizabeth. *Routes and Roots: Navigating Caribbean and Pacific Island Literatures*. Honolulu: University of Hawai'i Press, 2009.
De Roover, Jakob. *Europe, India, and the Limits of Secularism*. Oxford: Oxford University Press, 2015.
Derrida, Jacques. *The Beast and the Sovereign, Vol. I.* Translated by Geoffrey Bennington. Chicago: University of Chicago Press, 2009.
De Sousa Santos, Boaventura. *The End of the Cognitive Empire: The Coming of Age of Epistemologies of the South*. Durham, NC: Duke University Press, 2018.
Dessau, Adalbert. "Literatura y sociedad en las obras de Jose Carlos Mariategui." In *Mariategui: Tres estudios*, edited by Adalbert Dessau, Manfred Kossok, and Antonio Melis, 51–110. Lima: Biblioteca Amauta, 1971.
De Vries, Hent, and Lawrence Sullivan, eds. *Political Theologies: Public Religions in a Post-Secular World*. New York: Fordham University Press, 2006.
Diawara, Manthia. "One World in Relation: Édouard Glissant in Conversation with Manthia Diawara." *Journal of Contemporary African Art* 28 (2011): 4–9.
Dirlik, Arif. "The Postcolonial Aura: Third World Criticism in the Age of Global Capitalism." *Critical Inquiry* 20, no. 2 (1994): 328–56.
Drabinski, John. "Cesaire's Apocalyptic Word." *South Atlantic Quarterly* (July 2016): 567–84.
Drabinski, John. *Glissant and the Middle Passage: Philosophy, Beginning, Abyss*. Minneapolis: University of Minnesota Press, 2019.
Drabinski, John. "Shorelines: In Memory of Édouard Glissant." *Journal of French and Francophone Philosophy* 19, no. 1 (2011): 1–10.
Dressler, Markus, and Arvind-Pal Mandair, eds. *Secularism and Religion-Making*. Oxford: Oxford University Press, 2011.
Drexler-Dreis, Joseph. *Decolonial Love: Salvation in Colonial Modernity*. New York: Fordham University Press, 2018.
Dubey, Madhu. "The 'True Lie' of the Nation: Fanon and Feminism." *differences: A Journal of Feminist Cultural Studies* 10, no. 2 (1998): 1–29.
Dussel, Enrique. *Beyond Philosophy: Ethics, History, Marxism, and Liberation Theology*. Lanham, MD: Rowman and Littlefield, 2003.
Dussel, Enrique. *Desintegración de la cristiandad colonial y liberación: Perspectiva latinoamericana*. Salamanca: Ediciones Sigueme, 1978.
Dussel, Enrique. *Ethics and Theology of Liberation*. Maryknoll, NY: Orbis Books, 1979.
Dussel, Enrique. "Europe, Modernity, and Eurocentrism." *Nepantla: Views from South* 1, no. 3 (2000): 465–78.
Dussel, Enrique. *Filosofía de la liberación*. Mexico City: Edicol, 1977.
Dussel, Enrique. *The Invention of the Americas: Eclipse of "the Other" and the Myth of Modernity*. New York: Lexington, 1995.
Dussel, Enrique. *Philosophy of Liberation*. Maryknoll, NY: Orbis Books, 1985.
Dussel, Enrique. *Teología de la liberación: Un panorama de su desarrollo*. Mexico City: Potrerillos Editores, 1995.

Dussel, Enrique. *Towards an Unknown Marx: A Commentary on the Manuscripts of 1861–63*. London: Routledge, 2001.
Dussel, Enrique. *Twenty Theses on Politics*. Durham, NC: Duke University Press, 2008.
Dussel, Enrique. "World-System and 'Trans'-Modernity." *Nepantla: Views from South* 3, no 2 (2002): 221–44.
Eliade, Mircea. *The Sacred and the Profane: The Nature of Religion*. New York: Brace and World, 1959.
Esposito, Roberto. *Bios: Biopolitics and Philosophy*. Minneapolis: University of Minnesota Press, 2008.
Fanon, Frantz. *Alienation and Freedom*. Translated by Steven Corcoran. Edited by Jean Khalfa and Robert Young. London: Bloomsbury, 2018.
Fanon, Frantz. *Black Skin, White Masks*. Translated by Charles Lam Markmann. New York: Grove, 1967.
Fanon, Frantz. *A Dying Colonialism*. Translated by Haakon Chevalier. New York: Grove, 1967.
Fanon, Frantz. *The Wretched of the Earth*. Translated by Richard Philcox. New York: Grove, 1963.
Farred, Grant. *What's My Name? Black Vernacular Intellectuals*. Minneapolis: University of Minnesota, 2003.
Feretti, Pierina. "Del misticismo decadentista a la religiosidad revolucionaria: Estudio sobre el desarrollo de la dimensión religiosa en el pensamiento de José Carlos Mariátegui." M.A. thesis, University of Chile, 2016.
Fitzgerald, Timothy. *The Ideology of Religious Studies*. Oxford: Oxford University Press, 2003.
Fitzgerald, Timothy, ed. *Religion and the Secular: Historical and Colonial Formations*. New York: Routledge, 2007.
Frazer, Elizabeth, and Kimberley Hutchins. "On Politics and Violence: Arendt Contra Fanon." *Contemporary Political Theory* 7, no. 1 (2008): 90–108.
Freire, Paulo. *Pedagogia do oprimido*. Rio de Janeiro: Paz y Terra, 1968.
Fuss, Diana. *Identification Papers: Readings on Psychoanalysis, Sexuality, and Culture*. New York: Routledge, 1995.
Garraway, Doris. "What Is Mine: Cesairean Negritude between the Particular and the Universal." *Research in African Literatures* 41, no. 1 (2010): 71–86.
Gebara, Ivone. *Longing for Running Water: Ecofeminism and Liberation*. Minneapolis, MN: Fortress, 1999.
Gilroy, Paul. *The Black Atlantic: Modernity and Double Consciousness*. Cambridge, MA: Harvard University Press, 1993.
Girardi, Giulio. *Por una pedagogia revolucionaria*. Barcelona: Ediciones de Bolsillo, 1977.
Glissant, Édouard. "Aimé Césaire: The Poet's Passion." *Small Axe* 12, no. 3 (2008): 119–23.
Glissant, Édouard. *Caribbean Discourse: Selected Essays*. Charlottesville: University Press of Virginia, 1989.

Glissant, Édouard. "The Indies." Translated by Dominique O'Neill. Toronto: Editions de Gref, 1992.
Glissant, Édouard. *Introduction a une poetique du divers*. Paris: Gallimard, 1996.
Glissant, Édouard. *Philosophie de la relation: Poésie en éntendue*. Paris: Gallimard, 2009.
Glissant, Édouard *Poetic Intention*. New York: Nightboat Books, 2010.
Glissant, Édouard. *Poetics of Relation*. Ann Arbor: University of Michigan Press, 1990.
Gole, Nilufer. *Islam and Secularity: The Future of Europe's Public Sphere*. Durham, NC: Duke University Press, 2015.
Gomez-Barris, Macarena. *The Extractive Zone: Social Ecologies and Decolonial Perspectives*. Durham, NC: Duke University Press, 2017.
Gordon, Lewis. *Existentia Africana: Understanding Africana Existential Thought*. London: Routledge, 2000.
Gordon, Lewis. "Fanon and Development: A Philosophical Look." *Africa Development* 29, no. 1 (2004): 71–94.
Gordon, Lewis. *Freedom, Justice, and Decolonization*. New York: Routledge, 2021.
Gordon, Lewis. "Through the Zone of Nonbeing: A Reading of *Black Skin, White Masks* in Celebration of Fanon's Eightieth Birthday." *C. L. R. James Journal* 11, no. 1 (2005): 1–43.
Gordon, Lewis. *What Fanon Said: A Philosophical Introduction to His Life and Thought*. New York: Fordham University Press, 2015.
Grosfoguel, Ramon. "Epistemic Extractivism: A Dialogue with Alberto Acosta, Leanne Betasamosake Simpson, and Silvia Rivera Cusicanqui." In *Knowledges Born in the Struggle: Constructing Epistemologies of the Global South*, edited by Boaventura de Sousa Santos and Maria Paula Meneses, 760–92. New York: Routledge, 2019.
Grove, Jairus. *Savage Ecology: War and Geopolitics at the End of the World*. Durham, NC: Duke University Press, 2019.
Guenther, Lisa. "Critical Phenomenology." In *50 Concepts in Critical Phenomenology*, edited by Gail Weiss, Gayle Salamon, and Ann Murphy, 11–16. Evanston, IL: Northwestern University Press, 2019.
Gutiérrez, Gustavo. *The Power of the Poor in History: Selected Writings*. Maryknoll, NY: Orbis Books, 1983.
Gutiérrez, Gustavo. *Teología de la liberación: Perspectivas*. Lima: Ediciones Sigueme, 1971.
Habermas, Jürgen. "Religion in the Public Sphere." *European Journal of Philosophy* Vol 14. Issue 1, 1–25.
Habermas, Jürgen. "Secularism's Crisis of Faith: Notes on a Post-Secular Society." Translated by Joseph Ratzinger. *New Perspectives Quarterly* (2008): 17–29.
Hage, Ghassan. "Comes a Time We Are All Enthusiasm: Understanding Palestinian Suicide Bombers in Times of Exighophobia." *Public Culture* 15, no. 1 (2003): 65–89.

Hallward, Peter. *Absolutely Postcolonial: Writing between the Singular and the Specific*. Manchester: Manchester University Press, 2002.
Hanke, Lewis. *Aristotle and the American Indians: A Study in Race Prejudice in the Modern World*. Bloomington: Indiana University Press, 1970.
Hanke, Lewis. *The Spanish Struggle for Justice in the Conquest of America*. Dallas: SMU Press, 2002.
Hantel, Max. "Rhizome and the Space of Translation: On Édouard Glissant's Spiral Retelling." *Small Axe* 17, no. 3 (2013): 100–12.
Haraway, Donna. "Anthropocene, Capitalocene, Plantationocene, Chthulucene: Making Kin." *Environmental Humanities* 6, no. 1 (2015): 159–65.
Haraway, Donna, Noboru Ishikawa, Scott Gilbert, Kenneth Olwig, Anna Tsing, and Nils Bubandt. "Anthropologists Are Talking—about the Anthropocene." *Ethnos* 81, no. 3 (2015): 535–64.
Harris, Wilson. "History, Fable and Myth in the Caribbean and Guianas." In *Selected Essays of Wilson Harris: The Unfinished Genesis of the Imagination*, edited by Andrew Bundy, 147–60. London: Routledge, 1999.
Hegel, G. W. F. *Phenomenology of Spirit*. Translated by A. V. Miller. Oxford: Oxford University Press, 1977.
Heng, Geraldine. *The Invention of Race in European Middle Ages*. Cambridge: Cambridge University Press, 2018.
Henry, Paget. "Africana Phenomenology: Its Philosophical Implications." *C. L. R. James Journal* 11, no. 1 (2005): 79–112.
Hiddleston, Jane. "Aimé Cesairé and Postcolonial Humanism." *Modern Language Review* 105, no. 1 (2010): 87–102.
Hinkelammert, Franz. "La crítica de la religión neoliberal del mercado y los derechos humanos." In Franz Hinkelammert, *La vida o el capital: Antología esencial*, edited by Estela Fernandez Nadal, 153–88. Buenos Aires: CLASCO, 2017.
Hinkelammert, Franz. *Las armas ideológicas de la muerte*. Salamanca: Sigueme, 1978.
Hinkelammert, Franz. "La visibilidad de lo invisible y la invisibilidad de lo visible: El análisis del fetichismo en Marx." In Franz Hinkelammert, *La vida o el capital: Antología esencial*, edited by Estela Fernandez Nadal, 45–116. Buenos Aires: CLASCO, 2017.
Hollywood, Amy. "Introduction." In *The Cambridge Companion to Christian Mysticism*, edited by Amy Hollywood and Patricia Beckman. 1–36. Cambridge: Cambridge University Press, 2012.
Hong, Grace Kyungwon. *Death beyond Disavowal: The Impossible Politics of Difference*. Minneapolis: University of Minnesota Press, 2016.
Irvine, Andrew. "Liberation Theology as a Postcolonial Critique of Theological Reason." *Journal for the Academic Study of Religion* 25, no. 2 (2012): 139–61.
Isasi-Diaz, Ada Maria, and Enduardo Mendieta, eds. *Decolonizing Epistemologies: Latina/o Theology and Philosophy*. New York: Fordham University Press, 2011.
Jakobson, Janet, and Ann Pellegrini, eds. *Secularisms*. Durham, NC: Duke University Press, 2008.

Jantzen, Grace. *Power, Gender, and Christian Mysticism*. Cambridge: Cambridge University Press, 1995.

Jennings. Willie. *The Christian Imagination: Theology and the Origins of Race*. New Haven, CT: Yale University Press, 2010.

Johnson, Sylvester. *African American Religions, 1500–2000: Colonialism, Democracy, and Freedom*. Cambridge: Cambridge University Press, 2015.

Josephson Storm, Jason. *The Myth of Disenchantment: Magic, Modernity, and the Birth of the Human Science*. Chicago: University of Chicago Press, 2017.

Kahn, Jonathan, and Vincent Lloyd. *Race and Secularism in America*. New York: Columbia University Press, 2016.

Kahn, Paul. *Political Theology: Four New Chapters on the Concept of Sovereignty*. New York: Columbia University Press, 2011.

Kahn, Paul. "Political Theology and Liberalism." *Immanent Frame*, June 22, 2011. https://tif.ssrc.org/2011/06/22/political-theology-and-liberalism/.

Kahn, Paul. *Sacred Violence: Torture, Terror, and Sovereignty*. Ann Arbor: University of Michigan Press, 2008.

Kamugisha, Aaron. "The Promise of Caribbean Intellectual History." *Small Axe* 25, no. 1 (2021): 47–60.

Kawash, Samira. "Terrorists and Vampires." In *Frantz Fanon: Critical Perspectives*, edited by Anthony Alessandrini, 235–57. London: Routledge, 1998.

Kearney, Richard. *Anatheism: Returning to God after God*. New York: Columbia University Press, 2010.

Keel, Terrence. *Divine Variations: How Christian Thought Became Racial Science*. Redwood City, CA: Stanford University Press, 2018.

Kelly, Robin D.G. "Preface." In *Discourse on Colonialism* by Aimé Césaire, 7–28. New York: Monthly Review Press, 2000.

King, Richard. *Religion and Orientalism: Postcolonial Theory, India, and the "Mystic East."* London: Routledge, 1999.

Koskenniemi, Martti. "Empire and International Law: The Real Spanish Contribution." *University of Toronto Law Journal* 61, no. 1 (2011): 1–36.

Lackey, Michael. "Frantz Fanon on the Theology of Colonization." *Journal of Colonialism and Colonial History* 3, no. 2 (2002): 1–29.

Lamming, George. "The Imperial Encirclement." In *The George Lamming Reader: The Aesthetics of Decolonisation*, edited by Anthony Bogues, 85–94. Kingston: Ian Randle Publishers, 2011.

Lamming, George. "Nationalism and Nation." In *The George Lamming Reader: The Aesthetics of Decolonisation*, edited by Anthony Bogues, 110–20. Kingston: Ian Randle Publishers, 2011.

Lefebvre, Henri. *The Production of Space*. Translated by Donald Nicholson Smith. Oxford: Blackwell, 1991.

Lloyd, Vincent. "Introduction." In *Race and Political Theology*, edited by Vincent Lloyd, 1–21. Redwood City, CA: Stanford University Press, 2012.

Loichot, Valérie. *Water Graves: The Art of the Unritual in the Greater Caribbean*. Charlottesville: University Press of Virginia, 2020.

Long, Charles. *Significations: Signs, Symbols, and Images in the Interpretation of Religion*. Aurora, CO: Davies Group, 1986.

Lopez Hernandez, Eleazar. *Teología India: Antología*. Cochabamba: Verbo Divino, 2000.

Lugones, Maria. "The Coloniality of Gender." *Words and Knowledges Otherwise* 2 (2008): 1–17.

Lugones, Maria. "Toward a Decolonial Feminism." *Hypatia* 25, no. 4 (2010): 742–59.

Mahmood, Saba. *Religious Difference in a Secular Age: A Minority Report*. Princeton, NJ: Princeton University Press, 2015.

Mahmood, Saba. "Secularism, Hermeneutics, and Empire: The Politics of Islamic Reformation." *Public Culture* 18, no. 2 (2006): 323–47.

Maia, Filipe. *Trading Futures: A Theological Critique of Financialized Capitalism*. Durham, NC: Duke University Press, 2022.

Makalani, Minkah. "The Politically Unimaginable in Black Marxist Thought." *Small Axe* 22, no. 2 (2018): 18–34.

Maldonado-Torres, Nelson. "AAR Centennial Roundtable: Religion, Conquest, and Race in the Formations of the Modern/Colonial World." *Journal of the American Academy of Religion* 82, no. 3 (2014): 636–65.

Maldonado-Torres, Nelson. *Against War: Views from the Underside of Modernity*. Durham, NC: Duke University Press, 2008.

Maldonado-Torres, Nelson. "Liberation Theology and the Search for the Lost Paradigm: From Radical Orthodoxy to Radical Diversality." In *Latin American Liberation Theology: The Next Generation*, edited by Ivan Petrella, 69–117. Maryknoll, NY: Orbis Books, 2005.

Maldonado-Torres, Nelson. "Race, Religion, and Ethics in the Modern/Colonial World." *Journal of Religious Ethics* 42, no. 4 (2014): 691–711.

Maldonado-Torres, Nelson. "Religion, Modernity, and Coloniality." In *Religion, Theory, and Critique: Classic and Contemporary Approaches and Methodologies*, edited by Richard King, 547–54. New York: Columbia University Press, 2017.

Malpas, Jeff. *Place and Experience: A Philosophical Topography*. Cambridge: Cambridge University Press, 1999.

Mandair, Arvind-Pal. *Religion and the Specter of the West: Sikhism, India, Postcoloniality, and the Politics of Translation*. New York: Columbia University Press, 2016.

Marcos, Sylvia. "Beyond Binary Categories: Mesoamerican Religious Sexuality." In *Religion and Sexuality in Cross-Cultural Perspective*, edited by Stephen Ellingson and M. Christian Green, 111–36. New York: Routledge, 2002.

Marcos, Sylvia. "Mesoamerican Women's Indigenous Spirituality: Decolonizing Religious Beliefs." *Journal of Feminist Studies in Religion* 25, no. 2 (2009): 25–45.

Marcos, Sylvia. *Taken from the Lips: Gender and Eros in Mesoamerican Religions*. Leiden: Brill, 2006.

Mariátegui, José Carlos. *José Carlos Mariátegui: An Anthology*. Edited by Harry E. Vanden and Marc Becker. New York: Monthly Review Press, 2011.
Mariátegui, José Carlos. *Siete ensayos de interpretación de la realidad Peruana*. Caracas: Fundacion Biblioteca Ayacucho, 2007.
Marriott, D. S. *Whither Fanon? Studies in the Blackness of Being*. Redwood City, CA: Stanford University Press, 2018.
Mastnak, Tomaž. *Crusading Peace: Christendom, the Muslim World, and Western Political Order*. Berkeley: University of California Press, 2002.
Masuzawa, Tomoko. *In Search of Dreamtime: The Quest for the Origin of Religion*. Chicago: University of Chicago, 1993.
Masuzawa, Tomoko. *The Invention of World Religions: Or, How European Universalism Was Preserved in the Language of Pluralism*. Chicago: University of Chicago Press, 2005.
Mbembe, Achille. *Critique of Black Reason*. Translated by Laurent Dubois. Durham, NC: Duke University Press, 2017.
Mbembe, Achille. "Necropolitics." *Public Culture* 15, no. 1 (2003): 11–40.
Mbembe, Achille. *Necropolitics*. Durham, NC: Duke University Press, 2019.
Mbembe, Achille. *On the Postcolony*. Berkeley: University of California Press, 2001.
Mbembe, Achille. *Out of the Dark Night: Essays on Decolonization*. New York: Columbia University Press, 2021.
McClintock, Anne. *Imperial Leather: Race, Gender, and Sexuality in the Colonial Conquest*. New York: Routledge, 1995.
McCutcheon, Russell. *Manufacturing Religion: The Discourse on Sui Generis Religion and the Politics of Nostalgia*. Oxford: Oxford University Press, 2003.
McKittrick, Katherine. *Sylvia Wynter: On Being Human as Praxis*. Durham, NC: Duke University Press, 2014.
McKittrick, Katherine, Frances O'Shaughnessy, and Kendall Wiltaszek. "Rhythm or on Wynter's Science of the Word." *American Quarterly* 70, no. 4 (2018): 867–74.
Mendoza, Breny. "Coloniality of Gender and Power: From Postcoloniality to Decoloniality." In *The Oxford Handbook of Feminist Theory*, edited by Lisa Disch and Mary Hawkesworth, 100–121. Oxford: Oxford University Press, 2015.
Mendoza, Breny. "Decolonial Theories in Comparison." In *Indigenous Knowledge in Taiwan and Beyond*, edited by Shu-mei Shih and Lin-Chin Tsai, 249–70. New York: Springer, 2021.
Merleau-Ponty, Maurice. *Phenomenology of Perception*. Translated by Colin Smith. New York: Routledge, 2012.
Merleau-Ponty, Maurice. *Sense and Non-sense*. Translated by Hubert L. Dreyfus and Patricia Allen Dreyfus. Evanston, IL: Northwestern University Press, 1964.
Merleau-Ponty, Maurice. *The Visible and the Invisible*. Translated by Alphonso Lingis. Evanston, IL: Northwestern University Press, 1968.
Messeguer, Diego. *José Carlos Mariátegui y su pensamiento revolucionario*. Lima: IEP Ediciones, 1974.

Miguez, Nestor, Joerg Rieger, and Jung Mo Sung. *Beyond the Spirit of Empire*. London: SCM Press, 2009.

Miguez Bonino, José. *Doing Theology in a Revolutionary Situation*. Minneapolis, MN: Fortress, 1975.

Mignolo, Walter. *The Darker Side of Western Modernity: Global Futures, Decolonial Options*. Durham, NC: Duke University Press, 2011.

Mignolo, Walter. "Decolonizing Western Epistemology: Building Decolonial Epistemologies." In *Decolonizing Epistemologies: Latina/o Theology and Philosophy*, edited by Ada Maria Isasi-Diaz and Eduardo Mendieta, 19–43. New York: Fordham University Press, 2012.

Mignolo, Walter. "I Am Where I Think: Epistemology and the Colonial Difference." *Journal of Latin American Cultural Studies* 8, no. 2 (1999): 235–45.

Mignolo, Walter. *Local Histories/Global Designs: Coloniality, Subaltern Knowledges, and Border Thinking*. Princeton, NJ: Princeton University Press, 2000.

Mignolo, Walter, and Catherine Walsh. *On Decoloniality: Concepts, Analytics, Praxis*. Durham, NC: Duke University Press, 2018.

Miller, Nicola. *Reinventing Modernity in Latin America: Intellectuals Imagine the Future 1990–1930*. New York: Palgrave, 2008.

Monahan, Michael. *The Creolizing Subject: Race, Reason, and the Politics of Purity*. New York: Fordham University Press, 2011.

Moore, Jason. "The Capitalocene, Part I: On the Nature and Origins of Our Ecological Crisis." *Journal of Peasant Studies* 44, no. 3 (2017): 594–630.

Moraña, Mabel, Enrique Dussel, and Carlos Jáuregui. "Colonialism and Its Replicants." In *Coloniality at Large: Latin America and the Postcolonial Debate*, edited by Mabel Moraña, Enrique Dussel, and Carlos Jáuregui, 1–22. Durham, NC: Duke University Press, 2008.

Morris, Glenn. "Vine Deloria, Jr., and the Development of a Decolonizing Critique of Indigenous Peoples and International Relations." In *Native Voices: Native American Identity and Resistance*, edited by Richard Grounds, George Tinker, and David Wilkins, 97–154. Lawrence: University of Kansas Press, 2003.

Moten, Fred. "Blackness and Nothingness (Mysticism in the Flesh)." *South Atlantic Quarterly* 112, no. 4 (2013): 737–80.

Moten, Fred. "The Case of Blackness." *Criticism* 50, no. 2 (2008): 177–218.

Nesbitt, Nick. "Deleuze, Glissant, and the Production of Postcolonial Concepts." In *Deleuze and the Postcolonial*, edited by Paul Patton and Simone Bignall, 103–18. Edinburgh: Edinburgh University Press, 2010.

Nichols, Robert. *Theft Is Property! Dispossession and Critical Theory*. Durham, NC: Duke University Press, 2019.

Nongbri, Brent. *Before Religion: A History of Modern Concept*. New Haven, CT: Yale University Press, 2013.

Nordlander, Andreas. "Figuring Flesh in Creation." PhD diss., Lund University, 2011.

Noudelmann, François. "Édouard Glissant's Legacy: Transmitting without Universals?" *Callaloo* 36, no. 4 (2013): 869–74.

Oakley, Seanna. "In Citations to the Chance: Glissant, Citation, Intention, and Interpretation." In *Theorizing Glissant: Sites and Citations*, edited by John Drabinski and Marisa Parham, 29–52. Lanham, MD: Rowman and Littlefield, 2015.

Orion, Edgard. *Things Seen and Unseen: The Logic of Incarnation in Merleau-Ponty's Metaphysics of Flesh*. Cambridge: James Clarke, 2016.

Ortega, Mariana. *In-Between: Latina Feminist Phenomenology, Multiplicity, and the Self*. Albany: State University of New York Press, 2016.

Pagden, Anthony. *The Fall of Natural Man: The American Indian and the Origin of Comparative Ethnology*. Cambridge: Cambridge University Press, 1982.

Pagden, Anthony. "Human Rights, Natural Rights, and Europe's Imperial Legacy." *Political Theory* 31, no. 2 (2003): 179–99.

Panotto, Nicolas. "A Critique of the Coloniality of Theological Knowledge: Rereading Latin American Liberation Theology as Thinking Otherwise." In *Decolonial Christianities: Latinx and Latin American Perspectives*, edited by Raimundo Barreto and Roberto Sirvent, 217–38. New York: Palgrave Press, 2019.

Paredes, Julieta. *Hilando fino desde el feminismo comunitario*. La Paz: Comunidad Mujeres Creando Comunidad, 2007.

Parham, Marisa. "Breadfruit, Time and Again: Glissant Reads Faulkner in the World Relation." In *Theorizing Glissant: Sites and Citations*, edited by John Drabinski and Marisa Parham, 129–38. Lanham, MD: Rowman and Littlefield, 2015.

Paris, Robert. *El Marxismo latinoamericano de Mariátegui*. Buenos Aires: Ediciones Crisis, 1977.

Pimentel-Chacon, Jonathan, ed. *Teologías latinoamericanas de la liberación*. San Jose: Editorial Sebila, 2010.

Quijano, Anibal. "Colonialidad, poder, cultura y conocimiento en America Latina." *Anuario Mariateguiano* 9, no. 9 (1998): 113–22.

Quijano, Anibal. "Colonialidad y modernidad/racionalidad." *Peru Indigena* 13, no. 29 (1992): 11–20.

Quijano, Anibal. "Coloniality of Power, Eurocentrism, and Latin America." *Nepantla: Views from South* 1, no. 3 (2000): 533–80.

Radovich, Stanka. "The Birthplace of Relation in Édouard Glissant's *Poetique de la Relation*." *Callaloo* 30, no. 2 (2007): 475–81.

Ray, Ros, and Shela Sheikh. "Introduction." Special issue, "The Wretched Earth: Botanical Conflicts and Artistic Interventions." *Third Text* 32, nos. 2–3 (2018): 163–75.

Reinaga, Fausto. *América india y el occidente*. La Paz, Bolivia: Ediciones PIB, 1974.

Reinaga, Fausto. *La razón y el indio*. La Paz, Bolivia: Ediciones PIB, 1978.

Renton, James, and Ben Gidley. *Antisemitism and Islamophobia in Europe: A Shared Story?* New York: Palgrave Press, 2016.

Rieger, Joerg. *Christ and Empire: From Paul to Postcolonial Times*. Minneapolis, MN: Fortress Press, 2007.

Rivera, Mayra. *Poetics of the Flesh*. Durham, NC: Duke University Press, 2015.
Rivera, Mayra. *The Touch of Transcendence: A Postcolonial Theology of God*. Louisville, KY: Westminster John Knox Press, 2007.
Rivera Cusicanqui, Silvia. *Ch'ixinakas Utxiwa: Una reflexión sobre prácticas y discursos descoloniales*. Buenos Aires: Tinta Limón y Retazos, 2010.
Rivera-Pagán, Luis. *A Violent Evangelism: The Political and Religious Conquest of the Americas*. Louisville, KY: Westminster John Knox Press, 1992.
Robbins, Jeffrey. *Radical Democracy and Political Theology*. New York: Columbia University Press, 2011.
Roberts, Brian Russell, and Michelle Anne Stephens. "Archipelagic American Studies: Decontinentalizing the Study of American Culture." In *Archipelagic American Studies*, edited by Brian Russell Roberts and Michelle Ann Stephens, 1–56. Durham, NC: Duke University Press, 2017.
Robinson, Cedric. *Black Marxism: The Making of the Black Radical Tradition*. London: Zed Press, 1983.
Rosaldo, Renato. "Imperialist Nostalgia." *Representations*, no. 26 (1989): 107–22.
Rouanet, S. P. "Irrationalism and Myth in George Sorel." *Review of Politics* 26, no. 1 (1964): 45–69.
Rubenstein, Mary-Jane. *Strange Wonder: The Closure of Metaphysics and the Opening of Awe*. New York: Columbia University Press, 2010.
Sack, Robert. *Conceptions of Space in Social Thought: A Geographic Perspective*. Minneapolis: University of Minnesota Press, 1980.
Said, Edward. *Orientalism*. New York: Pantheon, 1978.
Salazar Bondy, Augusto. *Existe una filosofía de nuestra america?* Mexico City: Siglo XXI Editores, 1968.
Saldaña-Portillo, Josefina. "Who's the Indian in Aztlan? Re-writing Mestizaje, Indianism, and Chicanismo from Lacandon." In *The Latin American Subaltern Studies Reader*, edited by Iliana Yamileth Rodriguez, 402–23. Durham, NC: Duke University Press, 2001.
Santos, Milton. *The Nature of Space*. Durham, NC: Duke University Press, 2021.
Sayyid, Salman, and Abdookarim Vakil. *Thinking through Islamophobia: Global Perspectives*. London: Hurst, 2010.
Scannone, Juan Carlos. "La filosofía de la liberación: Historia, características, vigencia actual." *Teología y vida* 50, nos. 1–2 (2009): 59–73.
Schiebinger, Londa. *Plants and Empire: Colonial Bioprospecting in the Atlantic World*. Cambridge, MA: Harvard University Press, 2004.
Schmitt, Carl. *Political Theology*. Cambridge, MA: MIT Press, 1985.
Schulman, George. "Pluralizing Political Theology." *Immanent Frame*, June 27, 2011. https://tif.ssrc.org/2011/06/27/pluralizing-political-theology/.
Schutte, Ofelia. *Cultural Identity and Social Liberation in Latin American Thought*. Albany: State University of New York Press, 1993.
Scott, David. "The Re-enchantment of Humanism: An Interview with Sylvia Wynter." *Small Axe* 8 (2000): 119–207.

Segal, Robert. "In Defense of Reductionism." *Journal of the American Academy of Religion* 51, no. 1 (1983): 97–124.

Segato, Rita. "Género y colonialidad en busca de claves de lectura y de un vocabulario estratégico descolonial." In *Feminismo y poscolonialidad: Descolonizando el feminismo desde y en America Latina*, edited by Karina Bidaseca and Vanesa Vazquez Laba, 17–48. Buenos Aires: Godot, 2011.

Segundo, Juan Luis. "Capitalism-Socialism: A Theological Crux." In *The Mystical and Political Dimension of the Christian Faith*, edited by Calude Geffre and Gustavo Gutierrez, 105–26. New York: Herder and Herder, 1974.

Seshadri-Crooks, Kalpana. "I Am a Master: Terrorism, Masculinity, and Political Violence in Frantz Fanon." *Parallax* 8, no. 2 (2002): 84–98.

Settler, Federico. "Religion in the Work of Frantz Fanon." PhD diss., University of Cape Town, 2009.

Sexton, Jared. *Amalgamation Schemes: Antiblackness and the Critique of Multiracialism*. Minneapolis: University of Minnesota Press, 2008.

Sharpe, Christina. *In the Wake: On Blackness and Being*. Durham, NC: Duke University Press, 2016.

Sharpley-Whiting, T. Denean. *Frantz Fanon: Conflicts and Feminisms*. Lanham, MD: Rowman and Littlefield, 1997.

Singh, Julieta. *Unthinking Mastery: Dehumanism and Decolonial Entanglements*. Durham, NC: Duke University Press, 2017.

Slabodsky, Santiago. *Decolonial Judaism: Triumphal Failures of Barbaric Thinking*. New York: Palgrave Press, 2014.

Slisli, Fouzi. "Islam: The Elephant in Fanon's *The Wretched of the Earth*." *Critique: Critical Middle Eastern Studies* 17, no. 1 (2008): 97–108.

Smith, Jonathan Z. *Map Is Not Territory: Studies in the History of Religion*. Chicago: University of Chicago Press, 1993.

Smith, Jonathan Z. "Religion, Religions, Religious." In *Critical Terms for Religious Studies*, edited by Mark C. Taylor, 269–84. Chicago: University of Chicago Press, 1998.

Smith, Wilfred Cantwell. *The Meaning and End of Religion*. Minneapolis, MN: Fortress Press, 1963.

Sorel, Georges. *Reflections on Violence*. Edited by Jeremy Jennings. Cambridge: Cambridge University Press, 1999.

Strenski, Ivan. *Religion in Relation: Method, Application, and Moral Location*. Columbia: University of South Carolina Press, 1992.

Suarez-Krabbe, Julia. "The Other Side of the Story: Human Rights, Race, and Gender from a Transatlantic Perspective." In *Decolonizing Enlightenment: Transnational Justice, Human Rights, and Democracy in a Postcolonial World*, edited by Nikita Dhawan 211–26. Opladen: Barbara Budrich Publisher, 2014.

Tager, Michael. "Myths and Politics in the Works of Sorel and Barthes." *Journal of the History of Ideas* 47, no. 4 (1986): 625–39.

Tamayo, Juan José. *La teología de la liberación en el nuevo espacio político y religioso.* Valencia: Tirant Lo Blanch, 2009.

Tamayo, Juan José. *Teología del Sur: El giro descolonizador.* Madrid: Editorial Trotta, 2017.

Tamez, Elsa. *Las mujeres en el movimiento de Jesús, el Cristo.* Quito: CLAI, 2003.

Taylor, Charles. *A Secular Age.* Cambridge, MA: Harvard University Press, 2007.

Tayob, Abdulkader. "Decolonizing the Study of Religions: Muslim Intellectuals and the Enlightenment Project of Religious Studies." *Journal for the Study of Religion* 31, no. 2 (2018): 7–35.

Thomas, Greg. "Afro-Blue Notes: The Death of Afro-pessimism (2.0)?" *Theory and Event* 21, no. 1 (2018): 282–317.

Tlostanova, Madina. *Gender Epistemologies and Eurasian Borderlands.* New York: Palgrave, 2010.

Topolski, Anya. "The Race-Religion Constellation: A European Contribution to the Critical Philosophy of Race." *Critical Philosophy of Race* 6, no. 1 (2018): 58–81.

Valiente Nunez, Javier. "Liberation Theology and Latin America's Testimonio and New Historical Novel: A Decolonial Perspective." PhD diss., Johns Hopkins University, 2016.

Van der Veer, Peter. *Imperial Encounters: Religion and Modernity in India and Britain.* Princeton, NJ: Princeton University Press, 2001.

Van der Veer, Peter. *The Modern Spirit of Asia: The Spiritual and the Secular in China and India.* Princeton, NJ: Princeton University Press, 2013.

Vernon, Richard. *Commitment and Change: Georges Sorel and the Idea of Revolution.* Toronto: University of Toronto Press, 1978.

Vincent, K. Stephen. "Interpreting Georges Sorel: Defender of Virtue or Apostle of Violence?" *History of European Ideas* 12, no. 2 (1990): 239–57.

Wagua, Aiban. *Principios de la teofanía guna.* Roma: Orientamendi Pedagogici, 1982.

Walcott, Derek. "The Caribbean: Culture or Mimicry." *Journal of Interamerican Studies and World Affairs* 16, no. 1 (1974): 3–13.

Walcott, Derek. "Isla Incognita." In *Caribbean Literature and the Environment: Between Nature and Culture,* edited by Elizabeth DeLoughrey, Renee Gosson, and George Handley, 51–57. Charlottesville: University Press of Virginia, 2005.

Walcott, Derek. "The Sea Is History." In *Collected Poems 1948–1984,* 364–67. New York: Farrar, Straus, and Giroux, 1987.

Walcott, Derek. *What the Twilight Says: Essays.* New York: Farrar, Straus, and Giroux, 1998.

Wallerstein, Immanuel. "The Insurmountable Contradictions of Liberalism: Human Rights and the Rights of Peoples in the Geoculture of the Modern World-System." In *Nations, Identities, Cultures,* edited by Valentin Mudimbe. Special Issue, *South Atlantic Quarterly* 94, no. 4 (1995): 1161–78.

Wallerstein, Immanuel. *The Modern World-System*. Vol. 1. *Capitalist Agriculture and the Origins of the European World-Economy in the Sixteenth Century*. Berkeley: University of California Press, 1974.

Wallerstein, Immanuel. *The Modern World-System*. Vol. 2. *Mercantilism and the Consolidation of the European World Economy, 1600–1750*. Berkeley: University of California Press, 1980.

Walsh, Catherine. "On Gender and Its Otherwise." In *The Palgrave Handbook of Gender and Development*, edited by Wendy Harcourt, 34–47. New York: Palgrave, 2016.

Ward, Graham. *Christ and Culture*. Malden, MA: Blackwell, 2005.

Warren, Calvin. "Black Mysticism: Fred Moten's Phenomenology of (Black) Spirit." *Zeitschrift fur Anglistik und Amerikanistik* 65, no. 2 (2017): 219–29.

Warren, Calvin. *Ontological Terror: Blackness, Nihilism, and Emancipation*. Durham, NC: Duke University Press, 2018.

Weheliye, Alexander. *Habeas Viscus: Racializing Assemblages, Biopolitics, and Black Feminist Theories of the Human*. Durham, NC: Duke University Press, 2014.

Wiebe, Donald. "The Failure of Nerve in the Academic Study of Religion." *Studies in Religion/Sciences Religieuses* (Fall 1984): 401–22.

Wiedorn, Michael. *Think Like an Archipelago: Paradox in the Work of Édouard Glissant*. Albany: State University of New York Press, 2018.

Wilderson, Frank. *Red, White, and Black: Cinema and the Structure of U.S. Antagonisms*. Durham, NC: Duke University Press, 2010.

Winters, Joseph. "The Sacred Gone Astray: Eliade, Fanon, Wynter, and the Terror of Colonial Settlement." In *Beyond Man: Race, Coloniality, and Philosophy of Religion*, edited by An Yountae and Eleanor Craig, 245–68. Durham, NC: Duke University Press, 2021.

Wynter, Sylvia. "Beyond the Word of Man: Glissant and the New Discourse of the Antilles." *World Literature Today* 63, no. 4 (1989): 637–48.

Wynter, Sylvia. "The Ceremony Must Be Found: After Humanism." *boundary 2* 12–13, nos. 3 and 1 (Spring–Autumn 1984): 19–70.

Wynter, Sylvia. "Columbus and the Poetics of Propter Nos." *Annals of Scholarship* 8, no. 2 (1991): 251–86.

Wynter, Sylvia. "Ethno or Sociopoetics." *Alcheringa/Ethnopoetics* 2, no. 2 (1976): 64–97.

Wynter, Sylvia. "On Disenchanting Discourse: 'Minority' Literary Criticism and Beyond." *Cultural Critique*, no. 7 (1987): 207–44.

Wynter, Sylvia. "Unsettling the Coloniality of Being/Power/Truth/Freedom: Towards the Human, after Man, Its Overrepresentation—an Argument." *CR: The New Centennial Review* 3, no. 3 (2003): 257–337.

Zea, Leopoldo. *América como conciencia*. Mexico City: UNAM, 1972.

Zea, Leopoldo. "En torno a una filosofía latinoamericana." *Jornadas* 52 (1945): 3–78.

Žižek, Slavoj, Eric Santner, and Kenneth Reinhard. *The Neighbor: Three Inquiries in Political Theology*. Chicago: University of Chicago Press, 2006.

Index

abyss: Caribbean poetics and, 171–76; in decolonial theory, 157–60
African American Religions, 1500–2000 (Johnson), 10
African Americans. *See* Black Americans
African religion: diversification in scholarship on, 187n78; Western scholarship on, 141–43
Afro-Caribbean intellectualism, religion and, 6–7, 50–52
Afropessimism, 53–56, 123
Agamben, Giorgio, 14, 110
Ahmed, Sara, 118
Alexander, M. Jacqui, 20, 126, 174
Allen, Paula Gunn, 38
Althaus-Reid, Marcella, 87–91
Anidjar, Gil, 16–17, 31
animality, in Anzaldúa's work, 36–38
Anthropocene, colonialism and, 150–55
anti-Blackness: Afropessimist view of, 123; creolization and, 155–60; in North American Black Studies, 53–56; sacred and, 126–27
anticolonialism: Caribbean poetics and, 152–55, 161–62; history in Latin America and the Caribbean of, 28–29; Indigenous intellectual traditions and, 41; religion and, 10–11; sacred in writings on, 20–21
Antilleanness, 46–47, 114–15, 140, 148–55, 164, 168. *See also* Caribbean decolonial scholarship and poetics
anti-Muslim campaigns, Christian Europe and, 31
Anzaldúa, Gloria, 3–4, 28, 35–41
Aparecido da Silva, Antônio, 87
archipelagic thinking, Glissant's concept of, 149–55, 163
Arendt, Hannah, 135–36
Aristotle, 33
Asad, Talal, 11, 15
Assmann, Hugo, 82–85
atheism, Dussel on, 69

Barad, Karen, 123
belief, secularization of, 11–12
Beliso-De Jesús, Aisha, 43
Bentíez-Rojo, Antonio, 99–100, 161
Benjamin, Walter, 85
Bernabé, Jean, 155–56

Bidault, George, 107, 130–31
Bilbao, Francisco, 28
Bingemer, Maria Clara, 87
biopower, Mbembe on, 110
Black Americans: religious scholarship and, 42–44; transatlantic studies and, 53–56
Black diaspora, decolonialism and, 42–44, 100
Blackness: Afropessimism and, 53–56; Césaire on, 114–15, 130–31; creolization and, 46–47; Fanon on, 19, 54, 100–102, 113; Latin American liberation theology and, 87–91; modernity and role of, 42; nothingness and, 123–27; phenomenology of, 115–22; poetics of, 113–38; religion and, 44–52, 127–28
Black religions, 16–17
Black Skin, White Mask (Fanon), 100, 110, 113, 124–25, 137
Blake, William, 48
Blumenberg, Hans, 14
body: Anzaldúa on coloniality and, 36–37; Fanon's racial embodiment and, 19, 114–22; Indigenous cosmovision and, 39–40; Merleau-Ponty on, 116–19
Bolivian Indigenous Revolution, 40
borderland, coloniality and, 36–37
Brathwaite, Kamau, 139, 165
Brazil, Muslim slave revolt in, 28
Brinkema, Eugenie, 123
Britton, Celia, 165, 173
Brown, Wendy, 3
Butler, Judith, 3, 125–26, 135–38

capitalism: Dussel on, 66–67; religion and, 85–93
capitalocene, 150, 198n33
Caribbean decolonial scholarship and poetics: abyss and poetics of place in, 143–55; Black and Indigenous religions and, 16–17, 51; Black diaspora and, 42–44; colonial modernity and, 99–102; counterritual and, 21–22; decolonial theory in relation to, 1–4, 10, 19–20, 129–34, 139–43; feminist theory and, 20–22; history of, 28–29; island as sacred in, 169–71; negritude movement and, 3, 132, 196n59; ocean in, 161–68; Pan-African orientation in, 197n1; religion and, 27, 44–52, 129–34, 154–55; sacred in, 114–15; world-making and, 139–76. *See also* Antilleanness
Caribbean Discourse (Glissant), 143, 159–60, 163–64
Carter, J. Kameron, 31, 107, 130–31, 181n3
cartography of struggle, religion and decoloniality and, 26–27, 150–55, 158–60, 163
Casey, Edward, 155
CEB (Brazilian grassroots movement), 82–83
CEHILA (Comisión para el Estudio de la Historia de las Iglesias en America Latina y el Caribe / Commission for Historical Studies of the Church in Latin America), 69, 83–84
Césaire, Aimé: on Blackness, 114–15, 125, 129–34; Caribbean poetics and, 1–4, 28, 129–34, 139–43, 164; on creolization, 155–56; on religion, 8, 107, 181n3; sacred in work of, 20
Chakrabarty, Dipesh, 6
Chamoiseau, Patrick, 155–56
Christianity: Black diaspora and, 42–44; colonialism and, 10; definition of religion and, 21; Deloria's critique of, 41; Eucharist and colonialism in, 2–3, 107, 131–34, 181n3; Fanon's treatment of, 103–4; Guadalupe figure and, 37; humanism and, 34–35; Indigenous religion and, 6–9, 16–17, 39–40; Mariátegui and, 74–75, 79–80; political theology and, 98–99; whiteness and, 31
class: Latin American liberation theology and, 61–62; Mariátegui's discussion of, 75–84
Coatlicue (Aztec deity), 37

coloniality/colonialism: Césaire on, 1–3, 107; Christianity and, 98–99; creolization and, 155–60; Dussel's discussion of, 71–72; ecological crisis and, 150–55; Fanon on, 44–46, 99–102, 108–12; gender and, 38–41; Latin American liberation theology and, 59–60; liberation philosophy and, 64–72; Mariátegui on, 72–84; modernity and, 28–35; political theology and, 1–3, 99–102; power and, 9–11, 28–35; religion and, 5–9, 15–17, 182n22, 183n23; sacred in, 20–22, 102–7; US scholarship on, 52–56
commodity fetishism: decolonial liberation theology and, 84–87; Dussel on, 68
"Concerning Violence" (Fanon), 100–102, 107–8, 110–11, 134–38
Condé, Maryse, 115
Confiant, Raphaël, 155–56
Connell, Raewyn, 43
Connolly, William, 12
continental thinking, Glissant's concept of, 148–55
Corio, Alessandro, 167–68
creolization, in Caribbean scholarship, 46–52, 152–60, 169–71, 173–76
Crusades, 31
Cuban Revolution, 28
Cultural Identity and Social Liberation in Latin American Thought (Mariátegui), 78
Cusicanqui, Silvia Rivera, 41

"Daily Life in the Douars" (Fanon), 106
Dash, Michael, 149
The Decolonial Abyss (An), 158
decolonial theory: American studies and, 52–56; Anzaldúa's contributions to, 36–38; Caribbean scholarship and poetics and, 1–4, 10, 19–20, 129–34, 139–43, 167–68; Césaire on, 130–31; Eurocentric knowledge and knowledge production and, 9–14; Fanon and, 103–7; feminism and, 35–41; Glissant and, 20, 157–58; Latin American liberation theology (LALT) and, 18–19, 61–62, 82–93; liberation philosophy and, 62–72; Mariátegui and, 72–84; modernity and, 29–35; ocean poetics and, 161–68; political theology and, 13–14; religion and, 1–11, 16–18; sacred and, 49–52, 107–12, 127–34; violence and revolution and, 134–38; Walcott and, 157–58; world-making and, 17–18; Wynter's contributions to, 32, 34–35, 38
DEI (Departamento Ecuménico de Investigación), 84–85, 87–88
de las Casas, Bartolomé, 28, 33
Deleuze, Gilles, 159, 171–72
Deloria, Vine, 41
DeLoughrey, Elizabeth, 151, 159
dependency theory: decolonialism and, 28; Latin American liberation theology and, 58–59
Derrida, Jacques, 14, 174–75
De Sousa Santos, Boaventura, 43
determinism, in Mariátegui's work, 76–77
Discourse on Colonialism (Césaire), 2–3, 130–33, 181n3
disenchantment, Weber's thesis of, 97, 111–12
diversion, decolonial resistance as, 159–60
dominium, slavery and Roman concept of, 33, 185n29
Drabinski, John, 132, 159–60, 170
Dressler, Markus, 15
duality, in Nahuatl culture, 39–40
Du Bois, W. E. B., 151
Dussel, Enrique: on capitalism, 85–86; Caribbean scholarship and, 28–29, 36; decolonial theory and, 3, 18–19; Latin American liberation theology and, 60–61, 82–84; Latin American philosophy and, 63–72; political theology and, 184n11; on religion, 67–68

ecological crisis, colonial modernity and, 150–55
Economic Manuscript (Marx), 65–66

Eliade, Mircea, 50, 126, 146–48, 199n56
Ellacuria, Ignacio, 191n68
Éloge de la créolité (Bernabé, Chamoiseau, and Confiant), 152–53, 155–56, 161, 170
The End of the Cognitive Empire (De Sousa Santos), 43
Enlightenment: modernity and, 29–30, 97; secularism and, 12
Esposito, Roberto, 167
Eurocene, Grove's concept of, 151
Eurocentric theory: Afro-Indigenous religion and, 141–43; Caribbean poetics and, 149–55; colonialism and modernity and, 30–35; Dussel's critique of, 70; gender and, 38–39; Glissant's challenge to, 144–45; *Indianismo* rejection of, 40; knowledge and knowledge production and, 9–17; Latin American liberation theology and, 58–59, 81–84; Latin American philosophy and, 62–65; liberation philosophy and, 29; Mariátegui on, 76–84; religion and, 5–9, 31; secularism and, 12–14
Existe una filosofía de nuestra américa? (Salazar Bondy), 62–63
exteriority/alterity, Dussel's concept of, 69–72

faith, phenomenology and, 120–21
Fanon, Frantz, 151; anticolonialism of, 28, 44; on Blackness, 19, 54, 100–102, 113–22; Caribbean decolonial scholarship and poetics and, 4, 19; coloniality and work of, 44–46, 99–102, 108–12; on decolonial poetics and the sacred, 127–34, 139–40; Eurocentric theory and, 8–9, 14; on nothingness and infinity, 122–27; phenomenology of, 100–102, 107–15; political theology and, 45–46, 99–102, 107–12; prayer of, 125–26, 137–38; on race and decolonialism, 44–46, 99; on racial embodiment, 19, 114–22; on violence and revolution, 100–102, 107–8, 124–27, 134–38; religion and work of, 45–46, 99–107
federal law, Indigenous challenge to, 41
feminist theory: coloniality and, 35–41; global south and north and, 43; Latin American liberation theology and, 87–91; racial embodiment and, 126–27; secularism and, 20–22; violence and, 135–38
Foucault, Michel, 109–10
Freire, Paulo, 82–83
French Revolution, coloniality and, 30

Garcilaso de laVega, Inca, 28
gardens, colonialism and, 150–51
gaze, Fanon on racialization of, 117–22
Gebara, Ivone, 87
gender: Anzaldúa's work on, 37–38; Fanon's issues with, 125–26; Latin American liberation theology and, 87–91; modernity/coloniality and, 38–41; power and, 35–36; violence and, 135
genealogy of the secular, 13–15
geography: colonialism and, 158–60; imperialism and, 151–55; space and, 145–46
Gilroy, Paul, 42
Glissant, Édouard: Caribbean poetics and, 56, 115, 129–30, 139–43, 163–68; decolonialism and work of, 3–4, 8, 20, 156–60; island as abyss in work of, 172–76; negritude and work of, 156; on creolization, 44, 46–49, 152–55; on poetics of place, 143–46, 148–55, 165–68; on sacred, 169–71
Gordon, Lewis, 108, 137–38
Grove, Jairus, 151
Guattari, Félix, 159
Guldberg, Horacio Cerruti, 60
Gutiérrez, Gustavo, 61, 81–82

Hage, Ghassan, 134
Haitian revolution, 28
Haraway, Donna, 150
Harris, Wilson, 161–62

Hegel, G. W. F., 64, 70–71, 189n38
Heidegger, Martin, 116, 174
Heng, Geraldine, 31
Henry, Paget, 128
Hinkelammert, Franz, 84–87
history, Caribbean poetics and, 163–68
Hong, Grace Kyungwon, 123–24, 195n45
humanity, colonial denial of, in Indigenous culture, 33–35, 184n29
Husserl, Edmund, 116–17
hypermasculinity, Fanon and, 125–26

Indecent Theology (Althaus-Reid), 89, 91
Indianismo, 40–41
Indigenous culture: Anzaldúa on religion and coloniality in, 37–41; decolonial resistance and, 39–41; Deloria's rejection of federal law and, 41; diversification in religious studies of, 187n78; Fanon on religion in, 103; gender and, 38–41; humanity in, colonial denial of, 33–35, 184n29; Latin American liberation theology and, 87–91; Mariátegui on the marginalization of, 73–74; religion and, 6–9, 16–17, 51–52, 141–43; Spanish colonialism and, 32–35
infinity, Fanon on nothingness and, 122–27
The Invention of Race in the European Middle Ages (Heng), 31
Is Critique Secular? (Brown, Butler, and Mahmood), 3
Islam: Fanon's treatment of, 104–6; political theology framing of, 31–32
island: as abyss, 171–76; as sacred, 169–71

Jennings, Willie, 8, 182n22
Johnson, Sylvester, 10, 48, 52–53
Judaism: liberation philosophy and, 63–64; political theology framing of, 31–32, 184n11
Justo, Juan B., 72

Kahn, Jonathan, 26
Kahn, Paul, 101, 109–11
Kamugisha, Aaron, 27, 140, 154

Kawash, Samira, 135
Kelly, Robin D.G., 133
knowledge and knowledge production: coloniality of, 28–29; decolonial theory and, 9–10; embodied self and, 36–37; Glissant on, 159–60; Latin American liberation theology and, 59–60; religion and, 16–17; violence and, 43–44
Kusch, Rodolfo, 60

labor: colonial power and, 28; Dussel's living labor, 65–67
Lackey, Michael, 106
Lamming, George, 115, 150, 171
land use, in Mariátegui's theory, 73–84
language and narrative, poetics and, 129–34
Latin American decolonial theory: Anzaldúa and, 37–38; Black and Indigenous religions and, 16–17; Black diaspora and, 42–44; cosmovision in, 39–40; European modernity and, 29; history of, 28–29; liberation philosophy and theology and, 18–19; religion and, 9–10
Latin American liberation theology (LALT): decolonial theory and, 59–93; Dussell and, 60–61, 67–72; history of, 18–19, 57–62; legacy of, 92–93; Mariátegui and, 79–84; market, commodity fetishism and utopic reason and, 84–87; race and indigeneity and, 87–91; sex, desire and economy and, 87–91
Latinx feminism, 37–38
Lefebvre, Henri, 146
Levinas, Emmanuel, 29, 63–65, 70, 184n11
liberation philosophy, 29; decolonization and, 62–72; Latin American liberation theology and, 60–61
liberation theology: decolonialism and, 18–19, 28; Mariátegui and, 61–62, 72–84
"The Lived Experience of the Black Man" (Fanon), 110–11, 115–22, 137–38

Lloyd, Vincent, 26
Loichot, Valérie, 21–22, 154–55, 166–67
Long, Charles, 11, 126, 170
Lopez Hernandez, Eleazar, 87
Lowith, Karl, 14
Lugones, María, 35, 38–39, 186n44
Luxemburg, Rosa, 87

Mahmood, Saba, 3
Makalani, Minkah, 132
Maldonado-Torres, Nelson, 3, 8, 32, 70, 127–28, 137
Mandair, Arvind-Pal, 15
Manichean dualism, Fanon on, 45, 108–12, 187n63
Marcos, Sylvia, 39
Mariátegui, José Carlos: Caribbean scholarship and, 28; decolonialism and, 18–19; decolonial theory and, 72–84; liberation theology and, 61–62
market capitalism, decolonial liberation theology and, 84–87, 93
maroon movement, 28
Marriott, David, 136
Martí, José, 28
Marx, Karl, 11; Black diaspora tradition and, 42–44; commodity fetishism of, 68, 84–87; Dussel on, 65–68; *Indianismo* and, 40; Latin American liberation theology and, 81–84; Mariátegui and, 72–84
Masuzawa, Tomoko, 148
Mbembe, Achille, 5–6, 55, 109–11, 161, 162–63
Mendieta, Eduardo, 67
Merleau-Ponty, Maurice, 19, 111, 116–21, 127, 138, 194n9, 195n29
mestizaje/mestiza, coloniality and, 36–37
Middle Passage: Caribbean poetics and, 46–47, 140; decolonial theory and, 20; Glissant on, 143–55, 158–60, 173–76
Mignolo, Walter, 17, 28–32, 36, 81–83
Miguez Bonino, José, 81–82
modernity: Black diaspora and, 42–44; Caribbean poetics and, 149–55; coloniality and, 5–10, 16–17, 28–35; Dussel's critique of, 67–68; Fanon's critique of, 19; secularism and religion and, 11–13, 15–18; totalitarian metaphysics and, 29
Moltmann, Jürgen, 81–82
Moten, Fred, 53–54, 123
Mu (nothingness), East Asian concept of, 54
"The Muse of History" (Walcott), 156–57, 169
mysticism: Blackness and, 54; decolonial theory and, 49
myth: Fanon on, 103; Mariátegui on, 74–84

Nahuatl culture, duality in, 39–40
negritude movement, 3, 132, 139, 155–56, 196n59
neocolonialism, secularism and, 12–13
Nishida Kitaro, 54
nonhistory, Glissant on, 143–45
Notebook of a Return to the Native Land (Cahier d'un retour au pays natal) (Césaire), 1–4, 129, 131–32
nothingness, Fanon on infinity and, 122–27
Noudelmann, François, 168

Of Age and Innocence (Lamming), 171
ontology, liberation philosophy and, 65
Orientalism (Said), 16
origin stories and myths, decolonial theory and, 38
Ortega, Mariana, 37
Out of the Dark Night (Mbembe), 5–6
Oyewumi, Oyeronke, 38

Patterson, Orlando, 53
peasants, in Mariátegui's theory, 73–84
Perse, St. John, 1
phenomenology: of Fanon, 100–102, 107–12; Merleau-Ponty on, 19; place and, 146; of race, 113–38; of race and Blackness, 115–22; religion and, 44–52; sacred in, 21–22, 50–52

Philosophie de la Relation (Glissant), 166–68
place, poetics of, 143–55
plantation life: in Caribbean poetics, 46–47, 140, 150, 158–60; decolonialism and, 20
plantationocene, 150, 198n33, 199n37
poetics. *See* Caribbean decolonial scholarship and poetics
Poetics of Relation (Glissant), 143–44, 159–60, 170
political theology: colonialism and, 1–3, 99–102; decoloniality and sacred and, 107–12; Fanon on, 45–46, 99–102, 107–12; of Mariátegui, 78–84; racial identity and, 31; religion and, 98–99; secularism and, 13, 183n32
Politics (Aristotle), 33
Poma de Ayala, Guamán, 28
postcolonial theory: decolonial theory vs., 9–10; Mariátegui and, 79–84; religion and, 3
power: American colonial articulation of, 53–56; coloniality of, 9–11, 28–35; Dussel on, 68–72; gender and, 35–41; Latin American liberation theology and, 59–62; Mariátegui on religion and, 76–84; Mbembe on, 109–10; of market capitalism, 86–87; mystical construction of, 49; religion and, 15–18, 32–35, 154–55, 162–63
praxis, liberation theology and philosophy and, 60–61
primitive accumulation, religion and, 86–87
Provincializing Europe (Chakrabarty), 6
purity of blood principle, 30–31

The Queer God (Althaus-Reid), 90
queer theory: coloniality and, 36–37; Latin American liberation theology and, 88–91
Quijano, Aníbal: Caribbean scholarship and work of, 28–29; decolonial theory and, 36, 39; liberation theology and philosophy and, 61; Mariátegui and, 73–74, 77, 79; on power, 9, 79

race: in American studies, 52–56; colonialization of power and, 28–35; Fanon on, 19, 99–102, 107–8, 124–27; gender and, 35, 39; *Indianismo* rejection of, 40; Latin American liberation theology and, 61–62, 87–91; in Mariátegui's theory, 73–84; phenomenology of, 113–38; religion and coloniality and, 5–9, 44–52; science and, 31
Race: A Theological Account (Carter), 31
Gray, Ros 150–51
reason: Latin American liberation theology and, 84–87; Western geography of, 5–6
refusal, decolonialism and, 3–4
Reinaga, Fausto, 40–41
relation, Glissant on colonialism and, 159–60, 166–68
religion: in American colonial studies, 53–56; anticolonialism and, 10–11; Anzaldúa's decolonial reading of, 37–41; capitalism and, 85–93; Caribbean decolonial theory and, 44–52, 129–34, 154–55, 161–71; colonialism and, 5–9, 15–17, 28–35, 182n22, 183n23; as cultural universal, 15; decolonial theory and, 1–11, 26–27; diversification of scholarship on, 187n78; Dussel on, 67–68, 71–72; Eliade on, 146–48; European construction of, 5–9; Fanon on, 19, 45–46, 99–107, 124–34; feminism and, 35–41; Glissant on, 140–43; Indigenous emancipation and, 41; Mariátegui on, 72–84; modernity and, 28–35, 97–98; non-Western religion scholarship and, 5–9; ocean aesthetics and, 161–68; origins of, 177–78, 203n2; power and, 15–18, 32–35; privatization of, 11; sacred in, 20–22; secular colonial order and, 10–11, 182n22; space and, 146–55. *See also* sacred

resource extraction, colonial power and, 28
Revolta dos Malês (Brazilian Muslim slave revolt), 28
revolutionary politics: Fanon on violence and, 134–38; of Mariátegui, 74–84
Reyes, Alfonso, 72
Richard, Pablo, 84–85
"Rights of the Man and of the Citizen" (France), 30
Rivera, Mayra, 125
Robinson, Cedric, 42
Rodó, José Enrique, 72
Roig, Arturo, 60
Rosaldo, Renato, 151
Rouanet, S. P., 75–76
Rubenstein, Mary-Jane, 120, 195n33

sacred: in Caribbean scholarship and poetics, 20–22, 142–43, 154–55; decolonial theory and, 49–52, 107–12, 127–34; Eliade on, 126, 147–48; Fanon on, 20, 102–7, 110, 114–15, 124–34, 138; Glissant on, 20, 140–43, 165–68; Indigenous concepts of, 41; island as symbol in, 169–71
The Sacred and the Profane (Eliade), 146–48
Said, Edward, 16
Salazar Bondy, Augusto, 62–63, 188n9
Saldaña-Portillo, Josefina, 37
Santos, Milton, 146
Sartre, Jean-Paul, 122–23, 135–36
Scannone, Juan Carlos, 60, 83–84
Schelling, Friedrich Wilhelm Joseph von, 65–66
Scheper-Hughes, Nancy, 126
Schmitt, Carl, 13–14, 98, 109–11, 183n32
Schutte, Ofelia, 70, 188n9
science, race and, 31
A Secular Age (Taylor), 11–12
secular humanism: colonialism in Americas and, 34–35; Fanon and, 126–27; sacred and, 114
secularism: Caribbean poetics and, 169–71; coloniality and, 10–11, 19, 32–35, 52, 101–2; decolonialism and, 3–4, 11–17, 103–4; disenchantment thesis and, 97–98; Dussel's critique of, 67–72; Latin American liberation theology and, 60; Mariátegui on, 72–84; market and, 84–87; modernity and, 11–12, 101–2; normative framework of, 26–27; Orientalism and, 16; postsecular scholarship on, 15, 182n13; theory of, 6–9; Western worldview and, 30–31
"Secularism" (Anidjar), 16
Secularism and Religion-Making (Dressler and Arvind-Pal), 15
Segundo, Juan Luis, 82–83
Senghor, Leopold, 165–66
Sepulveda, Juan Ginés de, 33
Settler, Federico, 102
sex: Latin American liberation theology and, 88–91. *See also* gender
Sharpe, Christina, 56
Sheikh, Shela, 150–51
shock, phenomenology and, 120, 195n33
Singh, Julietta, 137
Slabodsky, Santiago, 184n11
slavery: Aristotle's support for, 33; Glissant on, 143–55; ocean aesthetics and, 161
Slisli, Fouzi, 104–5
Smith, Wilfred, Cantwell, 183n23
sociogeny, Fanon's concept of, 119, 164
Sorel, George, 74–77
sovereignty: Blackness and, 56–56; political theology and, 13
space: critical geography of, 145–46; religion and, 146–48
Spanish imperialism: colonialism and modernity and, 30; Indigenous religion and, 37; Valladolid debates and, 33–35
Spanish Reconquista, 31

Tager, Michael, 75–76
Tamez, Elsa, 87
Tawantinsuyu-Kollasuyu (Inca state), 40
Taylor, Charles, 11–12
Teología de la liberación (Assmann), 82

theology, Latin American liberation theology and, 57
Thoreau, Henry David, 48
The Thoroughbred (Drabinski), 132
totalitarian metaphysics, modernity and, 29
totality, Dussel's concept of, 66–67, 70–72
transatlantic experience: Caribbean poetics and, 140; religion and, 44–52; US coloniality and, 52–56
Tupac Amaru rebellion, 28

United States: Black diaspora tradition and, 42–44; coloniality scholarship in, 52–56; decolonial theory in, 9–10; Latin American liberation theology and, 58–59, 62
Unthinking Mastery (Singh), 137
urgrund, Schelling's concept of, 65–66
US-Mexico border, coloniality and, 36–37
utopic reason, decolonial liberation theology and, 84–87

Valladolid debates, 30, 33
Verzauberung der Welt, Merleau-Ponty and, 120
violence: colonial legacy of, 1–2; Fanon on, 100–102, 107–8, 124–27, 197n79; knowledge production and, 43–44; revolution and, 134–38; secularism and, 13–14
The Visible and the Invisible (Merleau-Ponty), 120
Vitoria, Francisco de, 33, 185n29

Wagua, Aiban, 87
Walcott, Derek: Caribbean scholarship and poetics and, 1–3, 20, 47–49, 162; island as abyss in work of, 172–76; on creolization, 44, 153–54, 156–57; sacred in work of, 142, 167, 169–70
Wallerstein, Immanuel, 29–30, 64–65

Warren, Calvin, 56
Water Graves (Loichot), 154–55
Weber, Max, 11, 97
Weheliye, Alexander, 193n36
Western thought: colonialism and, 5–9; diversification in, 187n78; Dussel's critique of, 67–68; Fanon on religion in, 103–7; Glissant's challenge to, 144–45; *Indianismo* rejection of, 40; Latin American liberation theology and, 58–59, 81–84; liberation philosophy and, 64; political theology and, 13–14, 31–32; sacred in, 126; secularism and, 30–31
whiteness: Christianity, 31; normativity of, 26–27; religion and, 129–30
Whitman, Walt, 48
Winters, Joseph, 126
women, Latin American liberation theology and, 88–91
Word of Man (Wynter): Caribbean intellectual tradition and, 46, 111, 115, 131–34, 143–55, 162–68; decolonial theory and, 38; power and knowledge and, 129
world-making: Eliade's discussion of, 147–48; poetics and, 139–76; sacred and, 21–22
world-system theory, 64–65
The Wretched of the Earth (Fanon), 100, 134–35
Wynter, Sylvia: on Blackness, 54; Caribbean poetics and scholarship and, 3–4, 8, 111, 115, 139, 142, 164; decolonial theory of, 32, 34–35, 38; on Fanon's sociogeny, 164; on Glissant, 169; on humanness, 119; modernity and, 107–8; on poetics, 128–33; on political theology, 115; on religion and colonialism, 28, 107–8; on secularism, 20, 46, 107–8

Zapatista movement, 28
Zea, Leopoldo, 63
Žižek, Slavoj, 14

www.ingramcontent.com/pod-product-compliance
Lightning Source LLC
Chambersburg PA
CBHW020836160426
43192CB00007B/677